Stumbling Towards the Finish Line
The Best of Ironman Columnist Lee Gruenfeld

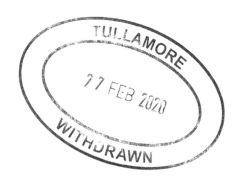

Lee Gruenfeld

Stumbling Towards the Finish Line

The Best of Ironman Columnist Lee Gruenfeld

Edited by Kevin Mackinnon

Meyer & Meyer Sport

British Library Cataloguing in Publication Data
A catalogue record for this book is available from the British Library

Lee Gruenfeld – Stumbling Towards the Finish Line
Maidenhead: Meyer & Meyer Sport (UK) Ltd., 2013
ISBN: 978-1-78255-005-1

© 2013 by Meyer & Meyer Sport (UK) Ltd.
Auckland, Beirut, Budapest, Cairo, Cape Town, Dubai, Hägendorf,
Indianapolis, Maidenhead, Singapore, Sydney, Tehran, Wien
Member of the World
Sports Publishers' Association (WSPA)
www.w-s-p-a.org
Printed by: Sprint-print
ISBN: 978-1-78255-005-1
E-Mail: info@m-m-sports.com
www.m-m-sports.com

Books by Lee Gruenfeld

Irreparable Harm

The Street

All Fall Down

The Halls of Justice

The Expert

Writing as "Troon McAllister"

The Green

The Foursome

Scratch

Barranca

The Kid Who Batted 1.000

Non-fiction

Confessions of a Master Jewel Thief, with Bill Mason

Becoming Holyfield: A Fighter's Journey, with Evander Holyfield

The Perfection Point, with John Brenkus

Stumbling Towards the Finish Line

To every athlete who has ever toed the start line at an Ironman (except the fat guy in the red Speedo at the 2007 World Championship in Kona; for him, there is no forgiveness)

Contents

FOREWORD

Most people who write about the Ironman and the sport of triathlon tend to be submerged in the lifestyle. They get up close and personal to a chlorinated pool five days a week and can't get through a typical day without spending a few hours on their bike, running the roads around their neighborhood and then emailing and Facebooking everyone they have ever met with the mind-numbing details of their mind-numbing workouts.

These people look at a few hours of spare time in their everyday life as the perfect opportunity to squeeze in a swim, bike, run, weight workout, yoga class or stretching session. Lee Gruenfeld, by contrast, would much rather use any spare time he might have to do something actually worthwhile, like catching a matinée, squeezing in a power nap, doing the *New York Times* crossword puzzle with a latte close by, or, if we're talking a larger window of time because his multiple-time Ironman age group champion wife Cherie happens to be out on a long bike ride, the perfect opportunity to hit the links and work on his long irons. In a cart, of course. In Lee's mind, any activity involving sweat is the devil.

Since Cherie is one of the greatest age group triathletes to ever grace this planet, and he is exposed to all things endurance 24 hours a day, seven days a week, Lee, like that Zen-enhanced dog walker who is somehow always able to avoid becoming one with the Hummer-sized St. Bernard droppings that are constantly in his life, has been able to steer clear of stepping into any of the endurance insanity that he is constantly exposed to.

Instead, he has become the ultimate outsider who prides himself on being able to document the craziness that surrounds him. He somehow, someway, has been able to survive in the eye of the hurricane with his 54" flat screen, remote control, Bear Claw and frosty mug always at the ready.

For the age group athlete and the professional, triathlon is serious business. Their training, racing and excessive behavior is how they identify themselves and how they connect with their training partners. To Lee Gruenfeld, one of the most accomplished humorists and authors around, these athletes and their quest to go farther and faster than ever before provide not only inspiration, but constant entertainment.

This collection of Lee's Ironman-related stories is guaranteed to give you insight into what makes the Ironman athlete remarkable.

When it comes to being an endurance athlete, Lee will tell you that he has no interest, and, even if he did, he would be totally hopeless. But as your trusted observer of the people in the sport of triathlon, he is not only incredibly insightful but also funny as hell.

Enjoy this book!

Bob Babbitt
Co-Founder Competitor Magazine
Co-Founder Challenged Athletes Foundation
10th Inductee Ironman Triathlon Hall of Fame
2012 Inductee USA Triathlon Hall of Fame

THE FIRST PART:

FUNNY STUFF

You People are Completely Nuts
(Why You Don't Want to do Ironman)

Last month in Kona someone asked me an interesting question.

"You obviously love everything about the sport," this person began, "so when are you going to do an Ironman yourself?" It was a reasonable question to ask, and I considered it carefully before replying.

"Imagine," I eventually began, "that the entire King Kamehameha hotel is made of solid lava. And imagine that, once every hundred years, a Hawaiian mongoose runs past and brushes it with its fur. When the hotel has been worn down to the size of a macadamia nut, that's when I'll do Ironman."

I've said it before, and I'll say it again: You people are completely nuts. Your rationales for doing Ironman are dangerously delusional. I guess it's understandable, since millions of words have been written about why you should do Ironman, but millions of words have also been written about extraterrestrials building the Parthenon and you didn't fall for that, so what's up with this?

Then it occurred to me: No words have been written about why you shouldn't do Ironman. Public-spirited guy that I am, I propose to correct that situation. Herewith, six reasons why you don't want to do this race.

1. **It hurts.** A considerable portion of the lengthy history of humankind has been spent searching for ways to alleviate pain. This year alone over $5 billion will be spent by researchers attempting to relieve physical suffering. So why in God's name would anyone want to deliberately hurt himself? What kind of sense does that make? If you have a little headache, you rush to the medicine cabinet and scarf down a handful of pills to make it go away, but you'll think nothing of running twenty-six miles on burning hot lava starting at high noon twenty-three degrees above the equator. Let me tell you something: There are cultures where running twenty-six miles on burning hot lava at high noon is how they punish people who commit murder.

2. **It's addictive.** A lot of Ironman athletes will tell you that doing one of these is like eating potato chips: Once you do it, you're hooked and powerless to resist the next one. You'll risk your family, your job and possibly your life trying to qualify, and then you'll think about nothing else until race day. Sound familiar? It should. This is the classic definition of addictive behavior. Addiction is bad. Everybody knows that. It's so bad the U.S. government has formally declared war on it, yet despite lavishing huge amount of resources fighting addiction, it's still losing, so what chance do you think you have?

3. **The food sucks.** I myself am partial to filet du boeuf au poivre, potatoes au mucho gratin and crème brûlée, accompanied by a nice '61 Beychevelle and perhaps an Ypres Sauterne to top it all off. Know

what you eat when you train for an Ironman? The same kind of things as when you're on chemotherapy or incarcerated in Abu Ghraib. I've seen paramedics put more appetizing stuff on open wounds. My wife blends up beverages that would violate fourteen different EPA regulations if you dumped them in a river. And it isn't a casual diet, either; I've known triathletes who have gone to confession after sneaking a few nanograms of Parmesan on their tofu burgers, so will somebody please tell me why anyone would go through all of that just so they can feel pain?

4. **You don't get anywhere.** Swimming, biking and running are modes of transportation. Look up *transportation* in the dictionary and you'll find that it means "going from one place to another." Swimming was invented to get across rivers, the bicycle let you go to the grocery store faster than walking, and running was good for escaping from lions or chasing down chickens. In each case, the point is to end up in a different place than where you started. But not Ironman, uh uh. In Ironman you swim, bike and run yourself into near exhaustion only to end up right where you began and, not only that, you don't even have a bag of groceries or a dead chicken to show for it. So, basically, by the time you finish you're back where you started and nothing has changed, except that you look like a drowned rat, feel like one, too, and you've lost an entire day of your life. And this is something you want to train for? You could get the same effect by falling asleep in a car wash.

5. **It's expensive.** I remember thinking once that Ironman might be worth doing if they paid you enough. Imagine my shock when I discovered that *I'd* have to pay *them*. That's unbelievable. I could get the same punishment by joining the Marines, and I'd at least get a couple hundred bucks a month for my trouble. And race fees are the least of it. My wife's bike cost more than my first car. Come to think of it, it cost more than my second car, and the tires cost more than mine do now. I can't understand why anyone would pay a hundred bucks for a carbon fiber bottle cage to save two ounces and then think nothing of slamming three pounds of water bottles into it. Yo! Put two fewer ounces of water in the bottles and save the hundred bucks! Why do you think they have aid stations?

6. **Bad weather.** I like to play golf. When the weather's bad, I don't play golf. If there's a tournament and the weather's bad, they postpone the tournament, even if it's a PGA major. This to me makes sense. Ironman races, however, don't get canceled unless lightning actually hits the starter gun or the surf is so high Laird Hamilton goes inside to watch reruns of "Sea Hunt" until it settles down. Doesn't matter how hot it is, or how cold or windy or humid, they do it anyway, even though entire industries have devoted themselves to protecting us from those very conditions. They don't just do it; they love it. Ironman athletes are like mountain climbers; the worse the conditions, the better the bragging rights. Please. If I spend a year training my butt off for an Ironman and it's a nasty day? I don't want to waste my one shot fighting elements that my ancestors had enough brains to run into caves to avoid. If Ironman got postponed on account of bad weather, then I might consider doing one.

Except for the other five reasons.

Visualizing Your Race

Blew it, didn't you?

Spent a whole year scheming and dreaming about The Big One, qualified on your third try, breathed several thousand miles of road dust and exhaust fumes, swallowed enough chlorine to disinfect Lake Superior and spent less time with your family than a Mir astronaut, then came to Kona and, just as you planned, left nothing out on the course but a stomach-full of PowerBars.

Except it was the swim course, because you never made it far enough up Pay 'n' Save Hill to make your first gear change before toppling over like Saddam's statue after the invasion. And now you have no idea why it happened.

Let's face it, folks: Athletes at the top of their games are all in basically the same shape. What sets them apart, what really allows one to triumph over the others (assuming that all of their sponsored supplements are equally useless), is the mental aspect.

And as elite athletes from Eddie "The Eagle" Edwards to Vinko "Agony of Defeat" Bogataj will tell you, the key is visualization, that uncanny ability to mentally place one's self smack in the middle of the event and feel as though it was happening right now.

It's no different for Ironman. So, for you amateurs—and especially you first-timers—here's a sure-fire, virtual reality guide to visualizing your race that is guaranteed to prepare you for what you'll encounter on race day. If you practice these exercises diligently, you'll happily discover that race day will hold few surprises for you.

Please note that many of these exercises require the assistance of two dedicated friends.

THE SWIM

Equipment Requirements: * Two twin-engine powerboats
* Four Merc-150 outboard engines

1. Tie the boats fast to a dock so that they are back-to-back and about 3 feet apart.
2. Rev all four engines up to top speed.
3. Jump in the water and have one buddy punch you in the mouth while the other rips your goggles off.
4. Remain positioned between the two sets of outboard engines and try not to touch any of the props. (For added realism, occasionally stick your arm in one.)
5. After your planned swim time has elapsed, continue for another half hour.

THE BIKE

Equipment Requirements: * Boeing 747

* StairMaster

1. Position the StairMaster in the backwash of the #2 engine of the 747.
2. Have your buddy crank the engine up to full power.
3. Commence climbing. Feel the burn.
4. After an hour, have your other buddy turn the StairMaster sideways to the left.
5. After two hours, have him turn the StairMaster sideways to the right.
6. When your planned bike time has elapsed, turn the StairMaster directly into the exhaust once again and continue for another hour. (First-timers please note: Unless you plan to finish the race in under 8 hours, tailwind simulations will be an irrelevant component of your training regimen.)

THE RUN

Equipment Requirements: * Treadmill

* Sauna

* Steambath

* 3000-watt searchlight

* MK3A2 concussion grenade

* Timex Indiglo watch (optional)

* Surplus WWII blackout curtains

1. Set up the treadmill in the sauna with the searchlight shining in your eyes.
2. Commence running. Feel the burn.
3. After an appropriate interval, have your buddies move the treadmill into the steambath, which has been rendered completely lightless using the blackout curtains. Illumination from the (optional) single Indiglo watch is permitted.
4. Continue running for what seems like a week, then add an extra day. Whenever death seems imminent, instruct your buddies to yell, "Looking strong!" and "Good job!" at the top of their lungs while averting their eyes in utter dismay.
5. At mile 24, strap the grenade to your chest.
6. At mile 25, pull the pin. Continue running following detonation.
7. For advanced training, have your buddies simulate your competitors thusly: As you continue running, have them shower; change clothes; have dinner, sex, and a nap; and then be fresh and alert to greet you at step 4 of the finish to tell you how terrific ("No, really!") you look.

Stumbling Towards the Finish Line

THE FINISH

Equipment Requirements: * Marine boot camp

                                              * Finish line banner

                                              * Large tent

                                              * Garish lighting

                                              * #2 pencil

1. Have your buddies set up that Marine training exercise where you crawl on your belly under barbed wire.
2. Commence exercise.
3. Have your buddies hold the banner up five miles away to simulate what it will look like when you're halfway down Ali'i Drive.
4. Once under the banner, have your buddies lift you and carry you to the garishly lit tent approximately 200 yards away. Time of trip: 40 minutes.
5. Once inside the tent, have one buddy jam the #2 pencil about three inches into your arm and mumble, "Damn...missed it." The other buddy should then reply, "I showed you once. You should have it down by now."
6. Repeat Step 5. Twice.
7. Once the pencil has been firmly implanted, buddies should mutter things like "fixed and dilated" and "flatlining" just above the threshold of your hearing.

* * *

Further simulations are unnecessary; humans are genetically programmed for the ability to lie deathly still for prolonged periods following the complete shutdown of all metabolic activity. Nature will see you through.

Good luck!

A Spectator's Guide to the Ironman

There are nine thousand books and ten times that many magazine articles telling you how to train for the Ironman. Remarkably, there is nothing anywhere telling you how to watch the Ironman.

What makes this so weird is that there are vastly greater numbers of people who watch the race than actually do it. Now, doesn't it strike you as odd that no one has yet seen fit to address the needs of this neglected yet vital component of the Ironman *ohana*?

Instead, tri magazine editors sit on the sidelines as tens of thousands of these poor bedraggled souls drift in and out of race venues the world over. The marketing possibilities alone are virtually limitless. Selling one or two chain polymerized, ergonomically designed, form-fitting and aerodynamically optimized hi-performance hydration systems (referred to by insiders as "water bottles") for a hundred bucks to gullible IM newbies is one thing. Selling their families dozens of double-death cheeseburgers, overpriced, genuine Kailua-Kona margaritas and custom-screened "Your-Athlete's-Name-Here Fan Club" T-shirts is potentially more rewarding. (You can trust my business acumen, even if I did buy Enron at $130.)

But, as magazine editors know all too well, you can't sell the ad space unless you have the readers, and to get the readers, you have to scatter some actual content among the ads for shoelaces that promise to put you on the podium.

Given that The Big One is only days away (I'm referring to the Ironman World Championship, not a repeat of 2006's 6.7 lava rocker), I'm going to kick things off by addressing myself to those unsung heroes who make the trek to Kona even though they get neither the glory nor the ink.

Loved ones, herewith a few tips to make your race day all you hoped it would be.

- **Don't forget to train**: It isn't easy being an Iron spectator. Believe me, I've done it many times and can tell you that, if you go into it cold, you're going to suffer. Your SPAM (Significant Participating Athlete Mate) is counting on you to smile and shout encouragement no matter how you're feeling, and let's be honest here: How you feel counts about as much on the Big Day as it did during ten months of training for the Big Day. So don't neglect your own training.

Your basic endurance-watching training should consist of slathering SPF 900 all over yourself and then sitting two feet from the business end of a flamethrower set to max power while staring forlornly into the distance as though waiting for something to happen. Remember how you used to sit by the fireplace for twelve hours waiting for Santa? It's a lot like that, except without the leftover eggnog you used to sneak to take the edge off. About every three hours, pick yourself up, walk around aimlessly for five or six miles, then sit back down in front of the flamethrower. Repeat endlessly, or until you lose count, whichever comes first.

Stumbling Towards the Finish Line

- **Don't peak too early**: This is a common mistake among amateur watchers. Another is to forget that spectating isn't just about watching the race; it's about being in Kona for a week or two beforehand. So you want to be sure that you work your way up to thirty-six holes a day slowly, rather than all at once.

  Thirty-six holes a day isn't just important; it's critical. Veterans can tell you that the last thing you want to be anywhere near while supporting your SPAM in Kona is your SPAM while he's in Kona. SPAMs in Kona are like badly constipated wild boars, which is to say, a little touchy to the extent of being perfectly willing to rip your liver out through your navel if you look at them the wrong way. As the Big Island is the single most isolated land mass on earth, there aren't that many places to hide. The Mountain Course at the Kona Country Club is one, and there are others.

- **Make checklists**: Triathlon-watching is too complicated to be left to the vagaries of memory. Rather than agonize over whether you've remembered everything and risk starting off your Hawaiian odyssey by fighting two thousand cruise ship passengers for the express lane at Wal-Mart, take a tip from airline pilots and make a checklist. Some items on my own list include a DVD player, a portable practice putting green, a towel (for when the race course gets close to the beach), a beach chair and matching umbrella, a cooler full of brewskies and pork rinds, and a good assortment of fine stogies, including some extras to hand out to natives, who have been known to let spectators slip into the lanai for a quick nap or a half hour of Dr. Phil in exchange for a primo Cohiba.

- **Sex the week before Ironman**: [this space intentionally left blank]

- **Negotiate the course**: The swim is fairly self-explanatory. The only tricky part is anticipating your SPAM's likely split. It's a good idea to give yourself a couple of minutes leeway in case she catches a good draft or dislocates a shoulder or has her jaw broken. Let's assume your best guess is 1:10 and you're staying at the Royal Kona. Since the gun won't go off any earlier than 6:55 am, make sure you don't sleep past 7:20 so you can get a nice shot of the swimmers stroking past the third buoy before you hit the rack again.

- **Understand the local lingo**: I'm not talking about the Hawaiian language. You can forget that. You'll hear a lot about how beautiful and musical and poetic and culturally vital Hawaiian is. What you'll never hear is anybody actually speaking Hawaiian. Nobody knows how, except one guy, and he doesn't have anybody to talk to.

  What I'm talking about is people blithely referring to places that don't exist. An example is the stretch of Palani between Kuakini Highway and the Queen K called "Pay 'n' Save Hill." There is no Pay 'n' Save there. There is no Pay 'n' Save within 2,800 miles of Pay 'n' Save Hill. There is a Sack 'n' Save across the street, and a Sizzler, but no Pay 'n' Save. Up until six years ago there was a Payless, and then there was a Ross store and now there's something else. But many years ago there was a Pay 'n' Save on the spot, and it's still called that because "Ross Stores Hill" doesn't cut it, and "Piss 'n' Moan Hill" is reserved for use by actual Ironman participants.

Knowing stuff like this separates the virgin watchers from the veterans. This is why "doing the Hilton" during swim training has been known to result in exhausted athletes being picked up somewhere in the vicinity of the Solomon Islands still stroking valiantly while waiting for the Hilton to show up because it's been the Royal Kona since 1986.

- **Don't eat anything on race day that you didn't eat while training**. This is age-old triathlon wisdom, or at least as age old as you can get in a sport that started after Nixon left office. It's doubly important for spectators whose constitutions are usually screwed up even on a good day, and for whom there are no sponsors plying them with products they've been using all year long anyway. In an exotic environment like Hawai'i where there are all kinds of strange and potentially lethal microorganisms, stick with packaged brands you trust, like Entenmann's, Frito-Lay and Hershey.

- **Use race course motivation**: Remember that you're there to help your SPAM. If you know that her nearest competitor is eight miles behind, don't hesitate to say, "You better step on it babe; she's right on your tail!" as a means of inducing higher performance. However, after you confess your little motivational cleverness while she's on her way into the medical tent, you are best advised to do so quickly and then step smartly away from the blast zone.

- **Take the time to learn new things**. Seek out expo vendors and learn how you can perkofry lactic acid, incarcerate free radicals, hydrosynclasticize oxygenated gluconodules and boost your nitrous infidibulum levels...all from products whose first four listed ingredients are water, fructose, red dye #2 and caffeine.

There's lots more I can tell you, but since another cardinal rule of IM-spectating is to pace yourself, I'll leave it for another time. Just remember to be disciplined: Plan the work and work the plan!

Good luck and see you at the finish. (That would be the bar at Pancho and Lefty's, where you might as well hang out while your SPAM is mainlining liter-bags of saline because spectators aren't allowed in the medical tent.)

EXOTIC NEW IRONMAN VENUES
Da Race'a Da Bums

Ed. note: The world of Ironman expanded dramatically in 1998. Lew Friedland, then the president of World Triathlon Corporation, began an ambitious expansion that saw Ironman races begin in Austria, Lake Placid, Florida, Malaysia and beyond. By 2003 there were seven full-distance events in North America alone—as opposed to the two that existed until 1999.

I know all this because, when I was hired as the managing editor of Ironman.com in 2003, I was responsible for 17 races. Now, in addition to having to try and keep Lee Gruenfeld in check, I am supposed to organize coverage for almost 120 events. (I am not sure which is more difficult).

In 2012, Ironman finally hosted an event in New York City, taking Lee's convincing advice. There were so many challenges in putting on that New York event that, as this book went to print, it wasn't clear that there would be another event in the Big Apple. Lee will no doubt be blamed for that, too.

It's nice to know that the Iron powers that be are always on the lookout for exciting new locations for races, and they've sure come up with some creatively off-the-beaten-path sites.

Of course, one man's exotic is another's ho-hum. Florida? Please. Their state bird is the Early Bird. And as for the championship of the world's #1 toughest endurance event, whose idea was it to put it in the world's #1 tourist destination? That's like having "Survivor" in Disney World. When you step off the plane on your way to an Ironman, you should be dodging rhinos or poison darts, not local women draping flowers around your neck.

Seems to me that if you're out to find new places to hold a notoriously tough sporting event, you should choose notoriously tough places. So as part of our ongoing commitment to see to it that Ironman doesn't get watered down into the athletic equivalent of an Oldsmobile, we'll be bringing you a series of carefully considered suggestions for truly exciting race locations.

Up first? Brooklyn, New York!

First, a little history. Once, dinosaurs roamed Brooklyn's gentle hills. Sixty million years later I was born there. That's pretty much everything of interest worth noting, so on to the race.

The swim would take place in the Gowanus Canal, a storied waterway off Upper New York Bay. This is what an Ironman swim was meant to look like, not some idyllic float along the warmest, bluest waters in the world. The theory when the Gowanus was built in 1869 was that tidal action would keep it flushed despite the lack of an outlet at one end. It didn't work. Instead, every single atom of over 200 industrial pollutants that poured into it in the last 140 years remains exactly where it was first deposited. Only three organic entities have ever emerged from the Gowanus intact enough to be identified. Two of them are under study at Area 51 in Nevada. The third was a guy named Guido, the canal being to mob squealers what the La Brea Tar Pits were to saber-toothed tigers. By the way, the Gowanus has the special distinction of being one of only two waterways in the U.S. that have ever caught fire. Regardless of water temperature on race day, wetsuits will not only be allowed but required. And not just some thin neoprene job, either, but a full industrial dive suit certified to underwater demolition standards including hard shoes and a metal helmet with an air hose to the surface. Volunteers assisting swimmers out of the water will not be working with rubber gloves but will be using remotely operated robotic arms like the ones used in processing fuel for atomic weapons.

In the early 1900s, the borough of Brooklyn was overlaid with so many trolley cars that it was almost impossible to cross a street without having to dodge a few, which is why the local baseball team was called the Dodgers. This tells you a little about what the bike leg of IM-Brooklyn might be like.

In addition to the standard equipment normally associated with a bicycle race, a Kryptonite chrome steel lock is highly recommended. This will be used to secure your bike to the rack while you're off doing the swim and, after T1, may be used as a defensive weapon by those participants who do not wish to add the weight of more formidable small-bore armaments tucked into a spare water bottle cage. Incidentally, the use of quick release wheel skewers will be discouraged. Those are mother's milk to many of the enthusiastic fans who will be lining the streets and who will be recognizable by their portable Mita diamond saws, which are capable of sawing through any kind of locking mechanism short of a chrome steel Kryptonite. Trust me when I tell you that any violation of the "no outside assistance" rule will have consequences never contemplated by USAT. (Old local joke: Q: What did the kid from Brooklyn get for Christmas? A: My bike.)

The borough being surprisngly small, three loops will be required to complete the full 112 miles, affording racers multiple glimpses of unique sights. One of these is Floyd Bennett Field, the airport from which Douglas "Wrong Way" Corrigan departed for California in 1938 but ended up in Ireland instead. Cyclists are advised not to dwell overly long on this as they will soon discover that all the bike course directional markers have been 'jacked and the volunteer traffic directors thrown into the Gowanus Canal. The good news is that it's likely to be the fastest bike leg in Ironman history. As an old African motto puts it: The slowest antelope has the shortest life. 'Nuff said.

The run portion should be historic. The last time this many people were seen running through Brooklyn was when the security guards at the Canarsie Wal-Mart went on strike. Local law enforcement authorities will be given special briefings to acquaint them with the low probability that people wearing Speedos, Spandex and wristbands are carrying concealed weapons.

And how's this for a benefit: You'll finally learn where the term "Carbo Party" comes from. Among the unique sights to be savored by runners weaving in and out of inner city neighborhoods are the boyhood homes of former Murder, Inc. members Abe "Kid Twist" Reles and Allie "Tick Tock" Tannenbaum. You'll also get a glimpse of the Half Moon Hotel in Coney Island where Reles performed the incredible feat of heaving himself through a window while his hands were tied, his subsequent death ruled a suicide and therefore rendering him unable to testify against mobster Frankie Carbo. When Carbo was released for lack of evidence, his pals threw a...you guessed it!

And speaking of Coney Island, if you make it through all 26 miles without getting shot, mugged or run down by a psychopathic bicycle messenger, you'll have the distinct pleasure of finishing the World's Most Dangerous Endurance Event at Nathan's, site of the annual International Hot Dog Eating Contest. This is another renowned endurance event except, unlike in Ironman, you get disqualified for throwing up.

A splendid time is guaranteed for all!

NEXT TIME: Ironman Antarctica.

SWT Seeks S/BWT For WOs, If You Know What I Mean

Last month the Director of Central Intelligence announced a new, proprietary Facebook-ish service designed exclusively for use by covert intelligence operatives. (Seriously. Google "facebook for spies" and check it out for yourself.)

It makes sense, when you think about it: Spies can't exactly get on your standard, public social website and just say, "GS13 black op's case officer on R&R from Afghanistan seeks 30-something mid-level staff spook for a bit of embedded input-output-input-output. Comfortable safe house with fully-vetted staff a must. Is Boris Badenov? Crack my code and find out. Please, no freaks, geeks or real names."

So now we have iAmTri.com, a social site especially for triathletes. If this isn't final confirmation that three-sporters are different from the rest of the world, I don't know what is. Think trying to talk to a technology snoid is difficult? Wait until you accidentally bump into a triathlete at the local Starbie's. Better yet, bump into one who's training for an Ironman and try to strike up a conversation.

"So what's up?"

"Not much. Except that I have this chronic defribiminulating myetomaceous dendriconifer that I just can't seem to—"

"A chronic what?"

"Uh, um...hangnail."

"Ah."

"And I think that it might be a result of too much gammacytonucloeones titrated into my—"

"Too much what?"

"Butterfat. Anyway, I tried adjusting the seat angle on my backup Orbea because I read in this Algerian cycling magazine that fifty-six degrees is the new fifty-five, and my orthopedist said that anything more than that would give me planetary fascism, which of course is what I'm sure I have, so—'scuse me a second—Make that a half-caf latte with 1.5 ounces of soy, two shots of wheat grass and a protein boost—sorry, where was I? Oh yeah, next year's race schedule. Well, I was thinking about Oceanside but I read that the water's too cold, so..."

Stumbling Towards the Finish Line

You get the picture. But there are people who would actually be absorbed by that arcane soliloquy. They're called "other triathletes." And a small subset of those would actually interrupt to ask follow-up questions. They're called "also-trying-to-qualify-for-Ironman triathletes."

These people don't just need their own social web space. They need their own galaxy. iAmTri.com is kind of like both in one, at least if you believe in alternate realities. (Being married to a triathlete, I can assure you that they exist.) Herewith a random walk through some recent postings.

- Recently divorced 40-something male seeks 30-something female interested in movies, romantic walks in the moonlight and 250-mile bicycle rides across the Sahara in the middle of July.

- I'm yours, except for the first two weeks of October and two of the following four times which I won't know until February unless I qualify in Kona or possibly until April when the Lottery results are announced...

- Many-times divorced but extremely buff amateur dominatrix seeks subservient male who's into macrobiotic cooking, doing laundry and only seeing me for two or three hours a day, generally around meal and laundry times.

- Many-times divorced male seeks compatible life partner with advanced bike mechanic skills. Knowledge of Shimano Di2 circuitry is a plus, own set of metric hex wrenches a must. M/F/Bi/whatever, I could care less.

- Interested in solitary walks on distant beaches, discussing the Western canon of essential literature and sampling private pours from prestigious vineyards? Good: Here's a quarter so you can call someone who gives a ****. I'm looking for someone who isn't interested in any activity that doesn't get your heart rate up to at least 160 bpm.

- Are you the uninhibited type who likes to groan and gasp, work up a sweat, pump your brains out, experience ecstasy and then take a shower and have sex? Call me ASAP.

- SBF who just loves to travel off the beaten path. Louisville, Lubbock, Muskoka, Penticton, Tempe, Langkawi, Busselton...been to all of them and eager for more! So if you're up for a hot time in Port MacQuarie, Haikou, Florianopolis Island or Klagenfurt, park your bike in my UPS-compatible box and let's hit the road!

- Do you have the self-confidence to hang with a chick who can grind your ass into pulp at any distance over 20K? Yeah, right. Don't even bother calling.

- Interested in uncomplicated, purely physical nooky with no attachments, resentments or guilt? If so, please call my wife and have all the fun you want, just so she gets off my back so I can train in peace. God bless you.

The 500th Anniversary Exxon-Mobile Ironman
October 19, 2477 Event Summary

You'll need the latest version of Internet Explorer installed in your brain-implanted chip in order to read this article by direct cerebral injection. If you don't yet have Internet Explorer 3467.2, please download it right away by sliding your credit crystal across your neck.

Well, it was hot, windy and humid.

And what a sight it was as the participants lined up in Kailua-Apple Bay for one of the greatest sights in the world of sports: over 85,000 athletes in a single mass swim start, representing 89 of 90 states (Fairfax-Chernobyl having no remaining population, of course), all 9 countries of the United Nations, 158 U.S. protectorates and 3 planets.

Owing to the lack of any significant ocean swells, the mortality rate was mercifully low this year, with a whopping 99.2% of the field managing to survive to the turnaround point abeam the Fairwind LXXIII and fully 89.7% making it all the way to the Apple Postal Service Launch Ramp adjacent to the pier. Aside from the usual blunt head traumas and drownings, there were four cases of barrier failure in the mandatory full-body wetsuits, allowing toxins from the once-living ocean to seep in and dissolve the swimmers. Furthermore, long waiting times at the TSA's metal-detecting stations rendered the entrances to the thirty-six changing tents somewhat more lethal than usual, with Buddhist Male-to-Female Transsexuals topping the carnage charts for a fifth straight year.

The newly-reconfigured, 230-acre Google Oil Company swim-to-run transition area was the scene of amiable and excited chaos as racers frantically GPS-located their bikes. Volunteers from the aircraft carrier USS President Shamiqua Goldberg moored off the new island of Lo'ihi efficiently repaired blown tires with laser-annealing tools before racers even knew there was a problem. Ensign Mustafa "Maverick" Lombardi marveled at how little bike geometry has changed since the old days of triathlon. "Hard to believe," he said, "that a bike weighing only a pound and a half could look just like a model from the original Ironman." Well, it cost over three hundred grand, Ensign, so there's a bit of a difference!

First out of the tents was perennial swim winner Lars Jorgensen 23rd, earning himself the Microsoft Leather Goods premium for breaking his own record of 26 minutes, 18 seconds. This time the rest of the elite field refused to get sucked into his game, knowing that the Norwegian had likely blown himself up winning the swim and would be toast once he hit the Disney Coast.

On his way up Pay 'n' Save Hill (and, for the hundredth time, we have no idea why it's called that; rumors of an ancient temple of that name having once occupied the site are just an old Internet hoax), Jorgensen

Stumbling Towards the Finish Line

made good use of his specially-built, chrono-synclastically infidibulized Huffy Snazzycycle, barely pausing for the traditional bow toward the last square foot of actual lava left on the Big Island lovingly preserved under glass in the front window of Bianelli's, before hitting the first of the 94 golf courses that make up the legendary Ironman bike course.

Not conversant in Spanish, Jorgensen at first couldn't make out what the raucous crowd was trying to tell him, and wasted precious seconds checking his pants. (Not unreasonable, given the unfortunate incident that ruined a previous race for a top contender following the introduction of high-bidder Dairy Queen's Mongoose Milkshakes as the new Official Ironman Energy Drink. Hey, we've said it again and again: Don't drink anything on race day you haven't been drinking in training.) Pretty soon, though, the message sank in: Jorgensen's old rival, Rock Bamm Whamm, was already pedaling his way up the sixth fairway of the Trump Golf and Polo Club, oblivious to the angry local golfers who had to move aside to let him pass. Less than two minutes later some 300 more hopefuls had cleared the sand traps and were bearing down on the fabled Kamanawannadoya water holes. Jorgensen gamely kicked it into high gear, but he ended up tripping alarms on the WTC's remote lactic acid detectors and was pulled from the course for his own safety. Commented race director Twinkie Falafel: "I need another lawsuit like a I need another whatever."

Spectators in Hawi were hanging out of every window of the massive skyscrapers lining Steve Jobs Boulevard as the first group of cyclists appeared. They were led by Natalie Fraser-Fuhr-Huddle-Badmann, whose great-grandmother was the female who ended forever the sport's domination by men. Wearing a flashy number from her new line of women's athletic and office wear, Natalie led a tight peloton consisting entirely of off-duty cops hired to Taser any photographers taking the Empress of Ironman's photo without having paid a license fee. Having successfully dodged legal action stemming from a mass poisoning of carbo-party attendees who'd eaten contaminated pierogies she once endorsed, Natalie dropped that sponsor and is now supported by her new corporate sugar daddies, Consolidated Lug Nuts ("If my bike used lug nuts, they'd be Consolidated Lug Nuts, by golly!"). Boy, you can see their 800-watt logo shining on her helmet a mile away.

Natalie hit the Queen K on the return trip just as the last bodies were being pulled from Apple Bay and methodically stretched her lead mile by mile until it seemed only an alien abduction could keep her from the victory stand. That abduction showed up in the form of Miranda Cosmota, a third-generation Martian Pilates instructor who broke the species barrier some years prior when she became the first entrant in the new and experimental ET category following several years of lobbying by the ACLU. Miranda failed in her first attempt, but a rules modification that allowed her to stock aid stations with a private supply of guava-flavored sulfuric acid and use every one of her limbs enabled her to finish under the wire the following year. If she ends up on the podium again tonight, Director Falafel promises to figure out how to prevent Miranda's Mother Ship from accidentally scooping up another wing of the King Kam Hotel along with Miranda at the conclusion of the ceremony. ("It did let us squeeze another 2,000 competitors into T1, though," Falafel huffed defensively at last year's somewhat heated press conference.)

Just before the Energy Lab, Natalie waved supportively to Novojard Tensing, the Nepalese Sherpa trying to become the oldest person to complete the grueling 140.6 mile course. "After climbing Everest without oxygen over thirty times," the spry 107-year old told us earlier, "you'd think this would be a piece of cake." Not so fast, Novo: There's no Starbucks at the 26,000 level of *this* event!

Pausing at the metal detectors and neutron sniffers at T2, Natalie turned briefly and got a shock as a race official ran up and drew a yellow X through her race number. "No way was I drafting!" she insisted to the official, but had she in fact failed to give way as another's racer front wheel came within 200 yards of her rear wheel? No; it turns out Natalie had used nail polish not licensed by the Ironman organization. An old veteran at these sorts of things, Natalie didn't waste energy grousing about it but used her time in the Sin Bin to sign a few autographs, ably assisted by race officials with satellite-linked credit card machines.

Once out on the run, Natalie found herself with some competition. German star Otto Govaster had reached way down and found something (hope it wasn't a hit of Durabol again, Otto! Just kidding...) and was now going stride for stride with the female leader as they rounded the Hot Corner, so named for the lava flow that destroyed this part of Pixar-Kona eight years ago following the wholly unexpected eruption of long-thought-to-be-dormant Hualalai Mountain. Tipping their hats at the monument to the 28 athletes who'd lost their lives that day because they thought they were hallucinating and refused to go around, Natalie and Otto made quite a pair as they headed out toward St. Dell's Basilica, the world's largest cathedral and the official house of worship of the Ironman. (The original, six-pew St. Peter's that once graced the site is carefully preserved as an authentic miniature reproduction in the Basilica's gift shop, and also available on-line.) Military spy satellites temporarily reassigned to provide aerial footage of the race beamed pictures of the pair to billions of telesets around the world, and viewers were able to see every drop of sweat on their faces as each struggled to shake the other.

But Otto proved no match for the genetic miracle that was Natalie Fraser-Fuhr-Huddle-Badmann. The not-so-Grand Teuton dropped farther and farther back, and could only watch helplessly as his distaff rival faded into the distance, her trademark pink Nike plutonium running shoes eventually disappearing altogether. Govaster would be passed by no fewer than three dozen other racers before posting a dismal overall time of 6:52:07, the victim of his own hubris and, did we mention, far too much pre-race partying in the Welchie Memorial Pub high atop the Mauna Lani Towers.

Natalie, of course, won it once again and was immediately rushed into the medical tent and hooked up to an IV. Natalie was fine, but three pints of blood had to be drawn, the minimum necessary to ensure that an accurate screen could be taken for the 38,000 substances currently on the Intergalactic Anti-Doping Agency's (slogan: "IADA smack you for using drugs") banned list. (The list is now species-specific, it having come to light only recently that water to a Venusian is like adrenaline to an Earthling.) At the award banquet along the airport's north-south runway the following evening, Natalie modestly shrugged off her achievement, attributing all of her success to Red Bull, flagship product of the company she bought following her victory here in 2473. As usual, Natalie donated her first prize of $134 million to a local charity; this year it was the Charles Schwab Home for Retired PGA Tour Professionals.

In closing remarks, Director Falafel predicted that next year's event was going to be "hot, windy and humid."

A splendid time was had by all.

IRONING OUT IRONMAN
How to Improve the World's Toughest Race

Don't get me wrong: I love Ironman. I wouldn't actually *do* one even if wild crows were pecking out my eyeballs, but I love the sport nonetheless, in much the same way I love, say, crocodile wrestling or *Fear Factor 13: Flirting with Plague*. Which is to say, as a spectator.

But I understand Ironman better than most active non-participating fans, being married to someone afflicted with MESS (Maniacal Endurance Sports Syndrome) and knowing an awful lot of MESS-ed up athletes. Having watched otherwise level-headed people compete in Ironman races around the world, I think I'm eminently qualified to comment on how the sport might be improved, if only those pig-iron-headed know-it-alls at WTC would wake up and smell the VOG.

Herewith a sure-fire set of ideas for ensuring that our favorite sport doesn't go the way of *Gigli*.

1 – The first idea is so absurdly obvious it's hard to fathom that no one's thought of it before:

Make it shorter.

I've thought about it a lot and have come to the conclusion that just about everything that's wrong with Ironman is due to its length. What kind of sense does it make to stage a race that's so long some people can't even finish it? *King Kong* is too long also, and there's nothing that can be done about that now because it's a one-shot deal (okay...one-shot and two remakes). But Ironman can still be edited. Just think of all the benefits.

For one thing, you can get rid of the medical tent, relieving psychic turmoil and buying back some finish line space. Upwards of 13% of all entrants end up in the medical tent, making the finale of the world's most prestigious athletic event look more like an airplane crash investigation than a sporting contest. A cot and a puncture wound in a M*A*S*H tent is why 90,000 people a year compete for a slot?

TThe cost savings alone would be enormous, starting with a lot fewer bananas, water bottles and support personnel. Then there's the reduction in wear and tear among spectators, something race directors have failed to take into consideration from the very beginning. Not to mention equivalent (and sometimes even more severe) wear and tear among the athletes, despite their much-ballyhooed conditioning. Basic corporate economics here, WTC: Why pummel your prime customer base so badly that they can only do business with you once or twice a year? Get the distance down low enough to where an athlete can do thirty, forty races a year and we're talking some serious entry fee revenue here, my friend.

Stumbling Towards the Finish Line

As an added benefit, you foster better relationships with the community. Let's be honest: Not everybody in the deceptively tranquil and purportedly Aloha-soaked Kailua-Kona looks at the annual World Championship the way Kirsti Alley looks at a Mallomar. For one thing, they don't like their main roads getting shut down, a frustration they like to vent by inventing their own sports, like the perennial, week-before-race-day favorite, "Let's see who can drive his 40-ton semi closest to a cyclist without getting a ticket." If the Ironman were entirely confined to a four-block area surrounding the corner of Ali'i and Kuakini Highway and set up so that access to the Blockbuster and Starbucks on Palani remained uninterrupted, why, I'm just guessing that there'd be one or two fewer dirty looks from the guy hawking timeshares from that little booth down by Pancho & Lefty's.

2 – Another one I can't believe no one's thought of yet:

Let's beef up the aid stations.

Mine is not a sophisticated palate and has been described by various snobby acquaintances as roughly akin to a hockey puck when it comes to culinary discrimination. But even I can see that slurping some sucrostic glop out of a foil packet hardly ranks among the world's great gustatory experiences (although I'm told that, when mixed with a goodly dollop of sweat, a certain intriguing piquancy may be achieved).

Try to imagine another event where you pay hundreds of dollars to enter, thousands more to travel there, and all they serve you on the "Big Freakin' Day" is glorified candy bars and sugar water. Out of *disposable bottles*, no less.

It doesn't have to be this way. What would be so hard about a slight upgrade of the menu? And speaking of menus, why does every athlete have to ingest the same stuff as every other athlete? We've got people from Ghana, Liberia, Ecuador and Detroit, and we feed them all the same stuff. What happened to this joyous celebration of multiculturalism the Ironman is supposed to represent?

At a lot of golf courses on the Big Island, there's a telephone mounted on the tee box of the ninth hole that's connected to the restaurant at the club house. There's also a printed menu where the phone book would normally go. You use the phone to place an order before teeing off, then pick up your food as you make the turn to the back nine. Simple, effective, and greatly appreciated by patrons.

So here's what I'm thinking. You know those giant Timex mileage markers? Replace them with menus. Then, a hundred yards later, have a bank of telephones. After athletes pass the menus, they'll have plenty of time to mull over their choices and be ready to call them in when they get to the phones. (Revenue-generating idea: Make them pay phones.) By the time they hit the aid station, their orders will be ready to go.

I keep reading in all these triathlon magazines that there's no reason a healthy diet can't be appealing and delicious as well, so even the kind of limited offerings one expects in the middle of a race should reflect that. What exhausted and numbed-out athlete wouldn't appreciate an appetizer of pâté de foie gras garnished with sprigs of parsley and radish curls, followed half a mile later by a little roast venison with mint sauce accompanied by julienne of potatoes and epinards d'Seville?

Which brings me to another thing: Is there anything in the Ironman rule book about alcohol out on the course? Because it seems to me that washing all of this down with a glass or two of '87 Montrachet would be just the ticket in more ways than I can count. The beneficial effects of red wine are well-established and need no elaboration here, and for athletes, the upside of quaffing in general is even more pronounced. You think PowerBars give you a nice glucose jolt? Slam down a few quick brewskis and you'll get an instant chemistry lesson in the three-step conversion of methyl alcohol into glycogen. There's a reason for that line-up of 5,700-litre beer trucks at the finish line of the Ironman European Championship in Frankfurt, and it isn't to keep the oompah band happy.

And, finally: You know how elite athletes don't worry too much about three-minute penalties anymore, having discovered that using the time to stretch a little and collect themselves can actually improve their overall times? Well, why not make the aid station meals sit-down affairs? White tablecloths, lightstick candles after sundown, table-side salad prep? If Ironman is eighty percent mental, I can't think of anything that would better prepare the mind for those last difficult miles than a relaxing dinner with fellow competitors, topped off with a short snifter of Hennessey and a choice Montecristo stogie.

3 – What's the biggest problem for Ironman racers other than not dying?

I'll tell you what it is: It's boredom. Mind-numbing, will-sapping tedium. Hawai'i is gorgeous, but when you're dragging your butt along the Queen K at barely the speed of smell, it's just one damned chunk of lava after another.

People play all sorts of weird mental games to keep themselves in the moment. Or out of it, depending upon your point of view. They count stripes in the road, or try to recall all the lyrics to "Louie, Louie," or attempt to resolve intricate scientific conundrums, like, "Why does my left quadriceps feel like I've just been bitten by a great white?"

None of this is necessary, which brings me to this suggestion: Issue every participant an iPod, a Blackberry and a Bluetooth headset.

Think of it: You're running along feeling like Dick Cheney in an aerobics class. You reach down to your belt and suddenly you've got Bob Marley wailing "You can make it if you really try..." right in your ear. Is that motivational or what?

Concerned that friends and family back home don't know how you're doing because Ironman.com is on the fritz and all they can get is an endless loop of Mark Allen doing Guido Sarducci impressions? Call 'em up! Or check in at the office! Or find out how Brad and Angelina are doing! A few years ago when my wife was having a particularly tough time at mile 9 of the run, I filled her in on the O.J. verdict. Boy, did she appreciate that timely update. Properly equipped, though, she wouldn't have to be so dependent on me for news.

Did you know you can play on-line poker on a Blackberry? Tell me there could be a greater rush in this world than going all-in with two-seven off suit while heading down into the Energy Lab.

And, hey...I just thought of something else: You wouldn't have to stop at those chintzy pay phones to call in your food order!

* * *

Next time: Neutralizing the unfair advantage of stronger and faster racers and other ideas for improving Ironman.

Ed. note: If editing a Gruenfeld column for Ironman.com is painful (which it is), "Ironing Out Ironman" set new records in pain management. In one quick and easy-to-read column he managed to piss off virtually the entire no-sense-of-humor triathlon community. "Make it shorter?" asked one reader. "It's an Ironman, it needs to be 140.6 miles." (I don't think they quite got Lee's humor.) Race officials were hardly impressed with his "take music and a phone" idea, while Ironman officials, who banned Chuckie Veylupek from the world championship for years because he took a few sips of beer from a spectator, were none-too-impressed with the concept of a "glass or two of '87 Montrachet."

Oh, and how'd you think PowerBar and Gatorade reacted to the "glorified candy bars and sugar water" comment?

It's a miracle I still have hair – although my wife says it started to go grey after Lee came on board with his column.

What's Latin for "Ironman"?

Ed. note: This was one of Lee's cleverest pieces, but you really have to work your way through the (ahem) "Latin" to get the full effect.

Every great sporting event tries for an extra touch of class to make the tailgaters think they're really at the opera. The Super Bowl uses Roman numerals in its name (which is going to be a little tough to unravel 43 years from now when it's "Super Bowl LXXXVIII"). Academy Award presenters are no longer permitted to say "The winner is..." because it sounds too much like a NASCAR event, so they say "The Oscar goes to..." instead, which I personally appreciate because every time I heard "And the winner is..." in the old days, I felt like throwing on a John Deere hat, popping a cold one and changing a tire in sixteen seconds flat.

WTC really needs to do something along those lines as well, and my suggestion is that they declare Latin to be the official language of the Ironman. All else aside, they'll get a license fee every time somebody says "nostrum" or "peccadillo" on television.

Once Latin is officially installed as the lingua franca of triathlon's crowning event, people are going to need some help getting used to it. We offer the following to get things kicked off right.

* * *

Non focus intensa, zephyr blasto á kiester.	"If you are not careful, the wind will knock you aside."
Non gustatoria competitum non gustatoria precompetitum.	"Don't eat anything when racing that you haven't eaten while training."
Competitum victoriat velocipedum.	"The race is won on the run."
Corrolary: Competitum non victoriat natatorium.	"The swim doesn't mean squat."
Initiatato supra velocito, morte rapide.	"It is not a good idea to start out too fast."
Voyagemus CCXXVII kilometers initiat cum obtainema locato.	"The journey of 140.6 miles begins with getting a slot."
Non dependas casino Ferrous; probablismus stratosphericus.	"Relying on the Ironman lottery for your slot should not be your sole strategy."
Non obscura logos adverteria con pedae. Sans "paters sucrose," admitta supra DDDM sistersas.	"Keep your feet off the banners at the swim start. If it wasn't for these 'sugar daddies,' your entry fee would be $16,000."
Certaintente thermo et zephyra et aquaticos— non vocalo par infante obnoxioumas.	"It's going to be hot, windy and humid—deal with it."
Non supra aero circolo—blastima á thermo.	"Do not overinflate your tires—they'll explode when it gets hot."
N'alia mephisto ontologia nymic "Mons Remitta et Retento." N'alia proviso merde.	"Nobody knows why the hell it's called 'Pay ,n' Save Hill.' Nobody gives a darn, either."
Admitta non proviso punctuta gratis.	"Your entry fee doesn't include a free IV."
Athletico psychopathalogicas extremis!	"This is a rather curious sport, is it not?"
Visio merde! Morte imminenta!	"You look great! Only a few miles to go!"
Telefonico IX-I-I immediamenta!	"Good job! Almost home! Hang in there!"
Musette del competitorum primum est sextet del Heineken.	"What on earth is that in Welchie's special-needs bag?"
Bitchem grindus toto munda.	"Toughest endurance race in the world."
Decorum officio zephyr-vacuuo-assisto nebuloso á vaporum. Disobediementos implicato disqualifactotum.	"The rules on drafting are quite clear. Compliance is advised."
Que filio caninas zephyr-vacuuo-assisto redux, rendus rectum novo.	"If that SOB drafts off me one more time, I'll tear him a new one."
Assistimi XVI ex nihilo aqua crocodillo.	"Aid station 16 just ran out of Gatorade."
Necessitum educatus urinario non discontinuum.	"One must learn to accommodate bodily needs without getting off the bike."
Pomme-pasta regurgitato continuum.	"Boy, I sure love these pierogies!"

WE THREE SPORTS OF TRIATHLON ARE
Kona Karols for Obsessed Competitors

When we landed in Kona last week, my wife said, "Boy, it's just like Christmas, isn't it?"

A lot of people who race Ironman think the World Championship is like Christmas in October. So why shouldn't The Big One have its very own Christmas-y songs?

SOMEONE DIDN'T FINISH TODAY
(to the tune of "Santa Claus is Coming to Town")

> *You drafted all day*
> *Cut corners, too*
> *Drank a bunch of stuff your girlfriend handed to you*
> *Someone didn't finish, today*
>
> *You shouldn't have blocked*
> *You had no excuse*
> *Your helmet came off "because the buckle was loose?"*
> *Someone didn't finish, today*
>
> > *The marshal saw you drafting*
> > *But that's no way to win*
> > *He knows that friends have jogged with you*
> > *And he's put you in the Bin*

Oh...

> *He's making an "X"*
> *He's marking it twice*
> *He just found out that you're not very nice*
> *Someone didn't finish, today*

Stumbling Towards the Finish Line

O, HOLEY TUBE
(to the tune of "O Holy Night")

O, holey tube
I can't believe you failed me
My tire's flat and I don't have a spare

Where are my tools?
I thought I had a sad-dle
I lost that too when I went flying through the air

I, trained so hard
And then
I hit a pot-hole
How dumb can you get?
I feel like I
Am such a schmuck.

Oh...I am screwed
Don't even have a cell
I'm hungry. I'm cold.
And I am eigh-ty miles from home.

Never again
I've had it with triathlon
It's much too hard and my butt is aflame

From now on
I think I'll stick to bowling
It's much more safe and it's just a dime a frame.

GOD HELP YE, BURNED-OUT TRIATHLETE
(to the tune of "God Rest Ye Merry Gentlemen")

God help ye, burned out triathlete, it's time to feel dismay
You trained your butt off all year long to make it to this day
But you forgot to taper and so now you're gonna pay
You're a mess, and you haven't got a prayer, got a prayer
You blew it and you haven't got a prayer.

You trained all year on yogurt, raisin bread and rice galore
On race day they serve stuff that you have never seen before
Your stomach will go into shock, it won't know what to do
You'll be sick as hell and puking up your guts, up your guts
You'll have cramps and you'll be puking up your guts.

A million guys have done this race a million times before
There are coaches, books and videos and training camps galore
You didn't want to spend the dough and now you're stiff and sore
You thought that you knew better than them all, than them all
You thought that you were smarter than them all.

God speed ye, panicked Ironman, let nothing you delay
You started in October, hope you finish before May
Your training sucked, your will is weak, you're sure you're gonna lose
And for once, you are definitely right, you are right
But don't worry, there is still a way to fight.

When marshals are all out of sight, just draft and block at will
If you don't do it, rest assured, your competition will
There's room up on the podium, there's hardware to be had
There is simply no excuse to finish late, finish late
You have no excuse, it's time to pull your weight.

Some people do the whole Lab, adding minutes to their race
Just duck inside some trees and find a snug and cozy place
To nap and rest your tired legs before you hit the K

Stumbling Towards the Finish Line

Grab the lead and your sponsors will be glad, will be glad
If you win it you'll find they're not even mad.

You know first place is in the bag if you just take the bait
C'mon, you moralistic twit, don't just accept your fate
Think Barry Bonds and Marion Jones, Canseco and McGwire
They're disgraced but every one of them is rich, very rich
They're disgraced but all of them are very rich.

Elsewhere in the songbook

O LITTLE TOWN OF KAILUA-KONA
GO TELL IT TO THE MARSHAL
ALL I WANT FOR CHRISTMAS IS A NEW FRONT WHEEL
HARK! THE SPONSOR'S CHECKS BUY BLING
IT CAME UPON A MEDICAL TENT
IT'S BEGINNING TO LOOK A LOT LIKE A LIGHT STICK
LITTLE AID STATION BOY
ROCKIN' AROUND THE FINISH LINE
GRANDMA GOT RUN OVER BY AN ORBEA
And Mike Reilly's new theme song: SILENT NOT

How to be Cool at a Triathlon

Never mind splits. Is more important how you look than how you feel. Here's how:

Wearing the official T-shirt of the race you're in is not cool. Wearing one from another race is. Cooler still is wearing one from the race you're in but from ten years ago, implying that you're a veteran out to protect the record you set in the early days and which has never been beaten.

Wearing a skimpy bathing suit is pretty cool, but wearing one seemingly woven from (a single strand of) dental floss is cooler. Wearing a suit that can only be detected with an electron microscope is really cool, but only if you look offended when people stare at you, since they should realize that the suit's minimalist design is solely in the interests of hydrodynamic functionality.

Wearing a helmet is totally uncool and strictly for wuss-burgers still living with their parents. It is much cooler to bike bare-headed. Even cooler is spending the rest of your life in a hospital being referred to by the spouse and kids you left behind as "Rutabaga," since that is now the life form you most closely resemble. Looking excited and pumped for your first long-distance triathlon used to be cool, but isn't any longer. Now it's cool to mope around with a grim and pensive look on your face that clearly says to onlookers, *If I don't shatter the course record, Nike's gonna take away my Gulfstream.*

Drafting is moderately cool, especially if, when you get caught, you yell "How the hell else am I supposed to get ready for Rio!" at the top of your lungs after surfing the slipstream of the athletes who dragged you from one end of the bike course to the other.

Saving a half dozen seats for your friends at the Ironman awards banquet is pretty cool. Snarfing up two entire tables with duct tape and your Uncle Nunzio standing guard is way cool.

Wave starts are uncool. Mass starts consisting of 2,500 over-trained and anxiety-stricken maniacs smashing each other in the face and gonads is cool as hell, but only for the spectators, many of whom gave up an NHL playoff game just to see it.

Wiping your magic marker'd age off the back of your leg so your competition can't tell who you are is cool. Replacing the number with one from two age groups down is even cooler. Replacing it with "Relay" is way cool, although not quite as cool as writing, "If you can read this, you're too damned close."

Dumping more water on your head than in your mouth at the aid stations is cool, but not as cool as wearing a time-release Prozac patch on your neck.

Getting off the bike to pee is as uncool as you can get. Peeing while riding is much cooler. Coolest of all is peeing standing up on the pedals while ascending a 20% grade in a headwind in front of a group of drafters.

Stumbling Towards the Finish Line

Winning an Ironman-qualifying race and then turning down your slot because you already have one is cool. Proposing to the second place finisher that you turn it down for a cash payment of a $1.000 is not cool. Doing it for $2,000 is.

Drinking two pots of black coffee before an Olympic distance tri is incredibly cool. (See also "Peeing on the bike" above.)

Coming into the bike-to-run transition area with your bike over your shoulder and a wheel bent in half is very cool, but not as cool as crossing the finish line with a broken arm while dragging an exhausted Doberman whose jaws are still clamped around your ankle.

Screaming at the aid station volunteers for "Two parts erg and one part water!" is sort of cool, but not as cool as throwing it at them if they didn't get the proportions right. The coolness of yelling for Gatorade and then dumping all of it over your head is still being hotly debated.

Running down a 55-59 competitor and then squeezing by her in the chute is mighty cool, but only if you're a 25-29 male.

Eating bagels and drinking ProOptibol before the Ironman is moderately cool, but not as cool as knocking back the "Tom Jones" special at Kona Amigos moments before the swim start and sticking a double-death bacon cheeseburger in your special-needs bag.

And you know you're a real triathlete if your favorite dessert is an IV drip.

If Ironman was like the Tour de France

After you!
No, after you!
No, please, you go ahead!
No, no, you go ahead!
No, really...!

I wasn't planning to watch this year's Tour de France.

It's not that I have a problem with an athletic event whose outcome is determined by which team has the cleverest doctor. It's just that, if you don't know in advance who's taking what, it's difficult to know whom to root for. Should I bet on the tried-and-true EPO guys, or maybe go with Team Transfusion, or throw caution to the wind and take a chance that Champs-de la-Androstenedione will ride in on this year's breakthrough pharmaceutical?

But my wife Cherie was glued to the Tour, as she is with any sporting event featuring athletes pushing themselves to the limit. (How many households do you know of where the Sports Illustrated subscription is in *her* name?) So I watched a little here and there, and it was occasionally exciting, but then I bet a wad of dough on Cavendish, and we all know how that ended up so I tuned out again.

Until I heard that the leader's margin over second place was twenty-three seconds going into the last day. Twenty-three seconds! And the guy in third was only a few seconds behind that! Cheating or no cheating, that was going to be one tremendous final day.

So I got up at 4:45 am, gathered together the requisite endurance supplies (soda pop, HoHos, pork rinds, etc.) and settled in on the couch to savor what was sure to be the best man-to-man athletic showdown since Ali v. Frazier.

"They're not racing," Cherie said as she came downstairs on her way to a swim workout.

"What?"

She pointed at the screen. "They're not racing."

"What?"

"They're not racing."

I looked at the television. There were Paul and Phil in the announcing booth, the weather looked beautiful, the riders were mounting their bikes...what the hell was she talking about? "What the hell are you talking about?"

"It's the last day," she said, stuffing a towel into her bag. "They don't race."

"What?"

"It's tradition." She slung the bag over her shoulder and headed for the garage. "Etiquette. Whoever's winning on the last day, they let him win."

Now I knew she was just kidding. These guys had dreamt about the Tour since they were kids, had spent years training, they'd just dragged themselves through a couple of thousand miles of hellish cycling, there were millions in endorsements riding on the outcome, and she was trying to get me to believe that they were going to concede the yellow jersey to a rider with a *twenty-three second* lead on the last day? Because of *etiquette*? No way I'm falling for that gag.

Then again, why was she leaving the house to go swimming instead of watching the last stage?

I'd always wanted to marry Miss Right. I just didn't know her first name would turn out to be "Always". Sure enough, a bunch of athletes whose idea of "etiquette" is swallowing enough steroids to turn a housefly into Mothra pedaled lazily in formation as they ushered the leader into Paris. I thought back to the year Lance Armstrong got his handlebars caught up in a spectator's tote bag. After he hit the pavement, another rider held everybody up to wait for him.

Excuse me? He did what? What a load of hooey. Imagine Janet Evans stopping mid-race to tread water so the swimmer in Lane Two can adjust her goggles, or Holyfield waiting up so Tyson can catch his breath. This is supposed to be athletic competition, not ballroom dancing. Yet the Tour is full of stories like that.

So as I munched away on the pork rinds, I got to thinking: What if other athletic events also had this kind of tradition?

What about Ironman?

* * *

Only a mile left in the run when a spectator yells out to Normann Stadler that Chris McCormack had to stop to tie his shoe.

Stadler, powering down Pay 'n' Save Hill, stumbles to a halt. *"Ach, du lieber Gott!"* he gasps. "What a terrible thing!"

Faris al-Sultan comes tearing around the corner. Stadler throws out an arm to stop him.

"What are you doing!" al-Sultan demands as he nearly falls to the pavement.

Stadler folds his arms and announce imperiously, "Macca has stopped to tie his shoe."

"You are kidding."

"I am not."

Al-Sultan's eyes grow wide. "You. Are. Kidding!"

"No. It is true."

Al-Sultan turns and looks toward the Queen K. He sees McCormack down on one knee, fiddling with something near the pavement. He turns back to Stadler:

"You're right, Normann. We must wait."

The crowd of spectators, utterly enchanted and moved nearly to tears, roars its approval. Less than six minutes later, Stadler, al-Sultan and McCormack cross the finish line holding hands.

* * *

Natascha Badmann does a hair-raisingly fast one-eighty at the bike turnaround up at Hawi, then stands on her pedals to gain even more speed as she storms through the aid station. She knows she's almost a minute behind leader Desiree Ficker and has to make up the time.

As she tops the rise leading out of town and begins heading downhill, Badmann suddenly screeches to a halt. There in front of her is Ficker, off her bike and scratching frantically at her fanny pack.

Re-mounting and pulling up close, Badmann asks her what's wrong.

"I though I had three GUs," Ficker replies, desperation in her eyes, "but I can only find two."

"No!" Badmann exclaims. As she gets off her bike, she notices Ficker looking back toward the turnaround. When she twists away to follow her gaze, Badmann sees Hillary Biscay powering her way over the top of the hill. The two women watch as Biscay slips into a higher gear and gathers speed. By the time she draws near she's doing almost fifty mile per hour.

Badmann throws out an arm and body slams Biscay to the pavement.

Her limbs splayed into awkward disarray, Biscay slowly opens her eyes and stares up at Badmann. "What the hell...?"

Badmann jerks a thumb to indicate Ficker and bends down, putting her face close to Biscay's. "Desiree's missing a GU," she intones solemnly.

Biscay, just beginning to focus again, looks over at Ficker. "Oh my God."

Badmann nods.

Newly stunned, Biscay puts her hands to her profusely bleeding head. "Oh! My! God!"

"Do you have an extra?"

Biscay, desolate, shakes her head.

"Here comes Michellie," Ficker says.

Sure enough, Michellie Jones is screaming down the hill. Thinking fast, Badmann grabs Biscay's shattered bike and hurls it beneath the 2006 champ's wheels, sending her arcing over the handlebars. Even before Jones is finished tumbling down the steep grade, Badmann is jogging along at her side. "Desiree needs a GU!" she calls out.

"Oh my God!" Jones shouts back as she continues to roll. "Give her one of mine!"

The footage, played over and over on the Larry King Show during an interview with the three women, eventually replaces the shot of Julie Moss crawling toward the finish as the iconic symbol of all that is great and good about Ironman.

Seventy-five-year-old Sister Madonna Buder, who sped past the three—and past 657 other women who stopped to lend assistance to Ficker—was the only female finisher and therefore the overall winner of the event. But after being righteously vilified by press and public alike, the nun had her medal taken away and was banned from the sport for life.

"Poor sportsmanship," sniffed WTC spokesperson Blair LaHaye.

Ed. note: Lee missed out on one real-life act of sportsmanship in 2000. David Bailey and Carlos Moleda, competing in the handcycle category, raced neck and neck for virtually the entire bike race. At the hot corner Bailey lost control of his cycle and fell. Rather than take off, Moleda waited for Bailey to get back on his cycle, then the two resumed their race. Bailey would eventually win.

Eight Things Ironman Can Learn From the Olympics

Having just pigged out on sixteen days of Vancouver glory (ask me anything about curling), I couldn't help but think about the parallels between the Olympics and the Ironman World Championship. There's much to be learned, so I offer these lessons:

1. **Indoors is better than outdoors.** This is as obvious as the 1260 double McTwist. Nearly a dozen Alpine skiing events were postponed in Vancouver, some by as much as a week, by bad weather. All of those events took place outside. None of the indoor events was affected, at least if you don't count the occasional failure of a battery-powered pseudo-Zamboni. Move the Ironman indoors, and it will make for a much fairer race, under repeatable conditions so records mean something year to year. If you're worried about tradition, don't be: There's plenty of tradition for ignoring tradition. Ice skating started out on rivers and lakes, resulting in all kinds of unfortunate incidents involving nature. Once they wised up and moved the rivers and lakes indoors, all that was left to get in the way of keeping to a brisk schedule was the need to clear the bodies off the short-track speed skating rink. So if moving indoors was good enough for Hans Brinker and the Edmonton Oilers, it ought to be good enough for Chrissie Wellington and Craig Alexander.

2. **Give medals to the winners.** Now they give wreaths and trophies. Even Miracle-Gro can't make wreaths last more than a week or two, and you can't wear a trophy. If you wear a medal going through the metal detector at the airport on the way home and set it off, you can slap your head and shout, "Oh, wait! I must have forgotten to take off my *Ironman World Championship medal*!" at the top of your lungs. Try doing that with a wooden bowl. And while we're on the subject, why not award silver and bronze as well? Under the current system, the race has one male and one female winner, with everyone else assigned the status of whale dung. Coming in second or third at Ironman should be pretty cool. (The only place I personally have ever been second or third is in line at Dunkin' Donuts.) Wouldn't it be nicer to refer to Chris Lieto as the 2009 "silver medalist" instead of "first loser"?

3. **Ignore the age groupers.** In fact, ignore everybody below fourth place overall. I grew up on Olympic television coverage. Until I was thirty-four, I thought there were only a few dozen competitors in the entire Games and only two or three who were allowed to compete in any one event. In 1984 I remember walking into the L.A. Coliseum and thinking, "Hey...who the hell are all these people!" Turns out, in case you didn't know, Lindsay Vonn and Julia Mancuso weren't the only skiers, Shaun White wasn't the only snowboarder, and there were actually more than three figure skaters in Vancouver. There are *thousands* of people in the Olympics, some of whom train for four years then travel eight or

nine thousand miles to the Games only to find themselves edited out, because it works very well for television. Ironman, on the other hand, insists on showing age groupers, which might explain why NBC paid the IOC $822 million for the rights to televise the Games while Ironman has to produce its own show which is then sandwiched in between infomercials for the Popeil Pocket Fisherman and reruns of "The Waltons." We'd do a lot better by pretending there are only four or five people in the whole race and then using some creative editing to create rivalries that can seemingly only be settled with knives.

4. **Pimp out the Carbo and Award banquets**. Contrary to popular belief, figure skating and gymnastics are not the hottest tickets at the Games. Figure skating used to be, but then ticket buyers started figuring out that there are more than three competitors, and they didn't feel like sitting through 150 renditions of "Feelings" or the theme from *Titanic* just to get to the two or three skaters who can actually remain upright for four minutes in a row. Now the hottest tickets at the Games are the Opening and Closing Ceremonies. Back in the old days, the Opening Ceremonies were used to introduce the athletes, and the Closing Ceremonies were for Americans to misbehave in front of the Queen. But sometime during the Cold War, the organizing committees decided to get into the competitive spirit and see if they could outdo one another in ways that would have made Nero hide in shame. All of these shows are characterized by three things: cramming as many cute, multi-ethnic schoolchildren as possible onto the floor, trotting out the indigenous peoples as a belated apology for having taken away their land in the first place, and raising obscure symbology to a high art to the point where a twig or a piece of burnt toast is claimed to represent man's inhumanity to man as expressed through the strivings of the proletariat in the early seventeenth century. And people pay hundreds to see it. So what Ironman needs is opening and closing ceremonies consisting of eight thousand Hawaiian dancers, musicians and fire-eaters; an Ironman eternal flame powered by a Saturn V rocket; and the Rolling Stones.

5. **Break up the event**. In our house, it's 24/7 Olympics-watching every two years. If you've got a good cable lineup and a fast Internet connection, you can watch any event you want from start to finish, with or without commentary, and it takes sixteen days to laugh and cry with the winners as all 27,000 medals are given out. During that time, we're exposed to 8,000 commercials and so many Up Close and Miserable features that the pimple on Lindsay Vonn's nose takes on more importance than earthquakes, tsunamis or the economy. Ironman, on the other hand, is a single day one-and-done. So the first thing we should do is break it up into three events, done on three different days, with gold, silver and bronze winners in each one. Then we come back on Day Four with the "Ironman Combined," where we do them all at once, except everybody gets four runs, just like in the bobsled, and there are multiple distances to boot: sprint, international, Grand Long Course and Super-I. If a speed skater can get five or six cracks at a medal at a single Games, why can't triathletes get a few, right? Hardware for everybody!

6. **Change WTC to FII**. That stands for *Fédération Internationale de Ironman*. Let's face it: Everything sounds classier in French.

7. **Add style points**. It shouldn't just be about who gets from here to, uh, *here*, faster. We should reward doing it with a little pizzazz. Ten seconds off your total time for the best looking bike, twenty for the coolest uniform, thirty for the slickest helmet, forty for the best crash of the day and fifty for not peeing while running.

8. **Add some new sports**. How about these:

   • Synchronized Ironman

   • Three-man team pursuit

   • Rhythmic Ironman

   • Freestyle (should be way cool on the bike course)

   • Bobsled

Give me a little more time to think about it and I can easily get this up to a two-week event.

Adding a Fourth Event

Anybody who runs a leading edge business will tell you the same thing: Innovate or die.

Steven Jobs invents the Apple computer, and by the time he's finished bragging about it, the company gets snatched away and given to some guy who used to sell soda. Took Jobs another ten years to figure out he needed an iPod a year to keep from losing it again.

Did Bill Gates sit on MS-DOS? NASA on the Mercury capsule?

No. They got creative and kept on going.

So you have to ask yourself: Just how long do the Ironman higher-ups figure they can get away with only three legs in the world's toughest triathlon? Are they really ready to let this great event go the way of film cameras and vinyl LPs?

It doesn't matter if it's still called a *tri*-athlon, either. We still "dial" telephones that have no dials and nobody cares about that, so they'll get used to this, too.

So what do we do for a fourth event? Here are a couple of ideas.

- **Archery**: You know that Winter Olympics biathlon where cross-country skiers have to stop and shoot guns at targets while their hearts are still doing about 195? (I love that event because it so mimics things we have to do in real life.) Suppose Ironman athletes had to come out of the water and then shoot half a dozen arrows at targets, with thirty seconds taken off their total time for each bull's-eye and thirty added if they miss the target altogether and hit something in the massage area. Can you imagine the intricate strategy in trying to figure out whether or not slowing down for the last hundred yards of the swim so you can steady yourself is worth it? Hey wait, here's a better idea: You have to get off the bike every ten miles and do it. (I love that because it so mimics the Olympic biathlon.)

- **Wheelbarrow racing**: That's the two-man event where one team member holds the other's legs in the air as he runs along on his hands. Takes two people, though, so for the professionals you make the second man the athlete's agent. I can just see the agent pushing as hard as he can even though his client is mostly running with her face rather than her hands. "She'll clean up later!" the agent shouts to concerned spectators as the sponsors he's signed up cheer lustily from the sidelines. Hey wait, here's a better idea: Let the athlete hold the agent's legs. My guess is we'd see faster times and possibly a few fatalities.

- **Boxing**: One of the problems I have with Ironman is that there's not enough head-to-head competition. Sure, once in a while you see two people running a few feet apart, but aside from playing with each other's minds there's not much one can do to materially affect the performance of the other. So what if we were to pair off competitors by whatever position they're in at, say, the Energy Lab exit, slap on 15-ounce gloves and let them duke it out for three rounds. (Age groupers would have to wear headgear, but not the pros.) That way you'd have a chance to, literally rather than figuratively, put some really serious hurt on your closest competitor, and knocking him out of the race would take on a whole new meaning.

- **Poker**: No Limit Texas Hold 'Em in T2. Everybody starts out with a hundred chips, each one worth ten seconds off the clock. It's up to the athlete how long he wants to stay in the game. Couple of all-in semi-bluffs with an ace-rag, score pocket rockets against an empty flush draw behind the big stack, and you could win the whole race without ever stepping foot on the run course.

- **Pool**: Something that's always been faintly annoying about Ironman is that a complete klutz could win it because there's hardly any hand-eye coordination involved. So let's set up a hundred pool tables in Hawi like that scene from *The Color of Money* and have a playing field that favors the finely coordinated for a change. Everybody starts with a full rack and doesn't leave the table until fourteen balls are down except the eight. We'd have to think about whether competitors could stash their own cue sticks in their special needs bags.

- **Fencing**: What a riot this would be with real swords and exhausted athletes! Of course, we should probably have it after the run so it's near the medical tent.

That's only a handful of the many possibilities. Another idea I considered was chess, but too many fights would break out and, besides, it's not very spectator friendly and would unfairly favor the Russians. Bass fishing came to mind but you couldn't do it at the world championship because, well, there are no bass in Hawai'i, and who'd want to train that hard just to get through a qualifier?

What about rhythmic gymnastics?

Hey wait: Figure skating!

Nah. The sport couldn't afford the scandals.

Advice for the New Owners

Anybody remember Victor Kiam? He's the guy whose wife bought him a Remington electric razor, a seemingly minor incident which led to one of the most famous catchphrases in modern advertising: "I liked it so much, I bought the company!"

True story, but not the last of its kind. I myself tried to buy Häagen-Dazs, Hostess and Sara Lee at various times in my career but wasn't able to put together a deal for several reasons, most having to do with an arcane financial concept called NSF which I learned about from reading a rubber-stamped imprint on one of my personal checks.

Just last month, though, a triathlete who apparently did not have this obscure "NSF" problem decided he liked Ironman so much that he bought that whole company. At least that's what he claimed. I have it on good authority that he needed an entry into the World Championship but all the community slots on eBay had been snapped up, so he snapped up WTC instead. (I have this recurring fantasy of doing something similar the next time I show up at an airport only to find that the airline "misplaced" my reservation. I make a phone call, then turn to the ticket agent and say, "I now own the airline. Find me a seat or find the door.")

Love of the sport notwithstanding, there's no reason not to make a buck at the same time. Victor Kiam got so rich off Remington that he had to buy the New England Patriots just to make sure he didn't have too much money. Ironman is perfectly poised to become a brand as well known among the masses as Coca-Cola, Remington and Enron, so my feeling is that the new owners should get themselves in gear to make that happen.

I've given WTC a lot of advice over the years. They've taken none of it. There are only two different meanings you can attach to that, and hey, I'm not the one who got sold, if you get my drift.

So I'm going to give the new owners the same opportunity I gave the old and see if they do a better job of paying attention when I offer up some free consulting. Starting right now.

The new owner is "Providence Equity Partners." You can tell a lot from a corporate name. It isn't voodoo science, either, like reading auras or body language. Companies spend millions on really smart consultants who help them craft corporate identities, so these names don't just come out of thin air. They're supposed to mean things.

A name like "Foundation for the Well-Being of Children All Over the Globe" tells you something. So does "Acme Radio Parts Company" and "Corleone Waste Disposal." You hear those names, you pretty much know what they do.

When you hear words like "equity" and "partners," you have no idea whatsoever what they do, but what you do know is that at least a few of the partners probably don't do Ironman (that the company's acronym spells "Pep" is pure coincidence) or even know what it is and are wondering why the heck they bought its owner. That, however, is plenty sufficient for me to start dispensing advice about how to make their latest investment throw off some serious shekels so that the partner behind the push to buy it ends up looking a lot better than if he was just trying to cop a free entry without qualifying.

I don't want to expose all my cards here—there's a concept called leverage I'll explain another time—so I'll just show the Pep company how a single event, the Ironman World Championship, can easily be re-engineered to take care of Providence Equity's short-term expectations.

Every year, some 90,000 athletes from all over the globe compete for about 2,000 Kona slots. I say let 'em all in. And while you're at it, double the entry fees.

Think about it. Right there you've got ninety million dollars in up-front revenue where you used to have less than a million. And you can forget about price elasticity and all that other macroeconomic hoohah you learned in college. Triathletes aren't like weekend 10K-ers who fret when their one pair of running shoes start to wear out. Triathletes think nothing of blowing a hundred bucks on a carbon fiber bottle cage to save three grams. You think someone with a $9,000 bike is going to balk at ponying up an extra $500 for a chance to compete in Mecca?

You might be asking yourself, "Why didn't the old owners think of that?" Well, they did, but they somehow convinced themselves that you couldn't cram more than 2,000 bikes onto the Kona pier. Used to be that they thought they couldn't cram 1,500, either, and before that it was 1,400 and before that 1,000.

See a pattern here? Human creativity is an amazing thing, and its primary stimulation is need. The new owners need to put 90,000 people into this race, and therefore they can. I know they can because I've already figured it out. Don't want to get into details but it involves leading-edge concepts such as "stacking" and doing away with unnecessary frills like showers, changing tents and aisles.

Now, obviously, not every spot can be considered primo, right? Well, where others see obstacles, I see lemonade. What you do is auction the bike locations. Highest bidder, best spot. Prime space will probably go to your pros, because their sponsors will put up the dough, but if some back-of-the-pack amateur wins himself a good row, so what? You've got a happy athlete and $15-20,000 in the bank with 29,999 bids yet to come. See where I'm heading with this?

It's a well-known fact of Ironman that race fees don't begin to cover the actual costs of putting on a race. We know because the old owners kept telling us that, so it's probably true and I believe them. Question I have is, what are you doing to make up the difference? I'm not a socialist, so this idea of equitable contribution and distribution bothers me. The model I like is the politically conservative philosophy of paying for what you use. So it should be with Ironman.

Stumbling Towards the Finish Line

Somebody who grabs a cup of water shouldn't suffer the same cost as someone who sweeps up three bottles of Gatorade, half a dozen PowerGels and some Fig Newtons. So let's put the aid stations on a cash basis. We can take ATM cards, too, and if you lose yours somewhere out on the course, I've got two words for you: micro loans.

T2 is going to be a bit of a problem, what with all those athletes speeding in and then running out on tired legs. What we should do is make the bike course a Figure 8, like those old demolition derbies in the Sixties. It'll give a whole new meaning to "Hot Corner" and should knock out about a third of the field.

Which brings us to the medical tent. There's no reason why someone who hydrates properly and manages not to get wiped out at the Hot Corner should subsidize the guy who drags himself in after 11:00 at night, slurps up three IV bags and gets enough medical attention from high-priced trauma physicians to start his own TV show. If the Mayo Clinic can charge for its services, why can't Ironman? And just to make sure there are no liability issues as a result of turning away disoriented athletes who didn't have enough sense to get their ATM cards back from the aid stations, the race can sell one-day insurance policies, just like USAT does. In fact, they should be mandatory. Who wouldn't pay fifty bucks for a top-notch insurance policy, especially if the deductible was only $500 with a $75 co-pay?

And what's with the free medals? Isn't anybody watching the bottom line here?

I got plenty more ideas, but it just occurred to me that I shouldn't be giving them away. This was just enough to whet their appetites.

I'm sure they'll get back to me for some more.

> *(Ed. note: I wouldn't wait by the phone. As a matter of fact, WTC did take Gruenfeld's advice. Once. It was called Ironman New York. How'd that work out for us, Lee?)*

Six Things We Don't Want to Hear at Triathlons Anymore

Awesome! Lookin' good! Whooohoooohooo!
Good job! Keep it up!

> —Aid station volunteer,
> Wildflower Triathlon,
> May 1, 1999,
> and I've got the videotape to prove it

Pushkin said that there are more ways to describe a sunset in Russian than in any other language, but what did he know? Surely English, the lingua franca of the civilized world (defined as those parts of the planet where English is spoken), sits atop the semantic ziggurat of expressive variety.

So how come we keep hearing the same words over and over? Have we become so complacent that we actually don't mind being repeatedly pummeled with such expressions as disgruntled, chilling effect, czar, slippery slope, partisanship and Anything-gate?

I hear this stuff and I'm all, like, what? (What scares me even more than cancer is that there are probably a few of you out there who actually understood that last sentence.)

To what do we attribute this explosion of uncreativity?

It's simple laziness, my friends. This is not too surprising, for reasons too numerous to mention, but where it doesn't make sense is among triathletes, probably the least lazy beasts since fish emerged from the primordial ooze and grew legs. So what better place to plant a seed for the tall oak of language rehabilitation?

Here are six things we ought not to hear at races anymore, along with some suggested substitutes.

1. **Awesome**: This is now probably the least awesome word in the language. It can apply equally to French fries, acts of God, a long course PR, Gummi Bears, great nooky and a subdural hematoma. If you hear someone yell "awesome" as you exit the water after a 2.4-mile, full-contact aquatic kickboxing match, think "not bad."

    How about: stupendous, outstanding, terrific, wonderful, awe-inspiring, astounding, fantastic, superb, splendid, sensational, marvelous, extraordinary, remarkable, magnificent or dazzling? Of course, those are just for the average performances, since all we're trying to do is find a replacement for "awesome," which we already know means "not bad." Next time, I'll come up with a few for truly over the top performances, but they'll likely be in Urdu, as there aren't any left in English.

2. **Give it up**: I'm not sure, but I think this means "let's have a round of applause." The reason I'm not sure is because, a mere handful of years ago, this phrase meant the same as, uh, well, "surrendering the pink," as Carrie Fisher put it. But what exactly do I give up when I "put my hands together," another idiom deserving of historical dustbinage?

"Let's hear it for…" is vastly preferable, as is "Let's make some noise for…" Come to think of it, "Put your hands together" is also hugely preferable to "Give it up."

3. **Good job**: This one is really interesting. The only people who ever hear it are back-of-the-packers, who are the ones specifically not doing a job when they're racing. Needless to say, I heard this one a lot before I got smart and gave it (in this case, triathlon) up. Whoever yells "Good job!" to a professional? What "Good job" really means is "We're amazed your heart is still beating," and there is not a thing even vaguely vocational about limping into the transition area entertaining a dehydration-induced fantasy of your PowerGels suddenly metamorphosing into Häagen Dazs rum raisin. Besides, "Good job" is more appropriate at the conclusion of an assigned task than at an intermediate step and might evoke in a delirious participant's mind the mistaken belief that she has in fact *done* a good job and is now free to enjoy the awesome six of Heineken back in the van.

How about, "There's at least one behind you" or "Keep it up"—the former a kind of left-handed motivational trick and the latter a subtle reminder that the soggy motel ice cubes within which nest the aforementioned Heinekens will have to hold out for another hour or two while you continue to do a good job.

4. **Whooohooohooo**: Not sure I spelled that correctly, but it's the same sound emitted at regular intervals by members of the Gabby Douglas Fan Club, hosts on *Saturday Night Live* when they're first introduced, and junior high school girls upon finding out that the last holdout among their friends just gave it up to the captain of the basketball team. I once suggested to my congressman that a bill be put forth to mandate that special chips be built into all U.S.-manufactured public address systems to automatically bleep this odious sound out, but it turned out his oldest daughter was an aerobics instructor whose livelihood depended on its periodic utterance and thus did my idea die aborning.

I'd considered "yippee," "yay" and "hooray" as substitutes, but was fearful that "way to go" or "go for it" might make untimely comebacks in the absence of some sound (as opposed to an actual word) requiring little in the way of rote memorization. So I think that *"eearooyurwheep!"* should do. It's difficult to phoneticize, but think of the sound that might result if you touched a red-hot poker to the anus of a wild boar.

5. **Lookin' good**: Let's face it—the only people who ever hear "Lookin' good!" are those who are decidedly *not* looking good, not looking good at all. "Lookin' good" means that the only thing awaiting you at the next aid station is the Angel of Death. "Lookin' good" means that, right now, you'd rather see Dr. Kevorkian with his medical bag than Raquel Welch naked.

   Of much more practical use would be "Almost there!" (inadvisable at mile 1 of the bike leg) or "How many fingers am I holding up?"

6. **Keep it up**. This is something I heard frequently when I was single (usually followed by "Dammit!") and I simply can't get used to hearing it shouted at females, so give it up, okay?

Living With an Injured Iron Psycho Beast

Ed. note: Hands down my favorite column. I am not sure if that's because I would never have the guts to write anything like this about my wife, or because it's just so funny. Oh, and in case you're wondering, Cherie is about the nicest woman on the planet. Lee, like myself, hears the words, "Why does she stay with him?" on a daily basis.

Needless to say, there is likely a tiny bit of exaggeration involved in this story. That said, though, when Cherie was laid low with an injury, I only called Lee's cell phone, never their land line. You know...just in case.

A few years ago I wrote an article for *Competitor Magazine* entitled "A Word to the Triathlon Widow(er)." It was a highly idealistic and somewhat romantic plea to the spouses or Significant Others of Ironman athletes, urging them to be as understanding as possible as their loved one pursues an idyllic and demanding dream.

A lot of people read that piece, copied it and passed it around, and to all of them I say this:

Please disregard it.

I've changed my mind.

You may have heard the old expression, "No captain ever proved himself on calm seas." Well, let me tell you, no Iron-spouse ever proved himself with a healthy triathlete.

If your Significant Other is a dedicated Ironman triathlete, at some point or other he or she is probably going to have a sidelining injury. Here's my suggestion if that should occur:

Shoot him. Immediately.

Trust me on this. It will be a mercy to both of you.

Some years ago my Iron Psycho Beast wife Cherie got creamed by another cyclist at Ironman Utah. It was to be the first time in eleven years she wouldn't be able to compete in Kona in October.

Let me explain something. Cherie is an accomplished woman. She has three college degrees and was a highly successful executive in the advanced technology industry making lots of dough.

One day she chucked it all into the *lua* so she could do Ironman. Now she eats, sleeps and dreams about it.

So when it sank in that she was going to have to skip a year, she was—how shall I put this—unamused. It went thusly:

DAY ONE: She's a little blue.

DAY TWO: The core melts down completely.

DAY THREE, MORNING: I hire a Mafia hit man to take her out in the parking lot of Trader Joe's.

DAY THREE, EVENING: I see on the news that some guy named Nunzio was beaten to death with his own leg in the parking lot of Trader Joe's.

But we eventually got through it, and Cherie recovered enough to do a few more world championships.

Last month she cracked up again, this time because some lady blew out of the DMV lot without looking. The guy who was pedaling just in front of Cherie stopped. My wife, who is genetically incapable of stopping until either the pre-determined workout time or the finish line arrives, didn't. Owing to some idiotic physical law concerning the impossibility of two objects occupying the same space at the same time, she ended up with a fractured hip, a separated shoulder and a torn rotator cuff.

Needless to say, she won't be doing Kona again this year.

Would you like to know what that's like?

Okay. If you could figure out a way to hook a generator up to gnashing teeth, my wife could fulfill all the electrical needs of Las Vegas for a year.

A recent house guest, while getting a fork and spoon out of a drawer in our kitchen, remarked that we really needed to stop letting our silverware slip down into the garbage disposal.

We don't have a garbage disposal.

The gardener waits across the street until he sees Cherie drive away before he'll tend to the lawn. Sometimes he has to sit there for five or six hours. The gardener, a six-foot-ten, 280-pound former tailback for the Detroit Lions, doesn't seem to mind.

Cherie coaches a lot of triathletes. Some days she spends a great deal of time on the phone listening to them gush about all these great workouts they had and how well their training is coming along and how terrific they feel and all these races they've scheduled. After several hours of this, she often feels the need to vent her frustration. The last time something vented that level of frustration, two-thirds of the island of Krakatoa was blown clear off the planet. That island is, of course, no longer near at hand to serve as the object of Cherie's frustration. I, however, am.

The fellow cyclist she smacked into, who emerged from the incident unscathed and didn't even fall over, now wishes he'd just run into that car and killed himself.

It's been an educational experience. One thing I learned is that the phrase "Snap out of it already!" often results in an entirely different reaction than the one you expected.

Believe me, you haven't lived until you've seen a perfectly innocent airport security officer picking his teeth up off the floor because of an exquisitely ill-timed and overly jaunty "So how's it going?" delivered to an Iron Psycho Beast limping through the metal detector.

I've had to take measures. Now, Cherie doesn't even get out of bed most days, because it just doesn't seem worth the effort to chew through the straps.

You think I'm exaggerating? Wait until it happens to you. We'll have dinner and talk about it.

I'll probably be sipping mine through a straw.

HOW TO KNOW IF YOU'RE A TRIATHLETE

You know you're a triathlete when:

✓ You used to drink water; now you re-hydrate.

✓ A rest day means just a swim workout. (You know you're a *real* triathlete when a rest day means the day after Ironman.)

✓ Good sex means quick-and-simple while you're still awake. (You know you're a *real* triathlete when great sex means no sex.)

✓ You draw a distinction between yourself and your body (e.g., "My body is tired").

✓ You used to have sympathy if your spouse was coming down with a cold; now it's "Go sleep in the other room." (You know you're a *real* triathlete when your reaction to your spouse's saying "But the kids are in the other room" is: "Your point being...?")

✓ Somebody asks your age and you answer "30-34."

✓ You ask the bartender to cut off your ProOptibol if you get too crazy.

✓ You reset the trip-odometer every time you go to the grocery store.

✓ Your car has a flat and you change it in 90 seconds. (You know you're a *real* triathlete when you leave the original tire on the side of the road and drive away.)

✓ You sustain a major concussion at 5:00 am before realizing that the pool had been drained the night before.

✓ You've got more running shoes in your closet right now than Jesse Owens went through in his lifetime.

✓ Road Runner has a phone line dedicated for your exclusive use.

✓ Even your cereal spoon is hydrodynamic.

✓ The opening page on your web browser is http://www.weather.com/Kailua-Kona.

✓ You buy a copy of Paula & Mark's exercise video...and you don't own a DVD player.

✓ You sand down the manufacturer's logos on your $1,800 rims to save weight.

✓ You can recite every one of your splits since 1981 but can't remember your license plate number.

✓ You're the keynote speaker at the Catalog Marketing Association's annual banquet.

✓ The question you hear most often is, "One right after the other?" (You know you're a *real* triathlete when the question you hear most often is, "All in one day?")

✓ Work is really starting to interfere with your training. (You know you're a real triathlete when your primary life's goal is to finish without a light stick.)

✓ You've spent a total of twenty weeks in Hawaii but have never sat on a beach.

✓ You can pack 60 cubic feet of junk in a 6-cubic-foot bike case. (You know you're a *real* triathlete when you back legislation that would make it possible for your bike to ride in a seat while your spouse rides in the bike case.)

✓ You begin to suspect that everyone who's faster than you is on steroids. (You know you're a *real* triathlete when suspicion turns to dead certainty. You know you've gone over the edge when you try to contact their sources.)

✓ You used to be an atheist, but now you worship Pelé.

Ironman: A Waste of Energy

'A time when condo associations order the stoning death of residents who water their lawns during daylight hours, it's a wonder Greenpeace hasn't Zodiac'd its way onto the swim course at the Ironman World Championship and 'jacked the turnaround boat. Could there possibly be a more blatantly nose-thumbing display of energy profligacy than the Ironman World Championship?

Two thousand of the world's fittest athletes churn, turn and burn their way over 140.6 miles, expending more energy in a day than Kilauea belches out in a year, only to wind up exactly where they started with nothing to show for it but a few blisters and some mumbo-jumbo about finding out who they really are. Oh, please. If you want to know who you are, ask yourself this: What happened to all that energy I just used only to end up where I started?

I'll tell you what happened to it. It got converted into heat, that's what, in an epic display of entropy. The net effect of all that effort was that you steamed up the ocean, fired up the air and nearly liquefied the pavement. In other words, thank you very much for your contribution to global warming, and now you know who you really are: Mr. Carbon Bigfoot Print, that's who you are. And you were so proud of yourself for not leaving foil tops from your PowerGels all over the Queen K Highway.

It doesn't have to be this way. You can still race Ironman even while doing your bit for the preservation of the planet while at the same time helping us to stop pretending we like people who hate us because we need their overpriced oil. It's easy. The technology exists. You can use your powers for good.

THE SWIM

Construction is already under way on devices to generate electricity from ocean waves. You have this big float resting on the surface hooked to a cable. The other end of the cable is wrapped around the axle of an undersea generator anchored to the ocean floor. Every time a wave pushes the float upward it pulls the cable which, yo-yo style, turns the generator.

"But Ironman swimmers don't generate big waves," I can already hear you saying.

Come on, people, think outside the box a little. What we do is unhook the cables from the floats and connect them to the swimmers using proprietary, WTC-licensed neoprene harnesses (complete with M-dot logo). As you swim, the cable turns the axle on the generator. The beauty part is that, unlike waves, which only generate electricity as the swell is cresting, the power output here is continuous, assuming the racer hadn't slacked off on his training and is paying for it now. Of course, a little energy is wasted because the athlete has to use some of it to overcome the weight of 2.4 miles of cable in order to, you know, stay on the surface (a major advantage in competitive swimming, so I'm told), but still, we're talking about enough surplus energy to run an Xbox through the first three levels of Grand Theft Auto IV.

THE BIKE

This one's even easier. Really, what's the point of actually pushing a 28-pound bike all over creation when we can use gadgets like Compu-Trainers to not only accurately simulate the course but recover energy instead of wasting it?

> (Ed. note: 28 pounds? Is he kidding? While this was the weight of Greg Welch's bike when he won the Ironman World Championship in 1994, no triathlete worth their salt would be caught dead on a bike that heavy.)

> (Auth. note: Bite me. When I wrote this piece you were still riding a tricycle.)

Trust me, the athletes will love this, especially the pros. One of their biggest problems is keeping track of where they are relative to the competition. With digital stationary bikes, there's no more guesswork. Real-time displays on every unit will show the precise (albeit virtual) "location" of anybody the athlete wants to look up, with a lot more information to boot. Just picture Chris McCormack punching up Craig Alexander and finding out that he's 240 yards behind and has been slowing down since mile 57 because he's getting a little sloppy on his left-side spin scan. Macca could even send Crowie an instant message, like, "You're fading a bit, mate. Come on, dig down deep and let's make this a real race!" which is about as close as I can come to what he'd *really* say and still get past the censors.

The benefit to spectators is almost too obvious to mention. The Ironman people have been wracking their brains for years trying to make the event more spectator friendly but, the fact is, nearly all of it takes place in locations accessible only to mountain goats and Mars rovers. Imagine instead two thousand stationary bikes cheek-by-jowl in the King K parking lot with giant, PGA-style leaderboards scattered all over town. Even better, spectators could actually walk in and around the athletes, up close and personal. What could be cooler than to stand three feet away from Chrissie Wellington as she (virtually) blows past her closest competitors, all the while cranking out enough electricity to run all the margarita blenders at Pancho and Lefty's?

I know what you're thinking: With today's technology, racers wouldn't need to be in the same parking lot. They wouldn't even need to be on the same continent. It's a good point, but there's no way around hooking the swimmers up to those cables, so they all have to be in Hawai'i anyway.

THE RUN

I have one word for you: Treadmills. Not the ridiculous kind where a motor moves the surface under the runner—seriously, what the hell is the point of that?—but ones where the runner moves the surface. Now, if you're picturing a treadmill like the ones in your local Sweat 'n' Strut, give it up. I'm talking about the kind in hamster cages, big wire wheels in which the runner stays in one place and the wheel turns around him. And, of course, the wheel shares an axle with a generator. What I love about this is that it gives us a chance to finally get rid of one of the silliest aspects of Ironman, namely T2. In a sporting event where just a few seconds can separate the winner from the first loser, what kind of sense does it make for the better athlete to end up sucking hind whatever just because the other guy could change his shirt faster?

If we put the hamster wheels right next to the stationary bikes, there's no need for T2. You hop off the bike and step right onto the wheel. Spectators can look out over a sea of these things and know precisely what the status of the race is, as well as the condition of individual athletes if we bleed off some of the generated electricity to power hundred-watt bulbs atop the wheels. The brighter the light, the faster they're running. (If the light isn't on at all, politely avert your eyes and summon the nearest *kokua*.)

THE FINISH

The Ironman finish line is the most exciting in all of sports. We can't possibly expect that watching numbers flick by on a display fed by thousands of hamster wheels is going to be able to duplicate that scene.

Well, we don't have to. You know that arcade horse racing game where people roll balls up a ramp and little horses move along the wall to show who's ahead? We can do the same thing at Ironman. With a little clever wiring we can have a wall of Mini-Me athletes wearing numbers that match the real athletes. As the digital equipment continuously computes each athlete's status, his plastic avatar moves accordingly, except now we don't have to watch grown people crawling toward the finish line because they can't stand up anymore. Alarm bells mounted on the hamster wheels will signal volunteer catchers in time for them to run over and get a towel around the exhausted competitors and march them over to the medical tent. (Injuries, of course, will be a thing of the past, unless you count accidentally sticking a finger in a moving wire wheel because you went all hypnotic running in one place for 26.2 miles.)

* * *

The energy recovered by this "green" approach to Ironman would be enough to power Cleveland for a year (assuming anyone would want to power Cleveland for a year). Do the same for all the Ironman and 70.3 events, as well as for all the training by the 90,000 triathletes trying to get to Kona, and we could send OPEC packing with enough cheap energy left over to bring back the Hummer.

Anything less is just plain irresponsible.

Iron-Lingo

Ever wonder where some of those great Ironman triathlon words and phrases come from?

Me neither.

But, amateur etymologist that I am, I decided to do a bit of research anyway and discovered that there is a great deal of misconception about the origins of some of the more popular terms in the sport. Here are a few examples, in no particular order:

Bonk:	An unfortunate and premature cessation to a planned bike ride. The term is onomatopoetic in origin, being eerily similar to the sound made when a bike helmet hits a telephone pole.
Brick:	A form of workout that, over time, maximizes volumetric uptake. From an old technique employed by Her Majesty's Middle Eastern Lancer Brigades in order to get a camel to drink 12 quarts of water prior to a desert crossing even though a camel can normally only drink 10 quarts. The technique involved inducing a gasp, and the consequent intake of the two extra quarts, by smartly bringing down on the poor beast's testicles a large brick whilst he's drinking. The effect of a "brick workout" on a triathlete is much the same.
Ali'i:	Incorrectly thought to mean "Avenue of the Royals," it is in fact another bit of onomatopoeia based on the condition of athletes entering the finishing stretch. When screamed with proper emphasis, it is a fairly accurate transliteration of the sound one might hear if one tried to iron a cat.
Energy lab:	Shorthand for "Lack of Energy Lab"
Paula Newby-Fraser:	Her real name is Florence Schwesterhosen, but a business partner suggested that this might not be the best moniker for selling women's athletic clothing. So Schwesterhosen hired a marketing firm (the same one that came up with "hydrate" instead of "drink") to devise a classier name. Rejected first attempts included "Tuffie McGraw," the "Wizard of Vog," and "Natascha Badmann."
DNF:	Florence Schwesterhosen's sister, Dora.
Fartlek:	Don't go there.

Runner's high:	*A myth perpetuated by a failing shoe manufacturer in a bid to boost sales. It worked for a while, but, like structured water, the giant squid, tasty health food and the benefits of fitness in general, it's a crock.*
Body marking:	*A term borrowed from the late-1990s/early-2000s teen craze of mutilating one's body with all manner of piercing and permanent graphic decoration, "body marking" is a euphemism intended to be less intimidating than "branding."*
Aerobars:	*Like energy bars, only lighter.*
Clipless pedals:	*Pedals that clip to your shoes. Go figure. (See "married bachelor" or "dry water" for related oxymoronica.)*
Drafting:	*Forced servitude in the military. Adapted to also include forced servitude in triathlon (e.g., "If you don't come to Lubbock with me, I'm going to make your life a living hell.").*
Negative split:	*A grammatical error (e.g., "I ain't going to no Lubbock, no way, no how.").*
Crank:	*Synonym for "draftee."*
Top tube:	*Australian nickname for the winner of an Ironman. ("Don't bet against Florence Schwesterhosen, mate. The little sheila was top tube for six bloody years!")*
The wall:	*An impenetrable barrier that's always located a half-mile before the finish line, regardless of the length of the race.*
Entry fee:	*In Middle Ages England, a prisoner condemned to death was required to pay the executioner for his services. It is much the same with Ironman.*
Number belt:	*A forensic device that enables the positive identification of bodies, obviating the necessity to match dental records following a race. Considered a backup to "body marking" (see above), which is unfortunately subject to erosion by contact with lava. (See "road rash".)*
Road rash:	*A light-hearted euphemism which, like "This might sting a little" or "Isn't it great you still have one kidney left?" is intended to cover over the fact that bare skin slamming into rough pavement at 40 mph isn't quite the same as a hot oil massage from Michelle Pfeiffer.*
Clydesdale:	*A male triathlete who has achieved oneness with gravity.*
Athena:	*A female triathlete who has achieved oneness with gravity.*

Lottery:	Avenue of admittance to the Ironman World Championship for those, male or female, who have achieved oneness with gravity.
GU:	Baby talk. Frequently heard being muttered by athletes proceeding down Ali'i Drive on all fours.
Speedo:	An item of extremely intimate apparel made from dental floss and worn primarily by dominatrixes in Sweden. Legislative proposals to ban its use by Clydesdales within the U.S. have thus far been unsuccessful.
Carbo loading:	Dinner at my house.
DQ:	Dairy Queen. Usually follows carbo loading at my house.
Draft off me one more time and I'll kill your children:	This is actually a slight mispronunciation of an ancient Hawaiian phrase meaning, "Stay right where you are and I'll be happy to pull you along for the next eighteen miles." So if you hear it while cycling out on the Queen K, don't be alarmed: Just settle in right behind that rear wheel and don't give it another thought.
Pre-registration:	Invented by state motor vehicle bureaus to alleviate excessive time spent in lines. The success of this concept in local triathlons is about the same as it has been in state motor vehicle bureaus.
Sprint distance:	A measurement applicable to a race participant who is competing while ingesting foods different from those employed during training. Defined as the distance separating said athlete from the closest unoccupied Porta-Potty. In the event of the added factor of overhydration or the drinking of unfiltered local water, it is referred to as the "ultra-sprint" distance or the "Holy-Mother-of-God-everybody-get-out-of-my-way" distance.
Transition:	Originally applied to werewolves, this is a rare form of human metamorphosis in which an otherwise normal weekend jogger turns into that special breed of psychopath known as a triathlete.
Wave:	A relief-filled gesture thrown to an athlete by a "draftee" (see above) at the commencement of the bike leg, signifying that the draftee is now free to go get a cold one and take a nap because cars aren't allowed on the bike course.
T2:	The period following the bike leg in which the draftee chases after an athlete while calling out the exact locations and physical conditions of every single person in her age group, whether they're in this particular race or not.

Chain ring:	*A group of bicycle thieves.*
Challenged athletes:	*People with physical deficits who nevertheless bike, swim and run much faster than most people can, which would seem to peg the derivation of the phrase as a challenge to the rest of us who complain that training is just too hard.*
On-line poker:	*An intense form of exercise that has been clinically proven to burn more calories, build greater muscle mass and boost volumetric uptake faster than any other physical activity known to humankind. Participants are strongly advised not to go to unhealthy extremes by the addition of swimming, biking and running. Walking is also highly discouraged, except as is absolutely necessary to service nutrition, hydration and elimination requirements while engaged in play.*
Mouse potato:	*A highly-conditioned on-line poker player.*

How to Win Ironman…Guaranteed

I don't see the point of advice columns by Ironman champions. Just because you won doesn't mean you know *how* to win, at least not in ways that you can explain to others. Kind of reminds me of reporters asking those people in the Andes how they lived to be 120 years old, as if one of those people actually knew the reason. ("I never drink, I drink every day, I don't smoke, I smoke three packs a day, yada yada yada.")

Qualified scientist that I am—I had a chemistry set when I was in grade school—I decided to give some thought to how people actually win The Big One, the Ironman World Championship, whether they know it themselves or not. Took a bit of digging and some research, but I'm ready to share the secrets with you. If you follow these simple steps to the letter and don't overcomplicate things with a lot of extraneous gobbledygook, you will win. I guarantee it.

Secret #1: Swim strategy. We all know that Ironman isn't won or lost on the swim. The idea is to get through it as efficiently as possible so you have plenty left for the bike and run. Then again, if you're a pro, there's a premium for winning the swim leg. So what you should do is this: Stay about half a body length behind the leader until the last 100 meters, and then sprint around him to the finish. That way you'll save energy, win the premium and have a comfortable head start on the bike.

Secret #2: Technique. The better your technique, the less drag you'll create, reducing the effort needed to move through the water. So make sure your technique is really, really good and the rest will take care of itself.

Secret #3: Okay, I have to introduce a little math here, but stick with me and we'll get through it together. The time required to finish is the distance divided by your rate of speed. Therefore, the shorter the distance, the faster your time. Now, the shortest distance between two points is a straight line. (Don't undertake the proof yourself, just trust me. Ignore Einsteinian space-time curvature, too. That only comes into play in longer races.) So the closer you stay to a straight line in the swim, the less distance you'll travel and (if you've been paying attention, you'll be way ahead of me here) the faster your swim time will be. Bottom line, even if you didn't follow all of that, is this: Swim in a straight line, and you'll come home a winner.

Secret #4: The work you do while pedaling accomplishes only two things: overcoming wind resistance and overcoming friction. This was dramatically demonstrated in 1984 when two-time Olympic cyclist and Ironman winner John Howard rigged up a contraption that eliminated all wind resistance and hit 152 mph using nothing but pedal power. So the first secret of the bike leg is this: Reduce wind resistance.

Secret #5: Reduce friction. Secret #4 dealt only with wind resistance. There's also friction to worry about, so make sure you reduce that as well.

Secret #6: Pedal faster. Sorry, we have to use some math again, but believe me, this is worth understanding. For any given gear setting, every turn of the pedals gives you exactly so much distance. This is fixed by the immutable laws of physics, and there's not much you can do about it. What you *can* do something about is "cadence," which is the rate at which you pedal. Now, here's where the math comes in. Let's say that, for a given gear setting, X turns of the pedal give you Y distance. (In technical terms, Y is a function of X, but let's not go there.) If that's the case, then aX gives you aY distance. Okay, I know I lost you, so let's get this down to practical terms with an example: Let's say that one turn of the pedals gets you 30 feet of distance, or Y=30X. Well, if you pedal 20% more, then you go 20% farther. Simple and obvious, but here's the good part: If you pedal 20% more in the same amount of time, you go 20% farther in the same amount of time. In other words—ready for this?—the faster you rotate the pedals, the faster you go! That's Secret #6: Pedal faster and you shorten the bike leg! Increase your cadence and you'll be a winner!

Secret #7: Know your target run time. If you give the run leg only cursory thought, you might think that your basic task is to run faster than your competitors. But it's not that simple. The problem is that one or more of your competitors (probably the ones that already know these secrets, even if they don't know that they know) might have gotten off the bike and onto the run ahead of you. Therefore, the job ahead of you is to run according to this formula: Tyr < Togr − (By − Bog), which can be read as "The time of your run has to be less than the time of the other guy's run less the difference between your bike finish time and the other guy's bike finish time." So let's say that she finished the bike ten minutes ahead of you. According to the formula, you have to run ten minutes and one second faster than she in order to win the race. As it turns out, any fairly sophisticated sports watch with a built-in programmable calculator can be used to perform the computation so you don't have to do it in your head while you're still dizzy from the long bike.

Secrets #8: Break it down. Just because you know the formula for computing your required run time doesn't mean you're home free. You still have to figure out how to accomplish it. This is a little tricky because calculations involving time are done in a "modulus 60" numbering system but, again, any fairly sophisticated sports watch with a built-in programmable calculator can do the job, as follows: The marathon is 26.2 miles. Take that number and divide it by the Tyr figure you computed above. The result is the amount of time per mile that your run must be faster than your competitor. If you didn't follow that logic, don't worry about it. Trust me, it works every time and can't fail. For example, if you came off the bike 9 minutes behind your competitor, all you need to do to wrap this baby up is run 21 seconds per mile faster than he does. Do that, and I absolutely guarantee that you'll win the race, even if you didn't grasp the underlying mathematics.

Stumbling Towards the Finish Line

(If that spun your head, just remember this: You have to run fast enough to overcome your opponent's lead plus a few seconds extra to get you out in front at the finish line. Here's a little shortcut mental trick: Make sure you pass your opponent on the run, and then get about fifteen feet in front. Hold that through to the finish and you're home free.)

Secret #9: Eat correctly. Your body is like any other engine: It needs fuel to run. So make sure you eat the right amount of what it requires so you don't "run out of gas" before the end of the race. While we're on the subject, there's also the matter of hydration. Your body needs water, and you have to replace whatever it is you lose while underway on the race course, including associated electrolytes. So it's critical that you do this by drinking the right amount of the right fluids. And don't cramp up or get sick, either, as this will only slow you down.

Secret #10: Be fit. I know what you're thinking, "All of this sounds great, but don't you need to have the strength and endurance to pull it all off?" Well, of course you do. That's why I saved the most important secret for last. You have to be as fit as possible coming into race day, so you should plan your workouts to accomplish that. Also, and this is mostly for the pros, your fitness level varies according to the intensity and duration of your workouts. You want to be as strong as possible on race day, so plan your workouts so you're at your very best at just the right moment. Olympians do this all the time and it works.

Summary: I didn't mean to overcomplicate the task at hand. All of these secrets are really just stepping stones to your major objective which, boiled down to its essentials, is to get from the start line to the finish line in less time than any of your competitors. But that's not as easy as it sounds, especially in a race as long as Ironman, and when it gets lost in the noise and hubbub of race day, just remember these ten essential secrets and you'll be amazed to discover yourself at the top of the podium at the end of the day.

I guarantee it!

Ironman Whatever

I recently got to thinking about what the plural of "Ironman" might be.

"Ironmans" doesn't do it for me. You don't need a lot of explanation there; just say it out loud and you sound like Damon Wayans doing "Men on Movies".

What about "Ironmen?" Not bad, at first blush, but:

Q: How many Ironmen have you done?

A: *Just a few, but they were really nice guys.*

You pretty much have to refer to multiples as "Ironman races" or, even better, as "Ironman triathlons." Which leads me to wonder why the adjective "Ironman" is necessarily confined to modification of the noun "triathlon." The word is a perfectly good euphemism for "endurance," so why not extend it to other athletic endeavors? After all, not everybody can swim, bike and run. Some people—and I'm not naming names—can't do any of those things.

In that spirit, I herewith offer the following suggestions.

- **Ironman Bowling**: Five hundred frames, without pause. One of the cool things about this sport is that, the better you bowl, the fewer balls you have to roll. Knock 'em all down on your first shot and you save yourself a second one. Your score is calculated by subtracting the total of each game from 300 and then adding in the time it took you to play, minus the cost of arm slings and Bengay. You don't have to wait for the pin machine to be ready, either. You can use several bowling balls and send them off whenever you're ready, except that there's a twenty-point penalty every time you hit the metal watchamacallit that protects the pins while they're being reset. Three "strikes" (no pun intended) and you're DQ'd. In keeping with time-honored traditions of the conventional version, there will be aid stations serving beer and wings after every ten frames.

- **Ironman Kayaking**: This strictly solo event starts at famed "Dig Me" Beach in Kailua-Kona, wends its way up the Kona Coast and around Kohala Mountain, then continues on to Seattle. Ninety-three thousand large orange buoys (don't bother to check; I did the calculation) evenly spaced every fifty yards will provide course guidance. Clydesdales and Athenas may use two-man kayaks.

- **Ironman Airplane Pylon Racing**: This is the LeMans of air racing, and a sport in which your equipment selection makes a real difference. The P-51 Mustang is the obvious craft of choice, but it's hell to land even when you haven't been flying in tight circles for twenty-four hours without a break. Use of an autopilot is grounds for lifetime disqualification, and, to reduce sponsor liability, no spectators are allowed anywhere near the course.

- **Ironman Snowboarding**: Racers will start at the summit of Mt. Everest and schuss their way to Lhasa Apso. Last one down is a rotten egg.

- **Ironman Golf**: This is a combination of speed golf and cross-country golf, two well-established sports, if by "well-established" you include "among the community of the mildly insane." Ironman golf consists of a single par-7,901 hole (don't bother to check that one, either), with the tee box situated in Des Moines and the green in Central Park. Your score is comprised of a combination of the number of strokes added to the total number of days required to complete the hole. The specific route taken is up to you, but event organizers suggest that, should you end up playing in from New Jersey anywhere near rush hour, you avoid the Holland Tunnel and take the George Washington Bridge instead. Participants are advised to exercise extreme caution in executing the final 11,000 yards, especially if you're laying up along Ninth Avenue.

- **Ironman Hopscotch**: Same rules as the time-honored original, but the layout is three miles long. Sponsored by the American Academy of Orthopedic Surgeons.

- **Ironman Hot Dog Eating**: Competitors in the classic at Coney Island eat as many hot dogs as they can in twelve minutes. In the Ironman version, it's twelve hours. We haven't quite worked out all the rules yet, but serious consideration is being given to waiving the "No Puking" provision.

I've got other ideas as well but have been asked by the U.S. Olympic Committee to hold off until after the Rio Games. Seems that one or two of my earlier suggestions resulted in injuries and a couple of fatalities. No specifics were provided, but undisclosed sources hinted they might have had to do with Ironman Gymnastics and Ironman Synchronized Swimming.

CHANGING COURSE
Fear Factor Meets the Ironman

I don't know about you, but I'm getting a little tired of hearing what a tough sport Ironman is, how the World Championship is one of the toughest endurance races in the world, and what an awful toll it takes on the body.

Come on. The only major injuries you ever see in the medical tent are exhaustion, dehydration and sunburn. Hate to point this out, but that's the same list the U.S. Health Department publishes under the heading "Dangers of Mowing Your Lawn." Maybe this is why Ironman is the 427th most popular spectator sport in the country, somewhere between lawn darts and trying on gloves at K-Mart. It certainly explains why rodeo riders who work 8.7 seconds a week earn millions while triathlon professionals have to bag groceries to make ends meet.

You know why the Ironman consists of swimming, biking and running? It's got nothing to do with the something-or-other Rough Water Swim or a bike race around Oahu or a standard marathon. It's because long-distance swimming, biking and running rank 1, 2 and 3 as the most boring sports in the history of Western civilization.

The spectators at an Ironman share something in common with the spectators at a Little League game: Every one of them has a friend or relative competing. Who would spend all day standing around watching strangers go numb with tedium? Isn't that what we have jobs for?

If this keeps up, Ironman is going to go the way of curling and rhythmic gymnastics.

Overcoming all of this might sound daunting but it really isn't, because the whole thing boils down to a single problem: The course is all wrong.

Think about it. First thing that happens, everybody swims into the ocean where nobody can see them and, candidly, who'd want to? Then they pedal off on a perfectly paved road where nobody can see them, and then they run along the same place they just biked. All the spectators cram into the finish area because, after 140.5 miles, the last 200 yards is the only thing worth watching, because it means your loved one is finally in and you can go get that shower and a cold beer.

Who designed this course...an accounts receivable clerk? Doesn't anybody at WTC watch reality TV?

The course needs a complete re-design. I'm talking serious out-of-the-box thinking here. The only elements worth preserving are the fixed distances, because of tradition. Nobody remembers just what those traditions are but, whatever they are, I'm sure they're swell.

Stumbling Towards the Finish Line

First thing we do, we put the swim last. Try to visualize this. They've just biked 112 miles and run a full marathon. Then they jump into the ocean. Now you've got some real drama when they swim away and disappear into the distance, because it's no longer a question of when they come back; it's a question of *if*. I'm just guessing here, but I'd lay some big money that you'd see a lot fewer double lattes and gin rummy games on the pier while that clock is ticking.

The run would go first, because there are few better ways to kick the living daylights out of your mind and body than with a full bore marathon. Which brings us to another sore point: Where did this business of "running through the brutal lava fields of the Big Island" come from? Did I miss a reel somewhere?

Nobody runs through lava fields in the Ironman. They run on a road so perfectly flat and smooth you could iron laundry on it. The only people on the lava fields are the spectators.

What I propose is putting the spectators on the paved road and the runners out on the lava. And not *pahoehoe*, either, that swirly, creamy Pollyana-smooth stuff. I'm talking *a'a*, those chunky rocks the size of Coleman coolers with edges so hard and sharp you could shape titanium fighter jet wings with it. Tell me you couldn't get a thirty share on Thursday prime time with 1,800 people doing 26.2 over that kind of terrain. Offhand I'd say the medical tent staff might have to seriously re-think the supply cabinet inventory.

Whoever's left now gets to hit the bike course, which brings up another bit of "literary license" in the Ironman media handouts. Who dreamed up this "athletes cycling up the side of a volcano" business... James Frey? I'm amazed Oprah didn't go all depressed and betrayed again. Kohala Mountain is a volcano like Barbara Bush is a Rockette. The last time Kohala erupted, Cro Magnon was the future of human development.

What the bike course needs is a real volcano, and wouldn't you know it: The most active volcano on Earth is right here on the Big Island and has been erupting continuously for over three decades.

Now, some people might think that dodging potholes, stray water bottles and overly-aggressive Italian cameramen on motorcycles is the height of excitement, but can it really compare to weaving your way around pools of magma hot enough to vaporize uranium? And, unlike potholes, this stuff doesn't stay still. An extra pound or two of subterranean pressure here or there and a white-hot jet of lava goes arcing into the sky, turning a pleasant little spin into flamethrower hell. This is made-for-television drama and gives a whole new meaning to "You're fired!"

Of course, it might require a little fiddling with the race schedule, because of the volatility of Kilauea's eruption cycle (not unlike my wife's). Back in the old days, the race date was selected to coincide as closely as possible with the full moon, because of how dark the Queen K gets. Now, we'd have to time it with the predicted flow rate of the race volcano.

Small price to pay. If they could move the entire race back a week to accommodate the S.S. Seventeen-Meals-A-Day in 2006, surely they can do it for a volcano.

Ed. Note: I feel obligated to provide some insight with regards to the "S.S. Seventeen-Meals-A-Day" comment. Here's part of the story we posted on Ironman.com about this:

Each year, World Triathlon Corporation (WTC) works with various government organizations in the Kailua-Kona community and throughout the state of Hawaii to finalize plans for the Ironman World Championship. Recently, WTC learned from the Department of Land and Natural Resources officials that there is a conflict with cruise ship operators and current permits for use of Kailua Pier with the event scheduled for October 14, 2006. WTC understands the need to be flexible and recognizes the importance of tourism to the Kona community and the Big Island of Hawaii. Therefore, WTC announces that the 2006 Ford Ironman World Championship will now take place on October 21.

Lee remains bent out of shape about this because he'd already organized numerous upgrades for his original trip for the week leading up to the 14th, including 18 holes on each of the Mauna Lani championship courses and a stateroom on one of the cruise ships in order to get a closer look at the swim course without getting out of bed.

Ambrosia

In case you're not familiar with the term from Greek mythology, "ambrosia" was the food of the gods, carried to Olympus by doves, a divine exhalation of Earth itself that conferred immortality upon whoever drank it.

Big deal. Pick up any triathlon magazine and you'll find ads for tons of stuff that's not only way cooler than that but available by mail order. There seems to be some sort of contest among manufacturers to see who can get away with the most outlandish claims, but nobody's won yet because there haven't been any rejections of submitted copy. (I once did a little asking around to try to find out just how absurd a claim would have to be for a magazine to reject it, and the only threshold I could find was whether the advertiser's check cleared.)

I wrote a whole book once about how golf equipment manufacturers long ago discovered that their customers will believe in, and pay big money for, anything they're told will improve their games, even though there was no evidence for it. So I got to thinking, "Why not try the same with triathletes?" People are already out there making tons of dough selling them supplements they don't need and equipment that makes no difference, so why not hop on the gravy train and cash in? If anyone is willing to put up some seed money to start operations, I've got some can't-miss ideas. Don't laugh. Anyone who believes that "oxygen-enhanced" water can improve performance will believe danged near any load of hoohah you can wrap in enough technical-sounding jargon.

Get a load of these babies:

- **Plutonium-infused energy bars**: Plutonium is the fuel that powers atomic bombs. Therefore, anything with plutonium in it will power you with the force of atoms themselves. Worried about radiation? No need. These energy bars are based on homeopathic medicine, which means that the "active ingredient" is repeatedly diluted to the point where there isn't actually any of it in the final product. But, as homoeopathists will tell you, it's the "echo" of the original substance that does the trick. Homeopathy has been around for 150 years and hasn't changed in all that time, so it has to be true. Of course, we might have a little trouble actually getting our hands on plutonium, but who cares? It's not like the FDA has a test for the presence of echoes.

- **Jamaican wheat grass**: Wheat grass, consumed yard by disgusting yard by legions of people who never took a few minutes to find out if it's doing them any good, isn't doing them any good. It's grass, f'cryin' out loud. Eventually, somebody's going to actually look in a book and figure this out, but we can be ready. Ready? Here goes: The reason it doesn't do any good, see, is because the wheat grass you're drinking is grown in places like Dubuque or somebody's back yard (or somebody's back yard in

Dubuque), where it used to be considered a nuisance until somebody figured out a way to get people to actually drink the awful stuff. But wheat grass from Jamaica, that's different. Jamaica is the home of sprinter Usain Bolt, the fastest man on the planet. So if you drink Jamaican wheat grass, you'll be faster, too. The best part is that "Jamaican" doesn't indicate where it comes from. It's just the name, like "Atlantic salmon" doesn't mean it comes from the Atlantic and "large" olives are actually the smallest size sold. This is perfectly legal under U.S. law. We can grow the stuff in places like Dubuque or somebody's back yard and we're, like, totally covered.

- **Magnetic GelPaks**: Gels in environmentally-hostile foil packs are so ubiquitous they're practically generic. What we need to do is spice them up a little by magnetizing the stuff. If you do that, then all the atoms of your body that it comes in contact with will have their magnetic spins aligned rather than knocking about in random chaos. Any physicist will verify this. Why having your atoms magnetically aligned makes any difference is utterly beyond me, but people have made a lot of money selling the concept to professional baseball players in the form of butt-ugly necklaces, so why not us?

- **Water infused with vitamins & anti-oxidants**: (Note to self: Someone is already doing this. And 7Up just announced their latest product: Cherry 7UP Antioxidant. Totally not a gag. Pay a little more attention in the future, okay?)

Stumbling Towards the Finish Line

- **Mountain gorilla gonads**: There's this stuff on the market named after bulls because it contains taurine, a grass supposedly munched on by bulls, hence the name "taurine," from the same root as "taurus," meaning "bull." It's an apt description, too, because eating the same grass that bulls eat and thinking you will therefore become bull-like is, well...you get the picture. But they sell this stuff by the warehouse load so why don't we cash in as well? If we grind up gorilla testicles and mix it into a concoction that contains caffeine, we can claim huge boosts in virility. At least for men. For women, it'd be a mustache, heavy thighs and a voice like the *basso profundo* in *La Traviata*. Still, if they think it'll get them to the finish line faster, they'll buy it anyway.

- **Dr. Whatsisname's chrono-synclasticized creatininic metastabotolic amino X complex**: Just trust me...this is great stuff. The literature is going to say that all you have to know is that the last two winners of the Ironman World Championship took it. What if someone asks about the 357 racers who took it and didn't win? Don't worry. The last time a claim like that ran in a tri mag, nobody asked. Besides, by then we will have been assured by no less an authority than Dr. Whatsisname himself that this was just noise in the data, and Dr. W got his PhD in psycho-ceramics* from the University of Our Lady of Perpetual Motion in Gottinhimmel, West Bavaria.

- **Homeopathic Gatorade**: Is this a great idea or what? Homoeopathy is like astrology: People believe in it because other people believe in it. It's completely unregulated, and there are no laws governing what you can call "homeopathic." So what we do is, we buy up millions of cases of Gatorade, slap "Homeopathic" stickers on the labels, then sell it at a 25% markup. Hey, wait a minute: We can call it "organic," too! No pesticides were used during manufacture, and...wait! It's also "sustainable" because if it runs out, we can make more!

I'm going to stop here because I'm already sorry I shared that last one with you. It's killer.

---

* the study of crackpots

Advice no ka oi
("You Can't Get Better Advice Than This")

I've never done an Ironman, or at least not a full one. But I have done pieces. There was the Romper Room One-Mile Fun Walk in Rahway, NJ, the Trike-Around-the-Block fundraiser for victims of psoriasis in Aruba, and I've been to the Splish 'n' Splash Family Water Park in Palm Springs not once but twice, my friend.

I therefore feel fully qualified to dispense Ironman advice, and while it's not my habit to do so for free, I've decided to open the contents of my private mailbag to the general triathloning public for the very first time.

Herewith some recent question from Ironman newbies, along with my responses.

Q: Dear DORK ["Dispenser of Racing Knowledge," I assume]:
I'm on mile 16 of the run. I've thrown up twice, my legs are cramping badly, I'm having hallucinations, and I don't feel I can run another step. What should I do?

A: Quit. Immediately.

This one is so obvious I can't believe you're even asking the question. There is absolutely no downside whatsoever to quitting, but the downside to continuing is horrific. The cramps are going to get worse, you're definitely going to throw up at least six more times, and you'll probably wind up in the medical tent where some first-year is going to treat you like a voodoo doll as he hunts around for a vein in which to jam a large-bore IV needle. Do these strike you as compelling reasons to go on?

Fuhgeddaboudit. Your hallucinations can't be that bad, but you have to really be painting behind your eyeballs to think there's any reason to finish the race. Just quit, and inside of twenty minutes you'll be sitting in some nice, comfy sag wagon being taken to the finish line the way God intended it, via piston-powered gasoline engine.

Soon you'll be happily ensconced in Kona Amigos slurping mai tais and watching all those sorry souls who never read my column drag their sagging butts down Ali'i Drive just so a sun-addled Mike Reilly can scream "You are an Ironman!" as they collapse across the finish line.

You want to hear Reilly yell "You are an Ironman"? I'll send you a ring tone, no charge, and you can listen to it twenty times a day. I hear it's especially popular in the New York City subways during the morning commute.

Q: What should I eat on race day? I've heard you should eat and drink the same stuff you've been eating and drinking during training. Is this true?

A: It may be true that you heard it. But that doesn't make it right.

Okay, let's break this one down. You're going to be doing a distance you've never done, on a course you've never seen, under conditions you've never experienced, alongside people you've never met. This is a day of firsts, and it's going to be tough out there, so why on earth would you eat and drink the same stuff you've been eating and drinking all along? You trying to jinx yourself? If everything else is going to be different, your food should be, too.

Now, the most important ingredients for getting you through an Ironman are carbohydrates, salt, glucose and something to help keep control of your anxiety. Taken as a group, these are known as "comfort foods," things that will give you the confidence and serenity to get through this race. Fortunately, everything you need is readily at hand. I recommend Twinkies, pretzels and beer.

There's no beer served in an Ironman, but most of the spectators lining the course will be drinking it, and those fans are only too happy to toss you a few cold ones. Just yell "Brewski!" as you pass by and you'll think a new aid station just materialized from outer space. But be careful: An overly pedantic reading of the rules might lead some marshal to conclude that sharing suds constitutes "outside assistance," which is forbidden. No problem. If confronted, pull out your own copy of the rules and refer him to the section entitled "special needs." The marshal, newly enlightened, will be sure to move you along with a cheery wave and a jaunty "Good luck!"

Q: Are there any sharks off the Kona coast?

A: No.

Q: What sunscreen do you recommend?

A: Hawaiian Tropic Thermonuclear Deep Tan Bronzing Oil.

Look, you're from like, what, Minnesota? You've been training all year at forty below wearing more layers than an astronaut ...are you really going to come all the way to Hawai'i to spend a week encased head to foot in some icky, white, full-body grease bath and then go home looking like Casper the freakin' Ghost? If you're going to do that, you might as well race in Anchorage.

Start slathering on that Hawaiian Tropic the instant you step off the plane, and keep it on all week. Strap a bottle to your race bike and follow this simple rule: Every time you sip some water, dab on some bronzing oil. Good race or bad, you'll go home looking like a million bucks.

And here's a little insider's tip: When you come out of T1, there are going to be some people there with buckets full of creamy white stuff. These people are going to try to rub that stuff all over you. Don't let them do it! That cream is full of a toxic chemical called "SPF" that will rob you of that great tan. The only reason the FDA allows it on the market is that it's used by veterinarians to induce vomiting in farm animals that accidentally ingest large quantities of industrial pesticides. You know those athletes you've seen doubled over by the side of the road, pale white and puking their guts up? 'Nuff said.

Q: What about hydration?

A: Not necessary. The air in Hawai'i is quite humid, and you can get all the water you need simply by breathing. Drinking more will only make you sick, because it sloshes around in your belly while you run. That's why you see all those people by the side of the road throwing up. If you should happen to get a little low, don't worry. That's what the medical tent is for. They've got it in little plastic bags hanging from poles. They'll pump it directly into your blood stream and have you off again in a jiffy.

Remember that too much water is poison to an endurance athlete. It'll flush potassium and sodium chloride out of your system faster than you can say "hyponatremia." And as for all of those people who keep telling you "Drink, drink, drink" all day? Let me put it this way: Gatorade is a major sponsor of the race. Need I say more?

Q: Any recommendations on running shoes?

A: Air Jordans. The best basketball player in the history of the sport designed them himself, and he ought to know.

Q: How do you handle all those marshals out on the course?

A: I actually have a lot of sympathy for those guys. It's a tough job that has to be done in order to keep the sport clean. Athletes who have their heads screwed on right understand and appreciate that. As a matter of fact, a lot of racers keep a $20 bill tucked under their bibs as a sign of appreciation to the marshals, in case one of them should happen to pull them over to the side to put that big red X on the race number. I've heard plenty of stories of how touched some marshals were by this display of generosity, and—I kid you not—they've even been known to refrain from assessing a penalty and simply wave the cyclist on with a jaunty "Good luck!" Now that's what I call the Aloha spirit!

Q: How long should I taper before an Ironman?

A: Glad you brought this up. In modern racing protocols, tapering has gone the way of carbo-loading, lost to history as an idea that sounded good on paper but turned out upon closer analysis to have no firm scientific footing. Tapering makes you bloated, sluggish and complacent.

A much better idea is to stay loose and in that all-important mental groove, so I recommend going out the day before and doing the entire course. Yes, you'll already have checked your bike in, but you can rent a perfectly adequate three-speed at the little kiosk directly opposite the King K. The best thing about those rentals is that you don't have to squeeze hand brakes to slow down. Just press backwards on the pedals and you'll come to a slow, smooth stop. My guess is that it won't be long before we see that remarkable innovation on triathlon bikes.

Q: Any special supplements I should be taking?

A: You bet. But I can't tell you which ones until my agent receives all the bids for my endorsement. However, I absolutely guarantee that you'll be very happy with the results, because they're the best ones on the market.

Q: I've been riding 5-600 hundred miles a week for nearly a year now. Everything within 18 inches of my groin is completely numb, and we're having trouble starting a family. Any idea what could be wrong?

A: Yes. You're not putting on enough miles.

That numbness you're experiencing is a cry of protest from your muscles that you're not giving them enough time to warm up. Just when they're starting to loosen up a little, you get off the bike and shut them back down. That's worse than never having gotten started at all.

As for that failure to start a family, well, that's just anxiety. Happens to a lot of guys, so don't worry about it. Double your bike mileage, work some of that tension out, and everything will be fine.

Q: I was recently diagnosed with multiple stress fractures in both of my tibias. What's the best way to deal with this?

A: Aggressively. Run through the pain.

Look, let's be honest with each other here. Ironman isn't a round of lawn bowling at some seaside resort in Brighton. It's the toughest endurance event in the world. Of course it's going to hurt. It's supposed to hurt! And you need to get used to looking past pain.

Q: I've seen a lot of pros wearing these really nifty-looking, knee-length tri-suits that appear to be very hydrodynamic and convenient. Should I consider getting one?

A: No. The problem with these suits is that they're black. From underwater you look like a seal, and that can attract sharks.

Q: Sharks? But I thought you said...

A: Whatever. Let's move on.

Q: I've heard that you should underpressurize your tires on race morning because they'll come back up to spec as the sun and hot road surface expand the air inside, but if you pump up to the right pressure to start with, the tire can explode as it heats up. Is that true?

A: No. In fact, you should overpressurize your tires on race morning.

Back when you were a 6-year-old riding your first Schwinn, do you ever remember pumping up your tires? Of course not. The only time you put air in was when you got a flat or turned eighteen. But now you've got one of those fancy-schmancy road bikes with tires the width of linguini that you have to pump back up before every ride because they leak so much.

Well, what do you think is happening to your bike while it's sitting in T1 for all those hours? The tires are leaking like sieves. And as the sun comes up and throws heat into the equation, the pressure inside jumps even higher and the leakage rate increase. Volunteers waiting in T1 can practically hear the hissing.

Now, since you don't want to take the time to pump your tires when you get out of the water, you want to make sure you've got plenty of extra pressure stored up to compensate. Here's a little chart to help you calibrate exactly how much is needed:

If your tires normally inflate to this psi:	Pump them up to this psi race morning:
100	230
120	260
140	280

When you arrive in T1, your tires will be nice and firm and ready to go. And don't worry about those popping noises you can hear all the way out to the swim turnaround. That's just local kids celebrating the day with a few harmless fireworks.

Q: What's the best single idea you've heard for what to put in the special needs bag?

A: A cappuccino machine.

Hands down, that's the best idea I've ever heard, and I'm not talking about one of those little stovetop pieces of junk you buy in a Parisian schlock shop for 15 Euros. I'm talking about one of those gigantic, copper clad Pasquini Liva numbers that can squirt six cups of espresso at a clip and has a foam-making nozzle like a fire hose. You'll not only give yourself a rip-roaring caffeine rocket boost, you'll be the hit of the race as your triathlon buddies line up for a crack at the next free spout.

And (but don't say you heard it here) you might even be able to snag a few bucks hawking fresh mocha lattes to the spectators huddled against the rain in Hawi. Just bear in mind that this is a health-conscious crowd, so be sure to also stash some fat-free creamer in that special needs bag.

Q: Is it possible to overtrain?

A: Overtrain? How can you possibly overtrain?

It's simple physics, so try to follow along here. Training makes you stronger and faster. The more you train, the stronger and faster you get. So what are you telling me? You're worried about getting too fast and too strong? Not bloody likely.

If you want to be the best, you have to work harder than everybody else, and no matter how hard you're already training, I guarantee you that somebody out there is working harder. Therefore, it's a mathematical certainty that, no matter what you're doing, you're undertraining.

And you're worried about overtraining? Please.

* * *

Well, that's it for now. If you follow these tips religiously, what could possibly go wrong?

WHO'S IN T1?
(with apologies to Abbott and Costello)

KEVIN MACKINNON: Well, here we are at the Ironman World Championship, Lee, and we've got a bunch of guys out of the water and in transition!

LEE GRUENFELD: Terrific! Hey, Kevin, listen: Will you tell me the guys' names in transition so when I see them get on the bike, I'll know who they are?

KEVIN: Sure. But you know, fans nowadays give a lot of the triathletes nicknames.

LEE: You mean like pet names?

KEVIN: Yeah, you know, like Crowie, Macca, Rinni. Sometimes they can get pretty peculiar.

LEE: What do you mean, peculiar?

KEVIN: Well, for example, among the Australians, Who is in the red swim trunks, What is wearing black, I Don't Know is in green—

LEE: That's what I want to find out; I want you to tell me the names of the guys on the Australian team.

KEVIN: I'm telling you: Who's in the red swim trunks, What's in the black, I Don't Know is in green—

LEE: You know the guys' names?

KEVIN: Yes.

LEE: Well, then, who's in the red trunks?

KEVIN: Yes.

LEE: I mean the athlete in the red trunks.

KEVIN: Who.

LEE: The guy in the red Speedo.

KEVIN: Who.

LEE: The guy wearing red.

KEVIN: Who is wearing red!

LEE: Well what are you askin' me for!

KEVIN: I'm not asking you—I'm telling you: Who is wearing red swim trunks.

LEE: I'm asking *you*—who's wearing red?

KEVIN: That's the man's name!

LEE: That's who's name?

KEVIN: Yes.

LEE: Well go ahead and tell me.

KEVIN: Who.

LEE: The guy in red.

KEVIN: Who.

LEE: The guy wearing red trunks!

KEVIN: Who is wearing red!

LEE: Is there an athlete wearing a red Speedo?

KEVIN: Certainly!

LEE: Then who's wearing red?

KEVIN: Absolutely!

LEE: When the sponsors pay the guy in red, who gets the money?

KEVIN: Every dollar of it! And why not, the man's entitled to it.

LEE: Who is?

KEVIN: Yes.

LEE: So who gets it?

KEVIN: Why shouldn't he? Sometimes his wife comes down and collects it.

LEE: Who's wife?

KEVIN: Yes. After all, the man earns it.

LEE: Who does?

Stumbling Towards the Finish Line

KEVIN: Absolutely.

LEE: All I'm trying to find out is what's the guy's name wearing red.

KEVIN: Oh, no, no, What is wearing black.

LEE: I'm not asking you who's wearing black!

KEVIN: Who's wearing red.

LEE: That's what I'm trying to find out!

KEVIN: Well, don't change the athletes around.

LEE: I'm not changing anybody!

KEVIN: Now, take it easy, take it easy.

LEE: What's the guy's name in red?

KEVIN: What is the guy's name in black!

LEE: I'm not askin' ya who's in black!

KEVIN: Who's in red.

LEE: I don't know.

KEVIN: He's wearing green. We're not talking about him.

LEE: How did we get to the guy in green?

KEVIN: You mentioned his name.

LEE: Okay, If I mentioned the green guy's name, who did I say is wearing green?

KEVIN: No, Who's wearing red.

LEE: Stay offa red, will ya!

KEVIN: Well, what do you want me to do?

LEE: I want you tell me what's the guy's name wearing green?

KEVIN: What's wearing black.

LEE: I'm not asking ya who's wearing black.

KEVIN: Who is wearing red.

LEE: I don't know.

KEVIN: *He's* in green.

LEE: There you go, back to green again.

KEVIN: Well, I can't change their names.

LEE: Will you please stay on the red guy?

KEVIN: Okay. What is it you want to know?

LEE: What is the fellow's name wearing the red trunks?

KEVIN: What is the fellow's name wearing black.

LEE: I'm not askin' ya who's wearing black!

KEVIN: Who's wearing red.

LEE: I don't know.

KEVIN & LEE: Green trunks!!

LEE: You got Japanese guys in this race?

KEVIN: Oh, sure. That guy in blue over there.

LEE: Japan has some good athletes?

KEVIN: Oh, absolutely.

LEE: The guy in blue's name?

KEVIN: Why.

LEE: I don't know, I just thought I'd ask you.

KEVIN: Well, I just thought I'd tell you.

LEE: Then tell me who's the guy in blue.

KEVIN: Who's in red!

LEE: Stay out of the Australian team! I want to know what's the fellow's name on the Japanese team.

KEVIN: What is the Australian guy in black.

LEE: I'm not askin' ya who's wearing black!

Stumbling Towards the Finish Line

KEVIN: Who is wearing red.

LEE: I don't know!

KEVIN & LEE: *Green trunks!*

KEVIN: Now take it easy, take it easy.

LEE: And the Japanese guy's name?

KEVIN: Why.

LEE: Because!

KEVIN: No, no, he's the German guy in orange.

LEE: Wait a minute. You got a Canadian in this field?

KEVIN: Wouldn't this be a fine race without Canadians!

LEE: I dunno. Tell me the Canadian's name.

KEVIN: Tomorrow.

LEE: You don't want to tell me today?

KEVIN: I'm telling you, man.

LEE: Then go ahead.

KEVIN: Tomorrow.

LEE: What time?

KEVIN: What time what?

LEE: What time tomorrow are you gonna tell me who's racing for Canada?

KEVIN: Now listen, Who is not racing for Canada. Who is the Australian wearing—

LEE: *I'll break your arm if you say who's wearing red!*

KEVIN: Then why'd you ask?

LEE: I want to know what's the Japanese guy's name!

KEVIN: What's an Australian.

LEE: I don't know.

KEVIN & LEE: *Green trunks!!*

LEE: You got a Brazilian?

KEVIN: Yes.

LEE: The Brazilian's name?

KEVIN: Today.

LEE: Today. And Tomorrow's Canadian.

KEVIN: Now you've got it.

LEE: I'm a good race reporter, you know.

KEVIN: I know that.

LEE: I'd like to report on this race.

KEVIN: Well I wish you would.

LEE: Okay. Let's say the Australian in the red Speedo is first out of the water.

KEVIN: Okay.

LEE: The Australian in the red Speedo is the first guy on the bike.

KEVIN: Okay.

LEE: Now me being a good race commentator, I want to make sure the camera is on the guy, right?

KEVIN: Right.

LEE: So I tell the camera guy to point the camera at who?

KEVIN: Now that's the first thing you've said right all day!

LEE: I DON'T EVEN KNOW WHAT I'M TALKING ABOUT!

KEVIN: Well, that's all you have to do.

LEE: Just point the camera at the Australian in the red Speedo?

KEVIN: Yes.

LEE: Now it's pointed at who?

KEVIN: Naturally.

Stumbling Towards the Finish Line

LEE: Who is on the TV screen?

KEVIN: Naturally.

LEE: Naturally.

KEVIN: Naturally.

LEE: O.K.

KEVIN: Now you've got it.

LEE: We point the camera at Naturally.

KEVIN: No you don't, you point it at the Australian in the red Speedo.

LEE: Then who's in the picture?

KEVIN: Naturally!

LEE: O.K.

KEVIN: All right.

LEE: I point the camera at Naturally.

KEVIN: You don't! You point it at Who!

LEE: Naturally!

KEVIN: Well, that's it. Say it that way.

LEE: That's what I said!

KEVIN: You did not.

LEE: I said I'd point it at Naturally.

KEVIN: You don't. You point it at Who.

LEE: Naturally.

KEVIN: Yes!

LEE: So I point the camera at the Australian in the red Speedo and Naturally is in the picture.

KEVIN: No! You point at the Australian—

LEE: Then who is in the picture?!

KEVIN: Naturally!

LEE: *That's what I'm saying!*

KEVIN: You're not saying that.

LEE: I point the camera at Naturally!

KEVIN: You point it at Who!

LEE: Naturally!

KEVIN: Naturally. Well, say it that way.

LEE: THAT'S WHAT I'M SAYING!

KEVIN: Now don't get excited, don't get excited.

LEE: I point the camera at the Australian in the red Speedo—

KEVIN: Then Who is in the picture!

LEE: He better be in the picture!

KEVIN: All right, now don't get excited. Take it easy.

LEE: Huh. Now I point the camera at the Australian in the red Speedo, so the first guy out of T1 is who. What passes who, I Don't Know passes what, Who falls behind tomorrow...they're running one two three.

KEVIN: Yeah. It could be.

LEE: Another guy comes out, he passes all three, he gets passed by Because. Why? I don't know. He's wearing green trunks and I have a *big headache*!

KEVIN: What was that?

LEE: I said, Big Headache!

KEVIN: Oh...that's the Swiss guy in purple!

> *(Ed.note: Lee and I recorded this a few years ago during race week in Kona. While we were rehearsing in the Ironmanlive studio, Ben Fertic was preparing his Welcome Dinner speech. I suggested that, since he had two writers in the room with him, one of whom was a best-selling author, maybe we could help him with his speech.*
>
> *"I want this to be funny," Fertic said. "You guys aren't funny.")*

THE SECOND PART:

NOT SO FUNNY STUFF

Things you probably didn't know

The Stone Walls of Kona

The first time I came to Kona, I was intrigued by all the hand-built lava walls in and around town. Many of them had no visible means of support that I could see, such as iron bars or cement, and seemed to maintain their structure by virtue of gravity acting on the intricately interlocked pieces. Not only that, but many of the walls had perfectly flat faces, yet the rocks didn't look like they had been cut or otherwise worked.

I thought this was pretty amazing, yet there was no mention of these walls in any of the tourist guides or brochures and, when I asked some locals, they'd just shrug. "It's just a wall, brah...what's the big deal?" So I figured that maybe I was making too big a deal about it. But I really didn't think so. I have trouble even making coral graffiti stay in place, so there had to be more to this than some guys picking up pre-fabricated lava walls at Home Depot and dropping them into place.

As it turns out, looking at these walls as "no big deal" just because there are so many of them in Kona is like looking at Michelangelo sculptures as "no big deal" just because there are so many of them in Florence. Unbeknownst to me until recently, and apparently to most people around here as well, Kona is the capital of the ancient and much admired Polynesian art of *pā pōhaku*, building stone walls by hand from natural rock, and there are more skilled artisans here than anywhere else.

In the best walls, the stones are used as is, with no cutting. There are two reasons for this. First, purists consider cutting to be cheating. Second, have you ever tried cutting lava? It isn't easy. I'm surprised someone hasn't figured out how to weaponize the stuff.

The advantage of building walls like these is obvious. The material is essentially free, aside from the cost of moving it from where you find it to where you're using it.

The disadvantage is that it's very labor intensive, and the craftsmen who select the stones and then fit them together like a three-dimensional jigsaw puzzle are a very busy bunch, as you can easily see just by checking out any new construction site. An incredible number of major building projects are underway all over the Kona Coast, and every one of them seems to involve huge stone walls.

The best of the stone wall artisans have traditionally been Tongans, although their small numbers in light of all the new construction have created openings being filled by others as well. (Not incidentally, there is a desperate shortage of all kinds of labor on the Big Island. One hotel up the coast currently has 145 unfilled positions and, like a number of other hotels, is importing chambermaids and housekeepers from Jamaica. Unskilled laborers are also pouring in from Mexico to take advantage of the job situation, and there are still not enough.)

From what I can see, there are several distinct types of walls. Some, like the ones I first noticed years ago, feature perfectly flat faces and have a very finished look to them. These tend to use lighter colored, bluish rock, which comes from the bottom layers of lava flows and is highly compressed, making them less porous and denser. Others have very rough surfaces and consist of much darker, reddish lava. These rocks are very porous and light.

This example of the latter is being built at the new Ted Weiskopf course at the Four Seasons Hualalai resort:

Stumbling Towards the Finish Line

Many walls are no more than three or four feet in height, but some are a good deal higher and, occasionally, there are some truly massive structures. These use huge, boulder-like blue stones at the bottom to support the weight above, fitted in fairly uninteresting, cinder block-like right angle patterns. It's only when you get above that level that the real artistry takes hold. Here's one example, and I figure this one is kind of a temple, since it's across the street from Wal-Mart:

You can get some idea of the scale by noting the standard-height fence at the bottom. If you're wondering what this beautiful wall is protecting, it's an empty lot, but part of it is a remnant of a five-mile long wall built by Big Island Governor Kuakini in the early 19th century to keep livestock from wandering off.

There are several methods used to ensure proper alignment during construction. One is to tightly stretch strings along the length of the wall to delineate the outer dimensions. Another, as shown here, uses wooden forms that are removed once the wall is complete:

The original Hawaiians were a little less concerned with form than with function, but keep in mind that all of these stones had to be hand carried to the building site. The Pu'ukohala Heiau in Kawaihae (about mile 34 of the Ironman bike course) was built using a hand-to-hand chain of over 20,000 men to get the stones up from Pololū Valley.

Stumbling Towards the Finish Line

This one crosses a fairway at Makalei:

By the way, does it seem to you that a lot of these walls seem to be on golf courses? I find that a fairly remarkable coincidence myself. Go figure.

> *(Ed. note: Probably has a lot to do with how much time Lee spends on golf courses on the Big Island. And how many walls he hits.)*

Some walls are built using a dark colored mortar, but others use a technique called *uhau humu pōhaku*, or "dry stacking." No cement of any kind, no metal joinery...just layers of raw rock held in place by intricate interlocking. That's the most visible feature of dry stacking, but what's harder to see is that many of the facades are tilted inward, which makes gravity act as a strengthener, in much the same way as with an arch. When done properly, you can jump up and down on one of these walls without jarring a single stone.

It's thought that this kind of construction began around 900 years ago by an "engineer of public works" named Chief Pa'ao, and the construction techniques were handed down from generation to generation. Since many of these walls were used as corrals or boundaries for grazing animals, building and repairing stone walls was as important to the early Hawaiian *paniolo* as building and repairing wooden fences was to cowboys in the American west.

If you come to Kona, take the time to have a look at these remarkable structures. You don't have to do anything to find them—they're everywhere. You just have to notice.

The Challenges of Being a Challenged Athlete in Kona

In 1992 when Cherie and I were here for her first Ironman World Championship, we stepped out onto our balcony at the King K on the first evening to watch the ocean as the sun set. On the balcony next door was a 30-ish guy doing the same thing. Before we even noticed his face we noticed a metal contraption where his leg should have been. Back then we had no idea how to behave around an amputee, what the proper etiquette was, and struggled to keep our eyes on his face so he wouldn't think we were looking at his leg. As we talked, he said he was there to race the Ironman, and Cherie and I both thought the same thing: *The poor guy will never make it out of T1.*

The "poor guy" was Jim MacLaren, and he knocked off the race in 10:42:50, which was about an hour-and-a-half better than the first time he did it back in 1989.

We've learned a lot about challenged athletes since then. One thing was that the proper "etiquette" upon meeting Jim would have been to say, "Whoa! What happened to you?" at which point he would have been perfectly happy to tell us as much as we'd care to know.

Jim's plight led directly to the founding of the Challenged Athletes Foundation. Much has been written about these people in the years since, with emphasis on the extraordinary strength of character it takes not only to try to make the most of their situation but to prevail over it and return to full-bore competition. Ironman represents the apotheosis of that determination. The most difficult mainstream endurance event in the world is tough for the able-bodied, so it doesn't take a great leap of imagination to realize that it borders on the miraculous for someone with unusable or missing limbs to do it.

I've written about these athletes myself, and hung out with them, and attended the annual CAF event in San Diego every year it's been in existence. But it was only recently that something odd occurred to me: I didn't know exactly *why* it was difficult for a challenged athlete to compete in Ironman. Sounds like the most obvious thing in the world, but when I began thinking about it, I wasn't sure I could explain it to someone if asked, at least not in any kind of detail.

So I decided to try to find out and hoped it wouldn't sound like a ridiculously dumb question. Turns out it wasn't, because when I started asking it of the athletes themselves, I got bombarded with explanations and descriptions of things that hadn't occurred to me in twenty years of watching them compete.

And that's what I want to share with you in the following two articles. You won't be reading about any of the heroics on display, which you have to see to believe anyway. What I was interested in was the mechanics of how they pull it off on race day (no pun intended), the kinds of obstacles we rarely get to see, and the kinds of things that can go wrong that the other athletes don't have to worry about.

Which brings us to why it's in two parts. The first thing I learned is that the world of challenged triathletes divides into two very different groups, generally referred to as Wheelies and Amps. (Kind of like Bloods and Crips, except the only people these guys beat up are themselves.) Amps are amputees, and the way they race is to essentially try to substitute plastic, carbon fiber and titanium for missing bone, muscle and joints. The idea is to simulate their original able bodies as closely as possible, then race the same way as everyone else: swim as best they can, ride a regular bicycle with pedals and handlebars, and run upright on two legs, whatever those legs happen to be made of. The division is called "Physically Challenged" and abbreviated PC in the race results.

Wheelies race what is essentially a different sport. These are people who don't have the use of their legs, usually because they're paralyzed but sometimes because of amputations that don't lend themselves well to race-worthy prosthetics. They still swim the swim, but instead of bicycles they use handcycles, and instead of running they use specialized racing wheelchairs. Equipment aside, though, they compete over every inch of the same Ironman course as everyone else. This division is known as "Handcycle," abbreviated HC. You might also see athletes competing in these divisions referred to as "Athletes With a Disability" (AWAD) or "Paratriathletes."

PART I: WHEELIES (HANDCYCLE)

I spoke with three athletes racing in handcycle and one former world champion.

David Bailey was a motocross champion before a training accident in 1987 left him a paraplegic. Eleven years later he placed third in the Ironman World Championship, the next year, second place, and then he won it all in 2000, besting course record holder Carlos Moleda in an epic battle. David isn't racing this year *(Ed. note: These two articles were written in 2010.)* but provided invaluable background to me in trying to understand what handcyclists are up against in this race.

Susan Katz was born with spina bifida but was ambulatory and athletic until the age of ten, when surgery to relieve pressure on her spine left her paralyzed. She took Paralympic Games gold in Athens as a member of the U.S. basketball team, and earlier this year raced Ironman Louisville. This is her first attempt in Kona, and she is the only female handcyclist entered.

Geoff Kennedy was shot eleven years ago in an attempted robbery in St. Thomas in the US Virgin Islands. (He was the victim, not the perp.) After moving to Puerto Rico and graduating college, he began racing. He qualified for Kona at the Buffalo Springs 70.3, and this will be his first full Ironman.

Andre Kajlich is an amputee but, owing to the nature of his injury—following a 2003 Metro accident in Prague, his right leg was amputated above the knee and a hip disarticulation left him without a femur on the left—he is able to walk with prostheses and a cane but can't run a step. So he's an amputee who races in the handcycle division.

LEE: David, it was news to me when you pointed out that differences in the nature and degree of the injury result in significant advantages and disadvantages on the race course. It's easy to see, among amputees, how one good leg versus none confers an advantage, but what can't we see with paraplegics?

DAVID: Thing is, you can't really "see" it unless you know what to look for. Spinal injuries are categorized by where along the spine the problem is: The higher up you go, the more stuff you lose. In my case, I'm paralyzed from the chest down.

LEE: You're only using your arms, so what difference does that make?

DAVID: The difference is basically in the abdominal muscles. If you have them, there's a lot more you can do in terms of leverage, seat position and so forth. If you don't, you can barely change a tire because you can't sit upright.

SUSAN: I'm kind of in between, an incomplete paraplegic: I've got some abs, but not all, and I've got a little bit of movement in my right leg but not enough to walk.

Stumbling Towards the Finish Line

LEE: How'd you do in Louisville?

SUSAN: Went real well. I felt good and managed energy and nutrition well. But there's plenty of room for improvement.

LEE: Just getting to the race must be difficult.

SUSAN: It is, and not just because it's tough for us to get around. Anybody would find it tough hauling around all the stuff we travel with.

LEE: Like the wheelchair?

SUSAN: That's the easy part, what we call the everyday chair. Then there's the racing chair, which is a completely separate piece of gear, and the handcycle, a big, awkward piece of equipment. Getting to the event site is like the first leg of the race, and it's expensive shipping all that stuff.

LEE: You can bring help for that, but once the race starts you're more limited in terms of assistance. So how does the swim work?

GEOFF: The rules tend to change as the sport gets smarter about dealing with wheelies. A new one says we have to bind our legs together—

LEE: Why?

SUSAN: To even the playing field. Some folks who have lower-level injuries might be able to kick, which would be a huge advantage over those with higher-level injuries who can't.

GEOFF: How you do that—Velcro straps, some kind of brace—depends on the extent of your injury and your own style.

DAVID: This is one of the times that having abs makes a difference. I don't have any core at all, and if I have any flotation on my legs, they pop up, and it makes my head go down, without a lot of good ways to bring it back up again. So I like to have my legs dangle down a little.

GEOFF: This may surprise you: Some of us have leg spasms—

DAVID: Yep. I sure do.

GEOFF: —and that can make your legs jump around when you don't want them to. I take medication to calm them down.

DAVID: Mine can get pretty bad so I borrowed an idea from Carlos Moleda: I made a brace out of PVC piping cut lengthwise and attached it along my legs with Velcro straps.

ANDRE: The biggest issue for me in the swim is body position. Since I've only got about half of one leg, my body wants to go vertical all the time, like walking, which doesn't make for very efficient swimming. I found that as long as I'm moving along at a good clip with good technique, I can stay horizontal. But then my wetsuit is more buoyant on one side, which tends to roll me sideways. For a long time I couldn't breathe on my left side so I had to learn to be able to breathe on both.

LEE: That reminds me of something I've always wondered about: wetsuits in Kona?

ANDRE: Challenged athletes are allowed to wear wetsuits in all races.

SUSAN: Which is good news and bad news both, because it can be awful to get it off after the swim. I ask for help from volunteers.

LEE: Let's back up. How do you get out of the water?

DAVID: I had a buddy carry me up the stairs.

SUSAN: I use two.

DAVID: I've found that two people can get out of sync really fast so one strong guy works best.

ANDRE: Took me a while to get used to the idea of being carried. We could hop, skip or crawl, but if we're all carried that means we all do it the same way and that's what counts.

LEE: What about getting into the handcycle?

GEOFF: I like to do as much as possible myself. Aside from wanting that independence, well-meaning people can mess things up because they might not know what you need.

DAVID: Very true. All I really need is for a friend to strap my legs in.

LEE: You can't do that yourself?

GEOFF: Abs again. You can't lean around the gears to get at the straps.

LEE: Lean around the gears...?

DAVID: A handcycle is like an upside down bicycle. The bottom bracket is sitting way up in the air right in front of the cyclist, who "pedals" with his hands.

LEE: Got it. Now, I've seen different people sitting in different positions, some nearly upright, some practically lying down...

SUSAN: A matter of preference, and there are a lot of factors. Most of the guys like to lean way back because it's more aerodynamic, but I sit more upright.

LG: Because...?

SUSAN: For one thing, you can see better. It also keeps your upper body farther from the road. You wouldn't believe the heat coming off the road in the middle of the day when you're down that low, and ten or twelve inches makes a big difference.

DAVID: It really does, and the aero advantage is over-rated. There aren't that many places where you're going fast enough for it to matter, and sitting more upright is easier. You get more power and leverage, which makes the uphills a little easier, and it's also a better position for eating and drinking. I went faster upright in 2000 than I did in 2009 lying down.

ANDRE: Heat is a problem for me as well. Being an amputee, I've got less surface area over which to shed heat.

SUSAN: I should also have mentioned making sure that the handcycle is correctly configured in the first place. When you have no sensation, there's no way to know if you're chafing and your skin is being rubbed raw. So you have to have enough cushioning and padding to make sure that doesn't happen.

ANDRE: You have to be careful about going through puddles, too. Moisture on the road means water and mud getting thrown up into your face because you're sitting right behind the front wheel.

LEE: What happens if you flat? David already said that it can be a real pain to deal with.

GEOFF: I need someone to unstrap my legs. The next problem is that I don't use a removable cushion, so I have to sit on the ground, which can be hot as blazes and very rough. Every time I change a flat, my legs and ankles get all scratched up.

DAVID: I use sew-ups to make flats less likely because if I get one, it's a nightmare. I have to put a cushion on the road, and then it's like working while sitting on a beach ball with no stomach muscles to balance me. Front flats are the worst because that's where the gears are. Rears are easier; you don't even have to take the wheels off to change the tire.

LEE: Didn't you flat in that historic battle with Carlos?

DAVID: Yes, right after the Hot Corner with six miles to go [on the old course], but I knew it would take longer to change than just ride it to T2. Sew-ups flare out a little when they go flat and keep rims from touching the ground, so I just rode it flat all the way to T2.

SUSAN: I don't even carry spares, just CO_2 cartridges and sealant.

LEE: Can you get help from the bike support vans?

DAVID: Problem is, they carry a standard complement of the most popular wheel sizes, and ours are different.

LEE: Even assuming that everything is going right mechanically, you're using only your arms. What's that like?

GEOFF: About what you'd expect: Your hands cramp, your shoulders hurt...

LEE: How do you steer?

ANDRE: You push the hand cranks left and right while cranking. Makes it kind of difficult to eat and drink because you have to take a hand off the crank, which is awkward and slows you down.

LEE: Can't you alternate left and right hand?

ANDRE: Then you wobble all over the place. I've actually had some practice at it because I once had a crank break off and had to pedal home one-handed, but it's still hard.

LEE: Just thought of something: How do you handle food that comes in wrappers?

ANDRE: It ain't easy! But I do use some energy gels just for a little diversity and extra calories.

LEE: Any problems mixing it up with the other cyclists?

ANDRE: Not for me. I love interacting with the other athletes. We motivate each other, and it just makes it a lot more fun out on the course.

LEE: Let's move over to the marathon. Different chair entirely, right?

GEOFF: Yes. It's a wheelchair, not a cycle. No gearing at all.

DAVID: Getting into it is the most difficult transition of the day for me.

ANDRE: Out of the handcycle and onto the ground, then up onto the racing chair ...

DAVID: And make sure you don't get more "help" than you need.

LEE: Sounds like you'd need a lot.

DAVID: Nope. Again, I like to do it all myself. Just need someone to hold the front end down while I'm getting in.

ANDRE: My chair was set up for a paraplegic and I modified it, but it's still difficult to get secure. I've got the advantage of having good core muscles, but my one limb takes the full brunt of countering each stroke. It gets fatigued even before my arms do.

SUSAN: And at this point in the race we need gloves, too.

LEE: Is that so you don't beat your hands up grabbing the wheel? I mean that metal pipe attached to the wheel?

GEOFF: Called a push rim, or hand rim, but there's a common bit of misunderstanding there: We don't actually "grab" the rims.

LEE: You don't?

DAVID: If you grabbed them you'd slow the chair down. The glove is kind of like a boxing glove. Your hand is in a fist, and what you do is hit the rims faster than they're moving, to speed them up.

LEE: That makes sense.

SUSAN: Doesn't work so well going up a steep hill.

LEE: (to David) I saw Carlos coming up from the Kona Surf backwards. Was it easier to pull then push in that situation?

DAVID: Can be, and it gives your arms a rest, but as soon as he saw me chasing him he flipped around and started pushing again!

LEE: How come you don't ever go backwards?

DAVID: As I said, I use sew-ups, and with the glue being warm in a place like Hawai'i, I'm afraid that twisting the tires like that could pull them off the rims.

GEOFF: There are other things to worry about on the run.

LEE: You call it "the run?"

ANDRE: Why not? Everyone else does.

SUSAN: Run, marathon, whatever.

GEOFF: Settling in on the chair is an issue for me. I've been down in the luge position on the handcycle for hours. Now I've got my legs tucked under me, and I'm hunched over like a Muslim on a prayer rug. Takes a few miles to get used to it.

SUSAN: I have a constant concern about my visibility.

GEOFF: We all do.

LEE: Because you're lower to the ground?

SUSAN: Somewhat, but the real problem is relative speed. The marathon is the one leg of the race in which wheelies have a real advantage. We're going to complete this leg in far less time than most runners.

ANDRE: For me, the marathon is redemption after the swim and bike. I'm dead tired but happy to be passing people.

LEE: So why is speed a concern?

SUSAN: Because runners just aren't used to people coming up from behind them at high speeds. Have you ever been in a race where you were passed by other runners?

LEE: Every race I've ever been in.

SUSAN: So you know that no matter how much faster they are then you, you can hear their footsteps and even their breathing well before they reach you, and the pass just isn't all that fast.

LEE: So...

GEOFF: So, now picture some guy out on the Queen K when it's dark and quiet and he's half delirious and barely moving. All of a sudden he hears me yell "Wheelchair on your left!" and before it even fully registers, he's startled and stumbles right into my path. He may have been passed by a hundred other runners already, but never by a wheeled machine going ten times faster than he is.

LEE: But what was he doing in front of you in the first place?

ANDRE: Had a faster bike or swim. That's why we're passing runners like crazy all the time.

SUSAN: I spend the whole marathon yelling, and it drains energy. It also doesn't work all the time, like if the runner doesn't speak English, or he does but his brain is just fried. If he whips his head around to see what's going on, half the time he's going to step right in front of me before he figures it out.

GEOFF: It's a little easier on uphills where we're going slower, but on downhills we have to go on full alert.

DAVID: The safety of other athletes is always in our minds. It has to be. It's like an obstacle course for us out there, and we can't depend on all of those people to be aware of us because they're just not used to it.

GEOFF: There are only six wheelchairs in the whole race this year.

SUSAN: Aid stations are the worst.

ALL: Absolutely. No question.

LEE: Because you have to slow down?

GEOFF: Because you're dodging runners left and right. People stopping suddenly, or darting across the street. I tried to steer a real wide path off to the side and give them all a lot of room.

ANDRE: I find it hard grabbing cups with the gloves. I have to use two hands and try to keep the gloves from getting wet. Since the marathon is relatively short for us, I try to do the whole thing on one Camelback I fill myself.

SUSAN: Aid stations are treacherous in other ways. The road can get slick from all the fluids being thrown around, there are cups and bottles all over the place...wet rims get slippery and difficult to push, and if your gloves get soaked they're probably never going to dry out. And here's something that might not have occurred to you: Once we're out of the water, we've got a helmet on for the entire rest of the race.

ANDRE: Do you get headaches?

SUSAN: I sure do.

ANDRE: Me, too. I don't even wear one when training.

LEE: Yogi Berra once said that it's amazing how much you can see by just watching, but I'm amazed at how much is involved that we observers can't see at all. If you could magically put one thought in people's minds that would make your races a little easier, what would it be?

SUSAN (without hesitation): No misters!

ALL: Amen to that!

LEE: Misters?

SUSAN: Those well-meaning people spraying the runners down with hoses?

LEE: What's the problem there? Sounds like some relief from the heat.

SUSAN: Not even close to being worth wet rims and gloves.

DAVID: I'd put it a little more generally: I appreciate all the gestures of support and goodwill, but please don't help unless I agree or ask for it.

LEE: Makes sense. Thanks, everybody, and best of luck Saturday. I'll be the guy out there with a hose—

SUSAN: What!

LEE: —pointed the other way.

* * *

PART II: AMPUTEES (PHYSICALLY CHALLENGED DIVISION)

I spoke with two athletes racing PC in Kona.

Scott Rigsby, 43, was the first double amputee to complete an Ironman. During his first attempt, in Coeur d'Alene, he crashed on the bike. Despite a cracked vertebra, he made it through twelve miles of the marathon before the injury overwhelmed him. A year later, in 2007, he did the "unthinkable" (which is also the title of his book) right here in Kona, finishing with eighteen minutes left on the cutoff clock.

André Szücs, 31, was born with a malformation that required surgery at the age of nine months to allow the fitting of a prosthetic lower right leg. He's also missing a couple of fingers and the first and second toes of his "good" left foot. Andre did Ironman Brazil in 2007, but this is his first trip to The Big One in Kona.

LEE: I learned a whole new language talking to the wheelchair guys, and it looks like I have to learn another one for the PC division.

SCOTT: Oh, yeah: Singles vs. doubles, above-the-knee vs. below-the-knee...but unlike with wheelies, you can tell with one glance what the extent of the injury is.

LEE: But only when you're wearing shorts. If you've got long pants on, I often can't see any sign at all that something's missing.

SCOTT: Neither can I. A lot of that has to do with technology.

LEE: André, was I hallucinating or did I see video of you surfing? And doing a lot better than I ever did?

ANDRÉ: That was me. I love the water. I was a competitive swimmer for eight years before I got into triathlon.

LEE: You don't wear a prosthetic in the water during a race, do you?

ANDRÉ: No. I leave my stump exposed or slip a liner over it.

LEE: With one leg, aren't you out of balance?

ANDRÉ: Yes, and that takes some getting used to. I also have to kick with my good leg, but there's no propulsion in it; I just do it to help me stay horizontal.

SCOTT: Propulsion is pretty much a non-issue for me, too. Even with four inches of leg below each knee, I don't get anything out of kicking because it's the foot that acts like a fin. So it's just about minimizing drag by not letting your legs flail around the water.

LEE: Can you wear any gear on your legs?

SCOTT: Depends on the rules of the race, but never anything that supplies propulsion. I'd like to wear something that will let me get out of the water and over to T1 more quickly, but I don't yet know what's going to be allowed here. Part of the problem is that there's a blanket rule against any kind of "add-on" at all. It was intended to prevent people from using things like flippers, but it's worded so broadly that it also covers things that could help you get out of the water but have no advantage while you're still in it.

LEE: Can you run or walk on your stumps?

SCOTT: Some people can, but it's tough for me, especially on a rough surface. I don't want to start a 140.6-mile race on scratched-up stumps. I also don't want to risk tripping up athletes who might not notice me because I'm down so low.

ANDRÉ: First thing I check out at a new venue is what the water exit looks like and how far it is to T1. Are we talking stairs, ramp, sand? A cycling leg is really no good for walking, but if it's a relatively short, easy trip to transition, I can put it on right out of the water.

LEE: How many legs do you have?

SCOTT: If you're a triathlete, you're going to have three sets: everyday walking, cycling and running.

ANDRÉ: And backups. Don't forget those.

SCOTT: Right. One of the things I'm a little concerned about is how T1 is going to be set up for challenged athletes. We've got our own tent on the pier, but Raj [triple-amputee Rajesh Durbal] and I alone have something like twelve legs. It's going to look like a prosthetics factory in there on race morning.

LEE: How difficult is it to get a leg on? I'm guessing you don't just step into it like a ski boot, snap a couple of buckles and head off.

ANDRÉ: It's a multi-step—

LEE: Is that a pun?

ANDRÉ: Unavoidable. Happens all the time. Anyway, it's a multi-step process involving silicon liners, fabric slip-ons, flexible carbon fiber, cups...

LEE: So what is that actually keeps the leg attached firmly to the stump?

SCOTT: Suction. The urethane liner fits tight around the stump and up along the thigh. Then, when you step into the prostheses and pull up an outer sleeve which creates a seal, the air is pumped out by an electric or mechanical pump, depending on the design, forming a vacuum seal that holds the whole thing on.

LEE: What keeps the vacuum intact?

ANDRÉ: A one-way valve. Every time you put pressure on your leg it forces air out through the valve, but it can't come back in.

SCOTT: The technology I use is an elevated-vacuum system. The processor in the electric pumps sense changes in the vacuum level. If it starts to weaken, the pump automatically restores the optimal vacuum level. The valve also expels sweat. Back in the old days—

LEE: Old, like...

SCOTT: Four or five years ago. Sweat was a huge problem. In '07 I was stopping every four miles on the run to take the leg off and pour cupfuls of sweat out. Blood, too.

LEE: Blood?

SCOTT: Yep. The old style legs were pure hell on stumps. I had rings of flesh ripped off and was in agony the last three miles. For five days afterward I was in a wheelchair.

ANDRÉ: Now there's a whole wicking system and the valve expels sweat automatically, which was a tremendous advance. Of course, if the liner gets punctured for some reason, the vacuum is compromised, and you wind up having to adjust things every few minutes.

LEE: Are we talking bike or run now?

ANDRÉ: Both. Expelling sweat is as important on the bike as the run, because all of that moisture breaks down skin. By the time you get to the run you can be in real trouble.

LEE: Now, is that the same system for both the cycling and running legs?

SCOTT: Yes, and walking, too. The interface between the stump and prosthetic is the same, but the prosthetic itself is completely different depending on the function. My cycling legs are an aerodynamic design. I don't even bother with any kind of shoe. There's just a pedal cleat at the bottom.

LEE: How tough is it to get out of the pedal quickly if you need to?

ANDRÉ: A fall to my right side is a bit of a problem. It's just not the same reflex to snap out.

LEE: I imagine that the bike is much less traumatic for you than the run.

ANDRÉ: Far less. There's a lot of rubbing, but no pounding. But there's also a balance issue for a single amputee, because one leg is working harder than the other and doing it on one side of the bike.

LEE: Bike legs look relatively straightforward, but there seems to be some real intricacy to run legs.

ANDRÉ: There is, and getting everything locked in correctly is critical. I take a lot of time in T2 to make sure everything is exactly right.

Stumbling Towards the Finish Line

LEE: Looks like a lot of complex hardware there. Are you talking about adjusting all those screws and bolts?

ANDRÉ: No. There are three main sections: foot, pylon and socket. You can pretty much figure out what each is.

LEE: Got it.

ANDRÉ: So the most important is the socket, because that's the comfort point. It's the part that every amputee struggles with in the beginning, not only because it's new, but because the stump changes a lot before it settles down. And, if you're an athlete, it changes in the middle of the race. It gets compressed from all the pressure and pounding, and it can swell from the trauma, so you have to make adjustments in the middle of the race.

LEE: Adjustments like...?

ANDRÉ: Slipping liners on and off to vary the thickness. But over time you figure things out, and the technology keeps getting better. I used to get terrible blisters that took weeks to recover from. At IM Brazil, I was down on the ground with the foot off after about six miles, and had no intention of getting back up. A friend came by and urged me back up, and I was able to block out the pain for a while. But with a few miles left I lied to him, told him I was fine and that he should go on, but the pain came back ten times worse.

LEE: And now?

ANDRÉ: This year I got a new socket and did a 20K run that was pure heaven. Now the only thing I'm worried about in the Ironman run is myself, because I think the leg is going to be just fine. Which isn't to say it's going to be smooth sailing. If the stump swells and I take off the leg to get a breather, I might not be able to get it back on. You need to decide on the right liner, too. If it's too tight, sweat will hurt you. If it's too loose, things move around and can rub you raw. But as long as you're not too beat up, you can stop in the middle of the race and pull liners on and off.

SCOTT: I've had the same problems. The run in '07 was just awful. The advantage of the new elevated-vacuum technology is that the high levels of vacuum create a stable environment that minimizes all that shrinking and swelling and trauma. Now, let's face it, I'm doing an Ironman. Even able-bodied athletes can't say that they feel great after 140.6 miles. But this time I'm looking forward to being able to concentrate on just running instead of struggling with the equipment and worrying about how badly my legs are getting trashed.

LEE: Has the foot part advanced much?

SCOTT: Interesting topic. There hadn't been a major advance over the C foot in thirteen years.

LEE: "C" refers to the shape of the carbon fiber arc?

SCOTT: Right, as opposed to the J. What a lot of people don't realize is that the fiber half-circle has only one purpose: to cushion the shock of each step. Other than that, there's no spring like you get from your back foot when walking or running. There's no mechanical advantage at all. In fact, it's a deficit.

LEE: You're referring to Oscar Pistorious.

SCOTT: Sort of. I don't really know that much about the specifics of his legs, but I do know that it's not like running on a set of springs. It's more complicated than that. People with one good leg use the momentum it generates to swing the prosthetic leg through. If you're missing both legs, you can't get it that smooth.

LEE: Rudy Garcia-Tolson doesn't swing them through at all.

SCOTT: Right. He kicks his legs out in a wide arc to clear the ground. But a little while back I got a call from a company called Freedom Innovations that came up with a new idea to return a little energy to more closely mimic an able-bodied pushoff from the rear foot. They put a strip of carbon fiber across the C arc. It acts like a crossbow. When you step onto the foot, the strip bends and stores energy; when you release pressure, it snaps back into shape and provides a little pushoff.

LEE: How effective is it?

SCOTT: Well, at first I kept breaking them one right after another! Took a lot of trial and error to get the right size strip for my weight and running style, but I think we have it nailed now.

ANDRÉ: Stuff breaking is an issue, by the way. The foot takes a terrific beating, and carbon fiber weakens and even delaminates over time. You've got to pay a lot of attention to make sure you spot it before it happens in a race.

SCOTT: I still don't know if we're even allowed to make repairs or replacements during the race. I'm hoping we find out at the race meeting.

LEE: Just thought of something: Where did you guys qualify?

ANDRÉ: Interesting topic.

SCOTT: We didn't. There's no qualifying for PC. It's all done by lottery.

LEE: Curious. The wheelchair people have two qualifying races. Is it because the range of possible amputations is so wide? It wouldn't really be fair to pit a double above-the-knee against a single below-the-knee with an Ironman slot hanging in the balance.

SCOTT: That's got a lot to do with it. You'd need a whole lot of categories to make it completely fair, and that's not practical. Not yet, anyway. But there are other ideas being discussed, like qualifying races where you can compete against people in similar condition, even though you might still lump the whole category together once you get to Kona.

LEE: You would need a lot of categories to cover everybody.

ANDRÉ: Compromises are inevitable. In my case, I'm missing some fingers, which makes it hard for me to brake on downhills, so I train with a time trial bike.

LEE: What about shifting?

ANDRÉ: Not a problem.

SCOTT: The lottery system isn't an unreasonable idea, but it's frustrating because it's so random. Everybody else can work harder and race their hearts out trying to win a slot. With us, you just roll the dice and hope.

ANDRÉ: Of course, that's unique to Ironman. There are all kinds of other races that you can plan for in advance.

SCOTT: And don't think I'm complaining. We've come a long way, baby.

A personal note:

When I first began speaking with challenged athletes in preparation for this piece, I thought I detected a little undercurrent of grumbling. There were thinly veiled references to inequities involving degrees of disability, race course rules that might not have been thought through fully, the frustrations of qualifying. It was nothing compared to the litany of complaints you get from able-bodied competitors, but it was there, and it was surprising, at least to me. I'd always thought that being allowed to compete alongside mainstream athletes was the acme of the challenged athlete's ambition, and once you made it to Kona, all you had to do is finish and you could ride off into the sunset, your life now complete.

Boy, was I stupid.

I've now done a complete one-eighty, and if you were to ask me what I thought was the single brightest indicator of the advances made by these remarkable athletes, I'd say it was the grousing, hands down. Why?

Because it says that they've moved beyond the Hallmark moment and into the rarefied territory of the genuine athlete. Carlos Moleda, Scott Rigsby, Sarah Reinertsen, Rudy Garcia-Tolson and other pioneers have already proven that it can be done. Step 1 (as André said...you can't avoid leg puns) is over and is, like, so last year. They've moved beyond breaking ground and are now into breaking records. Scott came in with eighteen minutes on the clock last time. This year? He wants to finish, take a shower and return to the pier in enough time to cheer the rest of the racers in.

> *[Ed. note: Scott finished in 16:22, thirty-eight minutes before the cutoff and twenty-one minutes faster than his first finish in 2007.]*

Andre Kajlich wants to crack eleven hours, and so does Geoff Kennedy. (Guess which race-within-a-race I'll be following.) So the griping is a sign of health, of acceptance not only by the larger community, but by themselves. The morph from anomaly to athlete occurs when the question changes from "Can I finish?" to "How fast can I go?" to "Can I be the best?" And anything that gets in the way, whether it's a qualifying inequity or an ill-considered rule, is just another obstacle to be overcome in a lifetime of overcome obstacles.

Let the games begin...

* * *

Special thanks to Bob "Funky Dude" Babbitt and Jill Prichard of the Challenged Athletes Foundation (www.challengedathletes.org)

Q & A With:

THE BIG ISLAND

The Big Island has been an integral part of the Ironman World Championship beginning with the third running of the event in 1981. Prior to that the race was held on Oahu, but the BIIMWC Organizing Committee put on a full-court press to bring the prestigious event to the island of Hawai'i, based on the supposition that this is where God intended it to be all along and the pupus were better. The Big Island had, of course, been around well before that and had hosted such notable events as the 1824 Holualoa Slip 'n' Slide and the 1742 beating death of Captain Cook.

LEE: First thing our readers want to know is whether you're male or female.

BIG ISLAND (BI): Can't believe you're even asking me that.

LEE: Well, there's that whole "Madame Pele" business...

BI: Listen, that ornery gal is just my girlfriend, savvy?

LEE: "Ornery" is a little mild, isn't it? I mean, aren't we talking—

BI: Worst case of PMS in the history of the Pacific Chain, yeah. This one time? When she put on Hilo and asked me if it made her look fat? Guess I gave the wrong answer because— [gestures to the North]

LEE: You mean Kohala Mountain?

BI: [nods ruefully]

LEE: What about it?

BI: Used to be seven thousand feet higher. Hadn't been for that little bit of thoughtlessness nobody would ever make the bike turnaround at Hawi.

LEE: She really blew her top, eh?

BI: Very funny.

LEE: Anyway, I see what you mean. So all that stuff about not taking home lava or coral...?

BI: OMG! Don't even say that out loud!

LEE: Sorry. But let's get back to you. Where were you born?

BI: Bottom of the ocean. Started out like every other little steam vent, no big deal, destined to be just another breeding ground for micro-organisms to be eaten by exotic deep-water vent-dwellers.

LEE: But something was going on that made you more than just another mid-tectonic plate hot spot. Tell us about that.

BI: Turned out that little steam vent was actually just the opening shot of upwelling plumes of lava from the base of the lower mantle.

LEE: So you turned into an undersea volcano.

BI: Couple of 'em, in fact. Kept growing and growing...did you know UNLV tried to recruit me right out of high school?

LEE: Yes, but I heard you couldn't go to your left or grab a rebound to save your—

BI: Whatever. Point is, the more lava that spewed out, the taller I got, and somewhere around 800,000 years ago I popped up out of the water. So one day I was a volcano, and suddenly I was an island.

LEE: Kind of like a geologic bar mitzvah.

BI: Such a party we had, you wouldn't believe it.

LEE: Now, most islands have a single primary volcano.

BI: A "shield" volcano, right, with gently sloping sides resulting from very fluid lava flows.

LEE: But you have...

BI: Five of 'em! [preens immodestly] And Mauna Loa is the biggest mountain on earth!

LEE: You mean biggest volcano.

BI: Listen to Mister Smarty-Pants. I said "mountain" and that's what I meant. Don't forget that it starts at the ocean floor, not the surface. Bottom to top, we're talking over 30,000 feet, pal, and that means she's looking *down* at Mt. Everest. And in terms of volume, it's not even close: Mauna Loa's base is over 1,800 square miles. She could eat Everest for breakfast and not even burp. Although, I must say, her burping is something to see.

LEE: But the other four volcanoes are dormant, right?

BI: Don't look so smug: You know what "dormant" means?

LEE: Inactive?

Stumbling Towards the Finish Line

BI: No. You're inactive. Dormant means "sleeping."

LEE: As in...

BI: Not dead. Just out for a while. Could wake up.

LEE: Yeah, but how long does it have to be dormant before you write it off?

BI: How long was St. Helens snoring before you people started building snack bars on her?

LEE: Well, let's see: Last major eruption was in 1800.

BI: Okay. See that there? [Points to the mountain east of Kailua-Kona that rises above the Ironman course.]

LEE: You mean Hualalai?

BI: Yep. Know the last time she jumped the shark?

LEE: Don't tell me...

BI: 1801. So the next time you're blithely sipping cappuccino at Lava Java, make sure your laces are tied.

LEE: You mean...?

BI: Just sayin'.

LEE: What about Kohala Mountain?

BI: You're safe. That was mostly an accident.

LEE: What kind of accident?

BI: I don't like to talk about it. We worked it out and the records were sealed. Hey, what are you writing there? That was off the record!

LEE: You should have said something earlier.

BI: You and the paparazzi. A hundred years I'm posing for postcards, and do I get a royalty check once in a while? No, I do not!

LEE: Is that why you threw a fit three years ago?

BI: You mean the earthquake. That was nothing.

LEE: Nothing? The guy in the place next to me lost a Sony big screen!

BI: Sorry about that. Fact of life when you're sitting on top of an active tectonic plate.

LEE: You mean there are going to be more?

BI: You better hope so.

LEE: Why?

BI: Because the longer you go without one, the worse the next one's going to be.

LEE: Kind of like when I've been eating barbecue and go for days without going to the—

BI: Whatever. Point is, it pays never to forget how I got here. Did you know that I'm the youngest bit of earth on this entire planet?

LEE: Way you've been behaving, I wouldn't doubt it. Probably why you're also the most remote bit of earth on the planet.

BI: Hey: Did I come to you or did you come to me?

LEE: Fair point.

BI: Thank you. When's your flight home?

"While you were racing…"

The greatest compliment we get is when
someone tells us they didn't even know we existed.

–John Bertsch, Director
Ironman Race Operations Center

Up until recently, I'd always assumed that the Ironman World Championship was run by elves. I could see the athletes and the volunteers but how did a fresh load of ice get to the aid station at mile 15? How did the trash that was building up at the turnaround disappear? How did sag wagons get to the bike crash near the airport so fast, and how did two new Port-a-Potties suddenly materialize on the Queen K near Waikoloa Village Road?

The only logical explanation was elves, and for the last twenty years that was good enough for me.

As it turns out, the real explanation is quite a bit more interesting than that. Have you ever seen footage of flight operations on an aircraft carrier? Aside from the awe-inspiring spectacle of dozens of noisy jets being violently flung off a floating airstrip, there's the more subtly fascinating sight of 5,000 people acting in intricate concert to make it possible.

What you might not know is that those carrier procedures are modeled after Ironman race operations. (If you're wondering how it's possible that a naval operation that has been going on for seventy years could be modeled after one that has only been in existence for four, you don't read enough science fiction.) The Race Operations Center, or ROC, is one of those things you hope you never need but are mighty glad are there if you do. In order to explain it, a little history is in order.

The original "race operations center" consisted of event director Diana Bertsch, a cell phone and a trailer full of radios. The people handling registration, aid stations, medical assistance, traffic control and a host of other functions knew their jobs and knew them well, but any unforeseen circumstance requiring coordination among two or more of them inevitably made its way to Diana's earpiece, through her brain and back out as a series of directives, but only to a small number of recipients. Others who might have been indirectly affected learned of the situation by happenstance, or not at all. The system worked, but its limitations nagged at the event director.

"I'd always thought there was a better way," Diana says, "but since things were working so well, there wasn't a lot of incentive to change. So while we made improvements every year, we didn't undertake a major overhaul."

That all changed on the morning of October 15, 2006. "The earthquake was a nasty wake-up call," Diana remembers. "I wondered what would have happened had it occurred on race day. How would we have marshaled and directed and communicated efficiently with all the resources that would have been required to deal with that situation?"

She went on to explain that they've always had critical incident plans, such as procedures to quickly move people to higher ground in the event of a tsunami. "But what we were missing was tight coordination with municipal authorities."

Fortunately, the answer was close at hand. Very close, as it happened. John Bertsch, ex-commissioner of both the fire and police departments on the Big Island, was a credentialed expert in public safety and was also intimately familiar with the inner workings of the World Championship.

"Diana gave us a clear mandate," he said of the team he eventually put together. "We had to come up with a single, centralized nerve center capable of coordinating and communicating with every facet of race-day operations and do it in a way that made it easier for people to do their jobs rather than layer on one more thing for them to worry about."

John knew that all the elements were already in place, but he also knew they were factionalized. "We had the medical team, aid station coordination, bike tech support, police, fire...but there was no good way of hooking people together and sharing information."

The first thing he did was involve every external agency that could play a part in the execution of the race, whether it was during the normal course of events or only during an emergency. This included not only police and fire officials, but the TSA, FBI, the Departments of Defense and Transportation, hotel security, SWAT, the Director of Civil Defense. "We even deal with the US Navy and the Coast Guard," John said, "although the Coast Guard's role pretty much ends when the last swimmer is out of the water."

Focus groups were conducted to gather ideas on developing a plan for how best to serve the athletes, volunteers and the community. As the plan started coming together, John brought in Stacey Aguiar. "We're going to need a room," he told her, one big enough to accommodate everybody who could conceivably be drawn in to deal with any of the myriad scenarios they were considering. "Why don't you figure out how to do that?"

What Stacey came up with was a configuration that provided a physical seat for each of the twelve race directors, every representative of the municipal agencies, three admins and three dispatch teams covering the main operational functions. That comes to over three dozen seats.

"The dispatch teams are the primary users of the ROC during normal operations," she says, "normal" meaning non-emergency. "Even when everything is going perfectly, it's still pretty frenetic, but it never gets chaotic. Those three teams, and the procedures they use, are what keep it that way."

Stumbling Towards the Finish Line

The three teams are medical, athlete (primarily bike) support and race operations. Each team consists of a dispatcher, who does the communicating, and a data logger, known as a "CAD operator," who is responsible for entering pertinent information into a computer system. The medical team also includes an ER physician.

While John is the director of the ROC, managing the room is Stacey's responsibility; she determines schedules and shifts based on anticipated workloads and is also responsible for training all of the participants in procedures and the use of the ROC's technology. While not all of the seats are occupied at one time—for one thing, most of the race directors are out on the course throughout the day—John and Diana have the ability to page any and all to the center should the need arise, as it might during a major emergency. (More about that later.)

At the heart of the operation is a computer system designed by Pat Riley, whose regular job is doing much the same for the Gig Harbor Fire Department in Washington State. A quintessential computer and electronics geek, Pat's first love is studying systems. "Complex interactions that form a smooth, well-integrated whole have always fascinated me," he says, "and creating one of those is an immensely gratifying undertaking."

Several years ago when the ROC was still being laid out, one of the chiefs from the Gig Harbor FD volunteered in the medical tent in Kona. John Bertsch walked by just as the chief opened his laptop during a break to check in on the situation back home. "I glanced at the screen and asked him what it was," John recalls. "*It's everything*, the guy answers, and he points to fire trucks, hydrants, incident reports, all overlaid onto a map. And the fire trucks were moving!"

It took John about two seconds to see the situational awareness possibilities for Ironman. "I got in touch with Pat and said, *I gotta have one of those.*"

"At first I thought, sure, an easy adaption" Pat said. But it wasn't that simple. For one thing, the event didn't own its own computers. And since all the vehicles were short-term rentals, nothing could be permanently mounted in them. "On top of that," he says, "the whole thing is over seventeen hours after it starts. You can't gradually phase it in; the entire enchilada has to be in place from minute one, and there are no second chances."

Intrigued with the possibility of creating a totally new system from scratch, Pat threw away the fire department template and started thinking about a fresh approach. "The first thing I decided is that we had to build this system in the cloud instead of housing it on a local platform. That meant it had to be entirely web-based, accessible from anywhere on anything that could host a browser."

And since there were going to be over five hundred separate touch points, using a computer for each one was financially and logistically impractical. "Ten years ago we would have been dead in the water on that one, but since the advent of the smart phone, there were all kinds of possibilities." He settled on Nextel phones as the primary device, then set about creating an app that could be downloaded into each of them.

"What we essentially did was turn these five hundred rented phones into five hundred handheld aircraft transponders. Each unit has its own unique code that identifies it in the central system."

The next step was to create a means of graphical presentation. A tidal wave of data is useless unless there's a way to filter and display it in a manner that doesn't overwhelm the user. "Anyone who's familiar with the 'Big Board' from movies like *Dr. Strangelove* and *Fail Safe* will recognize our display," Pat says, adding proudly, "except ours is light years ahead of those clunky, black-and-white visuals."

Color-coded icons dot a satellite map of the Kona course. "Depending on who needs to know what at any point in time," Pat says, "we can show aid stations, highway markers, medical vans, sag wagons, you name it. And when they move, the icons move." In addition, right-clicking on any icon calls up incident data entered by the CAD operators.

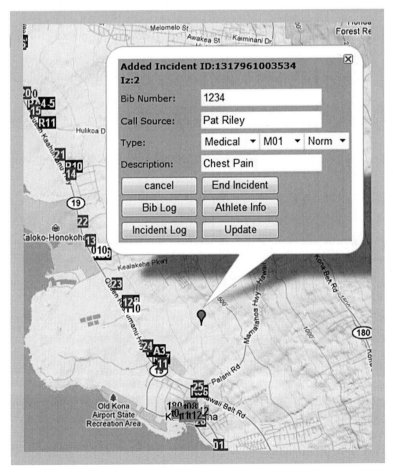

The ROC Board graphic display uses icons to provide a real-time snapshot of what's happening out on the race course.

Stumbling Towards the Finish Line

The ROC was rolled out in beta in 2008 and became fully operational in 2010. By that time it had gotten so sophisticated that not everyone was fully aware of all its capabilities.

"We were looking at the Board last year," John recalls, "and all of a sudden one of the medical van icons turned black. I thought maybe the system had a glitch and turned to ask Pat about it. He said no, he'd just forgotten to tell me about something new he'd added."

"There were occasional reports about drivers going too fast on the way to incidents," Pat continues. "So I added this feature that turns the icon black if the speed goes above sixty, and you can also see the exact speed."

"We want them to get there fast," John says, "but first of all we want them to get there. So we all smiled at each other and then I picked up a radio and called the driver and I said, *Hey, slow down! You're doing seventy-eight!* There was this big silence and up on the Board we watched the speed plummet and could practically feel him slamming on the brakes. About ten seconds later the guy gets on the radio and says, *How the* bleep *did you know that!*"

Back in the day, if there was a medical problem out on the course, someone would put out a general call until one of the medical vans picked it up and headed for the scene. The problem was that nobody had an overall picture, so there was no way to tell if that was really the best van to send. Now, a quick glance at the Board, along with the medical dispatcher's knowledge of what each of his teams is doing at the moment, allows him to call up the closest available team and get them on the case.

Spotting anomalies is a particular strength of the system. "We can do a lot," Pat explains. "If there are an unusual number of flats at mile 50, we're going to know it right away from the data that's been logged and get a crew out there to check the road. We've also got direct feeds from the Department of Transportation's street cameras and police surveillance cameras and can selectively put the images on the Board."

They can also log data on individual athletes. If a runner has a medical problem but gets going again, the information can be used to see whether he showed up at the next timing point. Nextel transponders are carried by every ice truck, every NBC crew, the motorcyclists accompanying the male and female race leaders, even the helicopters. All of their locations are tracked in real time, and any of them can be in two-way communication within seconds. There are other feeds into the center as well, including information on earthquake activity from the US Geological Survey, readings from the Pacific Tsunami Warning Center and detailed weather information from Doppler radar. Ten-minute briefings are held every ninety minutes to review overall status and incident reports.

"Our job isn't to tell the race directors how to do their jobs," John emphasizes. "What we do is give them the information and tools to do their jobs better. If you wanted to sum up the purpose of the center in a couple of sentences, you could say it's twofold: First, we gather information, cast it into useful form, and disseminate it back out to the people who need it. Second, we provide a central command facility in which relevant personnel can gather in the event of an emergency."

As an old-school systems pro myself, one of the things I find most impressive about the ROC is how it has reduced the amount of time wasted in deciding how to decide. The center conforms to the federal NIMS (National Incident Management System) protocol, as do many of the agencies it deals with, and so the procedures of gathering, interpreting and disseminating information are familiar to all the players. Equally important, there is a well-defined chain of command in place, with no need to spend a lot of time debating about who has the authority to do what. When incidents arise that need resolving, the individuals responsible for that resolution are able to focus on making the best decisions possible without getting distracted by the mechanics of decision-making.

The ultimate authority rests with Diana. "I used to get bombarded with things better handled by other people," she says. "Now, I'm able to concentrate on more critical matters while still keeping my finger on the overall pulse."

More correctly, the ultimate authority rests with Diana so long as the ROC stays the ROC. Should any of a number of pre-defined situations arise, the ROC turns into the EOC (Emergency Operations Center), and then life inside the room changes dramatically.

"Authority shifts depending on the nature of the emergency," John says. "This is an island, and our resources are strictly limited. If what we need isn't within fifteen minutes of us, it's going to be hours or maybe not at all. So if there's an earthquake and parts of the course become impassable, or if there's a brushfire that interferes with visibility to the point where safety is compromised, we're on our own, and if one of the agencies asks us to turn the center over to them, we'll do it. We're firm believers in continuity of operations and a unified command structure." In other words, only one person at a time can be the Big Kahuna, and who it is depends on what's going on.

And that, friends, is how fresh ice gets to the aid station at mile 15 and why no athlete in distress is alone for long and why you're in good hands if an earthquake in Japan threatens to swamp the finish line and why we'll probably have a lot of warning should a sixty-ton spacecraft with a badly decaying orbit decide to have its homecoming party in our vicinity.

At least that's what they tell me. Personally, I still think it's elves.

The Age Grouper's Race

One of the reasons for the exploding popularity of triathlon is that, unlike nearly every sport in the world except running, ordinary folk can not only compete but can do it in the very same events as the best in the world. This is like me teeing it up next to Phil Mickelson at the Masters. (I actually did tee it up once next to Phil Mickelson at the Masters, and it took nearly everything a dozen of my friends and family had to post my bail.)

At the Ironman World Championship, it's not unusual to see a 70-year-old nun wade into the start area next to eight-time world champion Paula Newby-Fraser. Once when my now 65-69 wife was 55-59, she was in the same helicopter television shot as Heather Fuhr. The fact that Heather was heading down Pay 'n' Save Hill at mile 25 while my wife was heading up Pay 'n' Save Hill at mile 10 is quite beside the point, the point being that they were still in the same race.

(A little side note here for those of you new to the World Championship: You might wonder why it's called Pay 'n' Save Hill when there isn't a Pay 'n' Save store within 2,800 miles of the place. To find out, see "A Spectator's Guide to the Ironman" elsewhere in this book.)

The non-professionals, known as age groupers, get a lot of attention in Ironman, because the World Triathlon Corporation considers every athlete to be the center of its mission. If you look at how the race is organized, you'll notice that this attention to every individual who competes is baked deep into the clockwork of the logistics. That's why the competitor who drags himself across the finish line at two minutes before midnight in 1,887th place gets the same reception and service as the one who came in nine hours earlier in first place. (Actually, now that I think about it, the reception is even more energetic.)

Yet, most of what's been written about the race seems to focus on the professional's experience. This isn't unreasonable. It's very exciting to read about epic battles like Scott vs. Allen, and less so about epic battles like Joe Blow vs. his exploding intestines. The professionals also photograph better, since one of the things that make for a nice picture is light, and there is a hell of a lot more of it at 3:00 pm on Ali'i Drive than there is at 11:00 pm on the Queen K Highway. It's also the case that press interviewers are fresh and alert when the pros come in but probably on their eighth mai tai at Pancho and Lefty's when the main body of age groupers starts drifting in.

So it occurred to me that, while Ironman fans seem to know a lot about what the race is like for a professional, they don't really have much appreciation for what it's like for an age grouper. Here are a couple of observations from hundreds of conversations with the-only-thing-I-ever-endorsed-was-a-check crowd.

BIKING THE QUEEN K: Professionals often comment on how hot it was out on the Queen K during the return portion of the bike leg. Part of the reason for this is that they usually have a tailwind. Herewith a little simple physics, well known to anybody who has ever sailed:

If you're doing 30 mph along the road with a 30 mph wind at your back, you don't feel the wind. As far as you're concerned, there *is* no wind. And if there's no wind, there's nothing cooling you down. Hence, you feel the heat.

Age groupers never complain about how hot it was out on the Queen K during the return portion of the bike leg. That's because, by the time they get back down from the turnaround at Hawi, the tailwind has shifted and become a headwind. The good news about a headwind is that it cools you down. The bad news is that it also slows you down. A lot. About 80% of the drag on a bicyclist comes from wind resistance. (The rest is from friction between the wheels and the road and the turning components of the bike.)

So the last 30+ miles of the bike leg is typically a howling hell for most age groupers. But, since the pros never mention it, a lot of people probably think that the age groupers are either making it up or making excuses.

And, in truth, it's even worse than that, because that wind that has become a tailwind on the way back is a headwind on the way out. This means that most of the age groupers have a headwind on the Queen K *in both directions*, and 68 miles of the 112-mile bike leg is on the Queen K.

If you ask me, the reason that most people turn pro is for no other reason than to get rid of that damned headwind.

THE ENERGY LAB: Nobody likes running in the Energy Lab, the main facility of a state-operated alternative research program about six miles out of town. Miles 15 through 19 of the marathon are in the Lab. It's four miles of hot, badly paved road of which the last mile is a relentless uphill pull. Worse still, it puts you tantalizingly close to the cool blue waters of the Kona Coast, so close that you can feel the spray if the wind is blowing right. Along with whatever other pains you're fighting, you also have to fight the urge to veer off the course and take a thirty-yard running jump into the biggest natural spa on the planet.

But, at least if you're a pro, you're doing all of this during *daylight*.

Doing it at night when you're already half-dead from dehydration and exhaustion is a whole 'nother smoke. As I said, the road is badly paved. It's also full of random chunks of lava and sandy spots that, to a dizzy, blind and semi-delusional age grouper seem like malevolent sprites dispatched by Madame Pele to teach a lesson to those who would presume to challenge her authority. Every step is a potential catastrophe, and it's hard for us non-racing mortals to fully appreciate the enormous psychic energy expended in dealing with this distraction. It takes a terrible toll at a time when the athletes have little left to give.

And when they leave the Energy Lab they have something else to look forward to:

Stumbling Towards the Finish Line

Night: I already said that. Once you get past 7:00 or so, yes, it's night, and everybody who hits the Lab after about six is going to do some portion of it at night. And it's pretty dark down there.

But night out on the Queen K is not just dark...it's really, *really* dark.

Back in the day, the World Championship was always scheduled for the Saturday closest to a full moon. This made sense. There are very few streetlamps out on the Queen K, so a full moon would provide a bit of illumination.

The problem was that night also brought an abrupt rise in humidity, which quickly threw up an overcast so thick you not only couldn't see the moon, you quite literally couldn't even tell where it was *supposed* to be. It provided about as much illumination as a Timex Ironman watch at 5,000 paces.

Most people in modern civilization really have little idea of what outdoor darkness is like, because it's rare for most of us ever to escape artificial illumination altogether.

About the darkest dark I've ever seen is the Queen K Highway at night. It's the damnedest thing you ever didn't see. You have to concentrate really hard to be able to make out your own feet, or even your hand, and as for other people out there somewhere in your vicinity, it's a good thing they're all breathing so hard and treading so heavily or you'd never know they were there. This is why the race gives out light sticks after sunset. It has nothing to do with helping you see where you're stepping. It's so you don't step on someone else.

Standing around in stuff like that is frightening. Running around in stuff like that is downright terrifying. To an age grouper, the aid station at mile 20 looks like an oasis to a desert traveler, not because of the Gatorade, but because of the *light*. However brief the respite, it's a moment of comforting illumination, then it quickly fades and then gets even worse. Like an escaping prisoner who thinks he has it made and is then recaptured, a bout of depression is in store for the athlete who plunges once again into a featureless sea.

Loneliness: Even if you can cope with the darkness, it's hard to fight the feeling of isolation. It's hard to keep in mind that there's actually a race going on when all you can hear is your own breathing and all you can see is nothing. It's quiet. Nothing moves. You run, but nothing seems to get closer so it's difficult to know if you're getting anywhere. There are no helicopters, no cameras, and absolutely nobody standing on the sidelines wishing you well, because what spectators would want to take up station where they can't even see the athletes?

It's one step, then another and another, and the only thing keeping you going is the knowledge that there truly is a finish line out there somewhere, and if you just keep putting one foot in front of the other, eventually you'll get there.

The last few miles out on the Queen K is where the Ironman veterans have it all over the first-timers: They know what's coming. They know it's going to be worth it.

The rest have to take it on faith.

Homeward Bound: Paula N-F once said that the reason you race the first 140 miles is just so you can do the last 300 yards. But there's one more psychic hand grenade thrown at you before you get to the good stuff.

It happens as you're running down Pay 'n' Save Hill (the one without the Pay 'n' Save on it). As you near Kuakini Highway, you can see bright lights in the distance down by the pier. You can hear music and celebrating and the voice of Mike Reilly conferring the title of Ironman over and over as weary athletes stumble to a stop with varying degrees of grace, relief, gratitude and new-found appreciation for the sport and for themselves.

At the bottom of Palani, you're back among cheering spectators and light and only a block away from the festivities, a handful of steps. It's right there, a seven-iron away but...

...you turn sharply left and, maddeningly, run away from the finish, to be swallowed up in the bleakness of Kuakini Highway, alone again. The reason is that you've only done 139.6 miles, and the full distance is 140.6. You have to add one more mile, and this is where you do it. The only thing that makes you feel a twinge better is that there are people just heading out on the run, twenty miles to go, and you can't comprehend what that must be like, so this last mile doesn't seem quite as bad. But it's still bad.

There are only two turns left. The first comes at Hualalai, and you wonder what it means. The mind races to put a label on it, to categorize the small maneuver, to fit it into some larger context, because at this point in your fatigue and disorientation those little milestones suddenly take on critical importance. It can't just be another mile notched onto your belt; it has to be the last mile before something, or the first of several something elses, some symbolic rite of passage to make the point that there is a point to all of this, that progress is occurring, that the list of things you have to check off is finite and getting smaller, and you've checked off another one. So what does that last turn onto Hualalai mean?

Once upon a time and for a number of years, hiding in the darkness at that corner was a man. A voice, really, because no one ever got a good look at his face. As each runner passed him he said quietly, "Welcome home." Nothing more. Just "Welcome home," but it's one of those phrases that seemed to glow with a quiet mysticism, dense with meaning and possessed of a kind of inarguable finality. You've been out "there" for thirteen, fifteen, sixteen hours, at times genuinely perplexed about what you were doing out there at all.

But now, all questions are answered and all questioning ceases. There's no more mystery. No more plunges into heartless darkness. No more heart-breaking detours.
Home is where you go when you go home. It's where they have to take you in, no matter what. That guy who welcomed athletes home knew all that, and in that instant when he said "Welcome home," you knew it, too.

I don't know who that fellow was. Nobody seems to, and I'm hoping he never actually existed, because just imagine what that would tell us about this race and these racers and about the kinds of things that are hard-wired into the human soul.

Stumbling Towards the Finish Line

ALI'I DRIVE: I'm going to shortchange you a little here and not even try to describe what it feels like for an Ironman finisher to run the final quarter mile. There are two reasons for this. The first is that I'm not an Ironman athlete, and I have no idea what it feels like. The second is that no Ironman athlete has ever been able to describe it, even though every single one of them has tried. Perhaps the fact that they all tried and failed tells you everything you need to know about what it feels like.

I do have a couple of observations, though.

The first is that Ali'i Drive on an ordinary day bears about as much resemblance to Ali'i Drive on Ironman night as Times Square on an ordinary day does to Times Square on New Year's Eve. There are thousands of people. There is singing and dancing. There is food and music and powerful lights and enough energy to power a nuclear submarine.

I'm not talking about mid-afternoon when the pros come in, either. I'm talking about midnight, when the last runner comes in, and all the hours that precede it. The place is a combination hoedown, riot, rave and Eminem concert, except without all the throwing up (at least if you don't count Joe Blow struggling to get to the finish line at the same time as his intestines).

Now that you've got that picture, picture this: You've been swimming, biking and running since seven that morning. You've been in the Pacific, up on Kohala Mountain, up and down the lava fields, all on your own power. You've seen the sun come up, seen it traverse the entire sky and seen it disappear again, and during all that time you never stopped moving. It's been hot, wet, windy, muggy, glaringly bright, blindingly dark, physically agonizing, psychically draining and unutterably lonely. You've seen God, you've seen the devil, and at times you couldn't tell them apart.

But at just about the point where you'd be willing to sell your soul for three minutes on a soft couch, you make the final turn onto Ali'i. Where there was darkness, there is now light. Where there was silence, there is now music. Where there was unbearable loneliness, there are now 2,000 of your closest friends holding the world's biggest frat party to celebrate the fact that you are in the final stretch of the Ironman World Championship.

As tired and hurting as you are, it feels as though some beatific spirit has just pumped 500 cc's of primo adrenaline into your sagging behind. You straighten up. You lift your shoulders. If you were walking, you now run, knees kicking up high. You adjust your race number and wipe away some sweat. You might even kick in a little speed, which a mere twenty minutes ago you would have thought about as likely as Jabba the Hutt making the Wimbledon finals.

All the demons in your head flee for cover under the onslaught of those 2,000 friends screaming their lungs out for you, and in the last few seconds as you close in on the finish line, everything suddenly becomes clear and you know why you're here. It took all day to figure it out, but it happens right smack in the nick of time, because one more second of delay and you might not be able to fully grasp the one voice that barrels

in over the rest because it's amplified by the public address system. The voice belongs to Mike Reilly or Whit Raymond, and it makes an official declaration every bit as profound as a papal bull from the Vatican:

"You are an *Ironman*!"

Welcome home.

Speaking Hawaiian

A tourist walks up to a native Hawaiian and says,
"So is it Hawai'i or Havai'i?"
The native answers, "Havai'i."
"Thank you," says the tourist.
"You're velcome," replies the native.

Actually, I should have called this "Pronouncing Hawaiian."

Kona locals are enraptured with the Hawaiian language. Everywhere you go you see words in Hawaiian: on posters, in newspaper editorials, on T-shirts, in the Aloha Airlines onboard magazine.

A few years ago I decided to study a little Hawaiian because, spending as much time here as I did, I thought it would be nice to converse with the indigenous population in their own lingo. That's when I discovered that, as much as people speak *about* Hawaiian, nobody actually *speaks* Hawaiian. The sole exception is the *kahu* who blesses the carbo and award dinners and, while I assume he actually knows what he's saying, nobody else does, including the locals, which is why he always provides a translation.

As it happens, my linguistic efforts weren't wasted, because I got enraptured with Hawaiian myself. It truly is musical, poetic and, in an odd way, reflective of the gentle island *gestalt* you start to feel as soon as you arrive. So what they say about Hawaiian is really true.

Except when they say it's a "rich" language. It isn't. It may be a lot of things, but rich isn't one of them. For one thing, there are only twelve letters in the entire alphabet (all five vowels plus h, k, l, m, n, p and w), making Hawaiian the ultimate minimalist character system. For another, there aren't that many words. Wal-Mart uses more words just to label its shelves than there are in the entire Hawaiian dictionary.

So why should race-week visitors to the Big Island consider learning anything about a language that hosts no great literature and nobody speaks?

Because even though the locals don't know much Hawaiian, they pronounce what they do know extremely well, and I've found over the years that making the attempt to do the same elevates you considerably in the eyes of native Hawaiians and makes interacting with them much more fun. Off-islanders rarely pronounce place names the right way, and the locals usually won't correct them. But if they sense that you've studied up a little and are making the attempt, they take great delight in helping you get it right which, to a linguistic pedant such as me, is terrific fun.

Speaking of which, Hawaiian words are a lot of fun to pronounce, because the language is so rhythmic and musical. Compare the word "humuhumunukunukuapua'a" with, say, "prestidigitate" or "atherosclerosis" or "turret-mounted anti-aircraft gun" and you'll see my point. It really is a cool language.

So let's get on with getting you up to speed.

* * *

One of the other things that makes Hawaiian so cool is that it has stuff English doesn't. Or French, or German, or just about any other language you can think of, except Zulu. (When you hear someone speaking Zulu, you want to smack him smartly between the shoulder blades to dislodge whatever is caught in his throat.)

One of these is the *okina*, which is written like this, `, a little smudge that looks like an upside-down apostrophe. Since that's kind of hard to type and I don't trust all of your web browsers to be able to reproduce it anyway, I'll use an apostrophe. Don't worry about confusing it with a real apostrophe because Hawaiian doesn't have any.

The *okina* is what linguists call a "glottal stop," a kind of catch in the throat. You see it all the time in written Hawaiian—in fact, it's right there in the word "Hawai'i"—but you probably ignore it.

You shouldn't. The *okina* is actually a consonant. You wouldn't drop a consonant in English, like turning "phone" into "own," and you shouldn't do it in Hawaiian either.

The *okina* tells you to come to a complete stop...and then start again. Take as an example the Hawaiian word "a'a." It's not pronounced "ahhhh," as a prolonged sigh, but rather "ah ah." It's two distinct syllables, such as you'd use when trying to admonish a child, as in "Ah! Ah! Don't stab your little brother in the eye with those scissors!"

Speaking of a'a, here's an interesting factoid for you. You know how Eskimos have thirty-six different words for snow? Well, they don't, but Hawaiians have several different words for lava. Look around the island and you'll see that some lava has hardened into big, creamy looking swirls, kind of like Carvel soft-serve ice cream, only black. Other lava lies around in rough, craggy chunks. The smooth-looking swirly stuff has a smooth-sounding swirly name, which is "pahoehoe" (pa-HOE-eh-HOE-eh). The rough, craggy stuff has a rough, craggy name, "a'a" ("Ah! Ah!").

One nice thing about Hawaiian is that, like French, it's completely phonetic. (Unlike French, however, Hawaiian actually makes some sense phonetically, unless you think "soixante" is a reasonable way to spell "swasont.") There are just a few basic rules and you're off and running.

One rule is that not only is every consonant pronounced, but so is every vowel. So the name of the local airport, Keahole, has four syllables, not two, rhyming with "Way to go, eh?"

Stumbling Towards the Finish Line

An exception is when two vowels are run together, forming a *diphthong*, like "ai." You run them together smoothly and pronounce it like "aye-ee," except not as two completely distinct syllables, but more like drawing out the "i" sound in "thigh." Thus, you might think "Kailua" is pronounced like "Hiya new ma," but because of the diphthong "ai," it's more like "Hi, new ma."

While we're at it: The accent is usually placed on the next to last syllable. So, for two-syllable words, the accent is on the first syllable—HU-la, LU-au, HI-lo—and for three-syllable words it's on the second—ko-HA-la (the mountain where the bike turnaround is), wa-HI-ni (a female), and two of the streets on the bike leg of the race, pa-LA-ni and ma-KA-la. But if there's a diphthong, that's what gets the stress: ma-KAI (meaning "on the seaside"), pa-LAU-nu ("brown"), and Ha-NAU-ma ("curved bay" or "hand-wrestling bay." Don't ask me).

Piece of cake right? Good. Now pronounce this out loud: *'Aiea.*

This is a good word to know because it's the only city in the entire United States composed entirely of vowels. (Okay, so it's only good to know if you get turned on by that sort of thing.) It's also probably the most frequently mispronounced city name in the entire United States, with the possible exceptions of Cle Elum (rhymes with "me TELL 'em") and Worcester ("Wooster"). The correct pronunciation is "Eye-YAY-yah," with that little okina catch in the throat at the beginning so that you don't so much *say* "Eye" as cough it.

See? Completely phonetic. Now try this: "humuhumunukunukuapua'a"

Just break it down, remembering that every Hawaiian syllable ends in a vowel—humu humu nuku nuku apu a'a—and you'll see that it rhymes with "WHO knew? WHO knew? YOU knew! YOU knew! Ah-choo! Ah! Ah!"

It's a real word, by the way, and means "little fish with a nose like a pig's." It's also the name of a Hawaiian bar drink. In some places it's free if you pronounce it correctly.

Here's another one: "Hualalai."

It goes "hu-WAH-la-LIE" and is the volcano on which Kailua-Kona is perched, as well as the name of the last street before the Ironman runners turn onto Ali'i Drive for the final quarter mile of the race. Incidentally, "Ali'i" is pronounced "ah-LEE-ee" and not "ah lee yee," because of the *okina* separating the i's. (It's also not "a-LEE-hee.")

The most mispronounced word in the Hawaiian language has to be "Hawai'i." It's not "huh-WAH-yee" or "huh-WAH-ee." It's "huh-WHY-ee," with the okina throat catch between diphthong "why" and "ee."

Here's one that might surprise you if you've ever been in a Waikiki tour group led by some guy who looks Samoan but is actually from Decatur or Worcester: "Aloha."

You know the guy. He's the one that makes you go "a-lo-HAH!" at the top of your lungs forty-seven times before he finally leaves you the hell alone. Well, it's not "a-lo-HAH." In Hawaiian, if there are no diphthongs or *kahako* (letters with a little hat ^ on them), it's always the next to last syllable that gets stressed. So it's "a-LO-ha" pure and simple, just like you always thought it was. When you hear somebody go "a-lo-HAH," you can be sure he's on the first day of a cruise.

An "e" not combined with another vowel is pronounced as in "left," not "bay." So a "haole," which means someone not of Hawaiian descent, is "HOW-leh," not "howly." (And note that it's two syllables, not three, because of the diphthong "ao"). But Makalei, which is a terrific golf course just above Kailua-Kona, is "MA-ka-lay."

One last thing: That big city on Oahu? It's not "Hah-na-LU-lu." It's "HO-no-LU-lu," as in "Oh no, Lulu!" That one alone will separate you from the people who save up all year for a Hawaiian vacation and then spend all of it at McDonald's and Wal-Mart.

I leave you with this ancient Hawaiian saying:

> *He lawai`a no ke kai papa`u, he pôkole ke aho;*
> *he lawai`a no ke kai hohonu he loa ke aho.*

If you think that's beautiful, it's only because the language is so cool. Translate it into English, and it doesn't exactly rank right up there with the best of Oscar Wilde:

> *A fisherman of the shallow sea uses only a short line;*
> *a fisherman of the deep sea has a long line.*

THE SECOND PART:

NOT SO FUNNY STUFF

Things you probably didn't know about people you probably know

Q & A with:
DIANA BERTSCH

Take it from a former professional management consultant: There's all kinds of executive talent, each with its own set of skills and capabilities, but the rarest is the operations manager who can successfully coordinate a wide array of disparate functions in pursuit of a single, time-specific goal. Do it right and you get the Normandy invasion, the opening ceremonies of the Olympic Games, or a shuttle launch. Screw it up and you get Mobile Me, Windows Vista or the Bay of Pigs. For those of you who have marveled at how the dizzyingly complex logistics of the Ironman World Championship seem, like DNA, to self-assemble effortlessly, be assured that it all starts at the top. Meet event director Diana "Will Work for Ulcers" Bertsch.

LEE: If memory serves, the 2010 event is your eighth time up at bat?

DIANA: That's correct.

LEE: Have you got it on autopilot yet?

DIANA: Don't I wish. Although actually I don't wish, because when we stop trying to make improvements, that's when I need to move on and do something else. It's gratifying when you introduce changes, and they make things better—they don't always—but that just motivates us to find more things that can be improved.

LEE: It's a cliché to say you can't get a degree in this kind of stuff, but you actually did, didn't you?

DIANA: Sort of, but not really. I've got a bachelor's in business from UNLV and several years of overseas graduate work in international management, but nothing in that schooling prepared me for this.

LEE: How'd you wind up going to college in Las Vegas?

DIANA: I lived there. When I was four and we were in Reseda [in the San Fernando Valley, west of Los Angeles], Dad decided that he'd had enough of the big city and moved us to Vegas, which in 1969 was a surprisingly small town.

LEE: So by the time you graduated in...

DIANA: 1988

LEE: ...you hadn't seen much of the world.

DIANA: True, so that's when I decided to move out of my comfort zone. I'd met [future husband] John at

UNLV, and his father was a kind of visiting professor at Brunel University in England. He persuaded me to go to grad school there.

LEE: Vegas to West London. That had to be abrupt.

DIANA: That was only part of it. I was not just the only female in the international management program and the only one who spoke only English, I was also the youngest student by fifteen years. Nearly everyone else was an experienced businessperson pursuing an advanced degree.

LEE: So much for your comfort zone.

DIANA: Exactly. But it was an intense learning experience. I remember one class in international law, the instructor would teach things out of this book and the students would roll their eyes and say, "No, no... let me tell you what happens in the real world."

LEE: Kind of like Rodney Dangerfield in *Back to School*.

DIANA: Huh?

LEE: Never mind. I seem to remember you once telling me you'd been to school in Switzerland.

DIANA: The program at Brunel was changing so I transferred to a school in Lausanne. Another eye-opening experience.

LEE: So what did you do with all this learning when you came back to the States?

DIANA: At first not much. I was back in Southern California and did some odd jobs, then went to work for an outfit that took people back and forth to Catalina Island by boat. I put on special events for groups, working with a marketing company called GMR. They now represent PowerBar, so that relationship kind of came full circle.

LEE: When was your first brush with Ironman?

DIANA: John and I honeymooned on the Big Island in 1990. We were at the Kona Surf and our last day was Ironman race day, so we decided to get up early and get a spot on the sea wall to watch the start. Neither of us had any idea what to expect, and I was totally unprepared.

LEE: What was it like for you?

DIANA: Utter shock and awe. To this day I remember every second of that magnificent spectacle. I was overwhelmed, and turned to John and said, "I want to do this someday." Somehow, I had to be a part of it.

LEE: But that day you had to go home.

DIANA: We did, but John was in construction, and two years later his company started building homes on the Big Island, and we jumped at the chance to move here. I got into the Ironman scene immediately, and for fours years we volunteered just about everywhere: finish line, aid stations, transition areas...we even helped set up the swim course. Anything to stay close to the sport.

LEE: Except doing it?

DIANA: Wasn't that easy to qualify, and then in '95 we had to move to Flagstaff, Arizona. I did the Keauhou Half Ironman that May, and wouldn't you know it: I got a slot in the roll down.

LEE: Four months to train for the Big One. Not a lot of time.

DIANA: No, but it was even less than that, because it wouldn't be until July that we were finally settled enough for me to start training. A friend of mine drew up a training plan designed to just get me to the finish line, and I got started. But it still wasn't easy, because I was traveling back and forth between Flagstaff and Vegas a lot.

LEE: Where did you swim?

DIANA: I didn't, hardly at all. I hadn't even learned to swim until we got to Hawai'i in '92, and only then because we discovered all these great events put on by Peaman [Sean Pagett]. The first time I swam a race in the ocean, I panicked when I put my head into the water and saw all those fish. The swim was only about 600 yards, but I hyperventilated my way through the whole thing. When I came out, runners were already finishing and I had to convince the race officials that, yes, I really did want to finish. Then a couple of days later John read in the paper that I'd placed in my division!

LEE: So back home your IM training was mostly biking and running.

DIANA: My Dad was worried about me doing that alone in Vegas so he'd grab coffee and newspapers and leapfrog me with his car. Some of my warmest memories are of him always appearing around the next bend. And John did the same for me in Flagstaff.

LEE: How was your Ironman race?

DIANA: What I remember most clearly was biking up Palani when it dawned on me, "I'm in the Ironman World Championship!" I couldn't believe it, people I knew cheering for me, the whole amazing spectacle.

LEE: And out on the highway?

DIANA: Reality set in quickly. I'd been told not to worry about the headwind going up because it would be a tailwind coming back. Well, maybe it was for Mark Allen [that year's winner], but not for those of us who were "slightly" farther back in the pack. By the time I came back down the Queen K, the wind had switched and that was a surprise. There were times I thought I might not be able to finish, but once I got out on the run I knew I'd finish...except one time.

LEE: Why? What happened?

DIANA: I saw a guy lying on the road, not moving, and people from a sag wagon had gotten out to help him. I felt bad for him, then it struck me: What if he'd felt as good as I was feeling now earlier in his race? Am I going to wind up the same way?

LEE: But you finished.

DIANA: And it was the experience of a lifetime. I wasn't too upbeat when I then had to go and start our new life in Flagstaff, but two years later I got a call from Ironman asking if I'd like to come work for the race. It took some doing and some luck to make that possible, but it worked out.

LEE: You only did it for three years, though.

DIANA: Yes, but as it turns out, that was a blessing. I became the spa manager at the Four Seasons/Hualalai, and when they decided to open Kukio next door, I was asked to help the spa get going there.

I was brought on even before ground was broken. It was the ideal training ground for learning how to manage a highly complex undertaking with a thousand details and a thousand opportunities for things to go wrong.

LEE: Kukio opened at the end of 2002.

DIANA: Right, and the timing couldn't have been better. A few weeks after it went operational I got another call from Ironman, this time offering me the job of event director.

LEE: Did you jump at it?

DIANA: I wanted to, but I was a little hesitant because it was the 25th anniversary of the event and it was a very big deal. Everything had to go perfectly. Also, I was concerned about the transition from the previous race director. In an atmosphere like gearing up for the Ironman World Championship, relationships mean everything and abrupt changes are hard.

LEE: So you took some time to think about it?

DIANA: Not a lot; I felt that if I could bring on two people who'd worked closely with me at Hualalai, I'd be up to the challenge.

LEE: And they were...?

DIANA: Mahea Akau and Kerri Love. We'd been through it all together and had rock solid faith in each other's abilities and in our working relationship. So in March of 2003 I jumped into Ironman heart and soul.

LEE: Was the transition as difficult as you'd feared?

DIANA: No, and one of the reasons was that everyone working for the race was, ahead of anything else, totally in love with the sport and not about to let anything interfere with the athletes' experience. I'm not saying the job was easy—far from it—but none of the problems and headaches ever stemmed from internal friction. I'd match this crew against any event team in the entire world of sports.

LEE: Has it been the same way since WTC was purchased?

DIANA: Thankfully, yes. The new owners are every bit as fiercely protective of the event as the original ones were. Attitude comes from the top, and with that kind of orientation I'm convinced there's nothing we can't handle.

LEE: You said earlier that nothing is on autopilot. Don't you think that there'll come a point where it's all nailed down and all you have to do is fight the occasional fire?

DIANA: Inconceivable, if for no other reason than we spend a lot of time trying to figure out how to improve things. We're always trying new ideas, some of which work, some don't. Unfortunately, there's no way to know if something's going to fly until you do it live, so it's a risk.

LEE: There's been some carping about previous changes. Altering the course itself, moving the transition area around...

DIANA: Sure. There's no way to get better without making some mistakes once in a while.

LEE: Does the criticism bother you?

DIANA: Only in one sense, but the criticism itself is actually welcome. Unless we hear from people, we don't know how they feel. We're intensely self-critical inside the organization, so getting flak from athletes and other involved parties is just part of the process.

LEE: But you mentioned that there was one sense in which you are bothered. What's that?

DIANA: When people think we were motivated by something other than trying to improve the race. Everyone on the crew loves Ironman and cares deeply about the athletes, so you can imagine how it feels when someone implies that we don't.

LEE: Any changes we should be looking for this year?

DIANA: Some, but few you'll notice, or so we hope. Most of the improvements we make are intended to be seamless, and people don't tend to notice when there are fewer problems or things just run smoother.

LEE: Kind of like the security business. If you do your job right, nothing goes wrong, but people hardly know you exist.

DIANA: And we're fine with that. If we're successful, at the end of the day participants should be talking about how they performed and what the race meant to them, not whether there was enough ice at the aid stations.

LEE: One last question: Seems that every year or two there are rumors about the race moving to another location. Any truth there?

DIANA: Can you imagine it being anywhere but the Big Island?

LEE: No.

DIANA: Me, neither. We're here to stay.

Q & A with
MIKE REILLY

Every major sporting event has its athlete heroes, but sometimes the public persona of the overall endeavor is represented by a different kind of participant. John Madden brought football alive by providing continuity and story lines across the season. For many people, baseball will forever be linked to the sound of Vin Scully's voice wafting out of radios on lazy summer nights. For boxing fans, it was Howard Cosell who anchored our perception even as champions of the ring came and went. For the Ironman World Championship, the iconic glue is Mike Reilly. It's his voice throughout the long day that pulls the pieces together, and it's his call across the finish line that stamps finality on a racer's day even more definitively than the last beep of the timing mat. Here's how it got to be that way...

LEE: So did you grow up in some exotic locale like Kailua-Kona?

MIKE: Pretty much. It was Toledo, Ohio.

LEE: But you live in Southern California, so what brought you there?

MIKE: My degree was in special education, and my brother Don had some pull in the San Diego school district. He got me an interview, and I got the job.

LEE: That was in a junior high, right?

MIKE: Yes, teaching kids with learning and physical disabilities. Very tough school in a very tough neighborhood.

LEE: I thought your brother had pull.

MIKE: So did I. When I called to tell him I got an offer to teach at a junior high there, he was thrilled until I told him which one. Apparently it didn't have the best reputation so he called his buddy and got me into a different one, then found it was twice as bad as the original.

LEE: I know your brother Don very well.

MIKE: I know.

LEE: What actually happened was that he thought the first place wasn't enough of a challenge, and that's when he made that phone call.

MIKE: Are you serious?

LEE: You'll never know. Your family is too tight, so I'm just trying to cause trouble. Anyway, you had nothing to do with triathlon at that point, right?

MIKE: Never even heard of it. But I'd wrestled in college so I was in pretty good shape, and I started running in Balboa Park. I met a few people there and heard about this bunch of athletes that were doing this weird three-sport thing on Fiesta Island.

LEE: Do you remember any of them?

MIKE: I remember all of them, but their names didn't mean anything to me then. Scott Tinley and his brother Jeff, Murphy Rheinschreiber...

LEE: This was when?

MIKE: About 1978.

LEE: The year of the first Ironman.

MIKE: Whatever that was. My first tri was the Horny Toad, and it was a half IM on Coronado Island. My goal was to pass some Navy SEALS on the run after they killed me on the swim and bike, and I did.

LEE: So you were a runner.

MIKE: I'd done some marathons in the 2:40's, and Don and I had opened up a bunch of running stores. I'd quit teaching to manage them.

LEE: When did the announcing thing start?

MIKE: I was signed up for a 10K in 1980 but was hurt and couldn't run. The guy who was supposed to be calling the race couldn't for some reason, and the race director, Lynn Flanagan [who staged running races for thirty years], asked me to step in at the last minute because I knew a lot of the people running. It was fun, but when she asked me to do it again at the next race, I turned her down because I wanted to run, not announce. Then at the race after that she offered me a hundred bucks. That was significant money at the time, so I did it, and I kept doing it all through the '80s: 10Ks, marathons, triathlons...

LEE: What happened to the running stores?

MIKE: We sold them. But I ended up as West Coast rep for a handful of vendors who used to call on me as a customer. The biggest was Saucony, but I also had PowerBar and some others. Nine major lines in all, with a crew of about fifteen.

LEE: And you were still calling races, too?

Stumbling Towards the Finish Line

MIKE: About two dozen a year.

LEE: But not Ironman. When did that start?

MIKE: In 1989 I got a call from Mike Plant, who was the Ironman announcer. He told me that Valerie Silk, who owned the race at the time, told him to bring me in.

LEE: The idea was for you two to work together?

MIKE: Yes, and we did for two years. Then I took over.

LEE: And called every World Championship since.

MIKE: Right, along with plenty of other Ironman and 70.3 races.

LEE: Aren't you creeping up on number 100?

MIKE: March in New Zealand will be my hundredth. Kona this week is number 97.

LEE: Okay, let's get to the heart of what people really want to hear: Where did the "You are an Ironman!" proclamation come from? And how did it get to rank up there with "Gentlemen, start your engines," and "Let's get ready to rumble!" as defining sonic emblems?

MIKE: It sure wasn't on purpose. In 1992 a friend of mine named Bob was doing the race for the first time. His confidence level wasn't very high, and he was going around kind of mopey and filled with self-doubt, so the day before the race I took him by the shoulders and said, "You *will* be an Ironman!"

LEE: And when he came across the finish line...

MIKE: I looked down at him from the tower and yelled into the mike, "Bob! You...are...an...*Ironman*!"

LEE: But that was just a very personal statement from you to a friend.

MIKE: Well, that's all it was supposed to be. But for some reason the crowd went absolutely nuts.

LEE: My guess is that they'd never heard that as a declaration before. They obviously knew that people were finishing a tough event, but maybe it hadn't dawned on them that, as soon as the athlete crossed the line, he was instantly transformed into a new kind of being.

MIKE: An Ironman.

LEE: Right. And no matter what else happens to them in life, that's one thing nobody can take away from them, ever.

MIKE: Bragging rights for life. I think that's right. So here was this ordinary guy and as he passed under the arch, this voice booms out over the PA and—

LEE: Officially confers the title.

MIKE: And people just went crazy. So the next guy that came across, I did it again: "You are an Ironman!"

LEE: And the crowd reacted again?

MIKE: Again, and again, and again. I started to get a little hesitant, because it was feeling pretty redundant, but then I realized that, hey, those people coming across the line were hearing it for the first time. And it was about them, not me, so I just kept on doing it.

LEE: And the crowd?

MIKE: Kept going berserk. I think they understood before I did how much significance it had for each athlete.

LEE: But that could easily have been a one-night phenomenon, quickly forgotten.

MIKE: Except that, at the next event, someone came up to me before the start and said, "Will you say that for me?" I asked her what she meant, and she said, "You know: *You are an Ironman!*" So I said, "Sure," and then it happened several dozen more times that morning.

LEE: I heard you actually recorded it for someone's wedding. True?

MIKE: Yes, but it was more than that. I recorded this whole thing, calling the walk down the aisle like it was a race, etc. I heard it was a big hit.

LEE: What happened in Wisconsin a few weeks ago?

MIKE: I wasn't on the mike when one guy came through, so when he ran into me at the airport, he said, "Man, you gotta say it! And do it right!" So I yelled it right there in the terminal.

LEE: That wasn't the first time.

MIKE: God, no. I've done it in stores, on the street, as anniversary gifts from one spouse to another...

LEE: There's something I always wanted to ask you. I've personally watched you call about two dozen races—

MIKE: And you've been in the tower with me a few times.

LEE: Right. An amazing experience, by the way, and that's what got me wondering: Your day starts at about 5:00 am, at least in Kona, and ends 19 hours later after you've yelled some 1,800 people across the line. Yet at midnight, you've got the same energy level as you did when the sun was coming up. How do you do that?

MIKE: First of all, it may seem like the same energy level, but believe me, it isn't.

LEE: Even more remarkable, then. What's the secret?

MIKE: I think it all stems from my passion for the sport and profound respect for the athletes. Who am I to claim fatigue at eleven at night when that guy coming across the line has been out swimming, biking and running all day without quitting?

LEE: Very romantic, but that kind of attitude will only get you so far.

MIKE: So long as it gets me to midnight. And it's more powerful than you might think. My biggest fear is missing an athlete or getting laryngitis, not running out of gas. By the way, Kona is actually easier than some other races.

LEE: How so?

MIKE: A lot of the U.S. races are nonstop, because after the swim I head out to spectator hot spots and announce athletes as they pass by. But Kona has one long bike loop so there's a lot of waiting once the swim is over.

LEE: So you get a nice break.

MIKE: It's a break, but I don't like it much. I get all this adrenaline pumping as a result of the start, and then I have to go down-tools. Once things get going in town again, I'm higher than a kite for the rest of the day.

LEE: How do you feel when the race ends?

MIKE: Like I've been hit by a freight train. I sleep about six hours, then have to somehow get out of bed and start working on the awards ceremony. At least in Kona I have the whole day. Most of the mainland races do the awards at noon. What's funny is, people who did the race express concern for me. They say, "How's your voice?" and I look at them in amazement: "How's my voice? Never mind that...how're your legs!"

LEE: It's a good question, though. How is your voice?

MIKE: Depends where I am. Kona is as good as it gets, because all that warmth and humidity feels great in the throat and it feels fine.

LEE: What's the worst?

MIKE: Arizona, hands down. That bone-dry air hurts like all get out. Two years ago, heading home, I pulled into this In-N-Out Burger after not having spoken for a couple of hours, and when I tried to talk into the speaker, nothing came out but this weak little rasp. I couldn't say a word. Kind of scary.

LEE: Do you use the same crew at every race?

MIKE: Tom Zebart is always with me at the U.S. races. He's a terrific announcer himself, and we have this routine where he steps in for about ten minutes every hour to give me a break. At Kona we add Whit Raymond, and that's fun because he speaks fluent Japanese, and there's a large contingent of racers from Japan.

LEE: Wait, back up: Tom relieves you for ten minutes at a time? What happens to all those athletes who don't get to hear you call them across?

MIKE: Why do you think I do so much yelling in airports!

Q & A with
STEVE BUTTERFIELD

"An army travels on its stomach." The general who uttered this famous observation was making an important point: Monumental heroics may have won battles at Agincourt and Normandy, but you can't mobilize an army without taking care of things like hauling and preparing food, providing toilet paper and toothbrushes, and getting the ammo to where it's supposed to be in time to be useful. The people who make sure all of that happens are truly unsung heroes, all the more so for their selfless devotion to carrying out a difficult and complex mission while realizing that the only time the recipients of their dedication are likely to notice them is if something goes wrong. What kind of person puts himself on that risky a line for little public reward? Meet Ironman warehouse director Steve "Butter" Butterfield.

LEE: First of all, you're crazy.

STEVE: Helps to be a little nuts to want to do this job.

LEE: How long have you been at it?

STEVE: As director, since 2003, but I started volunteering in 2000.

LEE: Where were you from originally?

STEVE: Southern California. I was an electrical engineer and co-founded a company that made imaging technology that we licensed to big laser printer manufacturers like HP, Ricoh, Canon...

LEE: Are you the guy responsible for all those paper jams?

STEVE: No, we just helped make the images. Feeding the paper was someone else's job.

LEE: Then you're forgiven. How'd you get to Hawai'i?

STEVE: My wife Rosalind and I visited the Big Island around 1980 and fell in love with the place. Spent the next twenty years figuring out how to move here, and retiring from my company allowed us to do that.

LEE: Retiring? You're only what...fifty-five?

STEVE: Fifty-eight. Yeah, things worked out well.

LEE: Not for me. I still have to write for a living. How did you get involved with Ironman?

STEVE: We didn't know too many people, and I was looking around for something to do. An acquaintance knew that Ironman was looking for someone to help out and asked if I happened to know anything about working in a warehouse. Well, I'd been a night foreman in a warehouse when I was going to engineering school.

LEE: Already knew how to drive a forklift?

STEVE: I did. So I volunteered, then a year later was asked to be a coordinator, then an assistant director and finally director, which I've been doing ever since.

LEE: Pretty nice career path. Just think: If you'd been doing that for GE or Ford, you could be retired now.

STEVE: I am retired now.

LEE: Oh, yeah. So what's the basic role of the warehouse director?

STEVE: We're essentially a service organization for all the other directors. It's our job to make sure that every material thing that's needed to put on the event is procured, housed and distributed to where it needs to be, when it needs to be.

LEE: When you say every material thing...

STEVE: I mean everything: barricades, fencing, tables, tents, timing equipment, racks, food, three different kinds of water, medical supplies, carpeting, banners, T-shirts, ice...it's a pretty long list.

LEE: Sounds like a tough job.

STEVE: It is, but I like working behind the scenes on complicated stuff that's critical to the success of the event, and I like working with people who feel the same way. And the tougher it is, the better the sense of accomplishment when it comes off smoothly. By the way, there are actually two organizations within the warehouse. The other is Supplies, and that's run by Vickie Ewing. The way we put it is that she's responsible for all the small stuff, and I do all the big stuff. So she worries about clipboards, paper towels and marker pens, and I worry about fencing, water and construction materials.

LEE: Hope you two get along.

STEVE: Oh, yeah. Vickie and I have been working together and with the other directors for ten years, and we take a lot of care in assessing their needs to make sure they get what they need. They're our customers, after all.

LEE: Is it a year-round job?

STEVE: Not full-time, but pretty close to year-round. Remember that we do two major events here.

LEE: Ironman 70.3 Hawai'i, also known as Honu, as well as the World Championship.

STEVE: And they're only four months apart. We start planning just a few weeks after the Ironman, at the end of October, but we're still pretty fried and don't start ordering in earnest until January. It gets pretty intense around April for the 70.3, then picks up again in August. September we're at it full time.

LEE: Is the warehouse shut down the other months?

STEVE: No, because we lend out equipment to various community organizations throughout the year. Things like tables, chairs, coolers...

LEE: What kind of organizations? What do they need the stuff for?

STEVE: Well, as an example, two weeks after the World Championship one of the elementary schools puts on a "Keiki" triathlon for kids. We give them flagging, markers, a lot of fluids and other consumables left over from Ironman. There are canoe club and other sporting club events, Pop Warner football, all kinds of things. A lot of the people who are involved with those events are Ironman volunteers, and this is another way for the Ironman organization to give back to the community and also say thanks to the local volunteers in a meaningful way.

LEE: Now, hard goods can sit there all year. When do the consumables start coming in?

STEVE: The warehouse is only about a third filled with hard goods, so you can imagine the volume of consumables that comes in, because the place is packed to the ceiling just before the race. A couple of months beforehand we start getting water, branded fluids, energy bars and gel. By the time it's all here, we'll have unloaded 225 pallets.

LEE: You mentioned three different kinds of water.

STEVE: Three different packaging forms, actually. We've got it in bike bottles with sports tops—this year it's Arrowhead water, from Costco on the mainland. Then we pour water into cups for the run course, and that comes from a bottler on Oahu. Then we also have single-serve bottles at the three banquets, for volunteers throughout race week, etc. Those come from a Coke distributor on Oahu.

LEE: Wait a minute, back up. You bring in water from the mainland?

STEVE: Thousands of cases.

LEE: And from Oahu? There's no water on the Big Island?

STEVE: One of the things you realize when you live here is that about 90% of everything we consume comes from off-island.

LEE: Yeah, but water?

STEVE: Listen, the bottled water you drink at home probably comes from hundreds of miles away, maybe even thousands. It's the same way here, except that yours comes by truck and ours comes by boat.

LEE: I'm amazed. You also mentioned branded fluids.

STEVE: This year PowerBar is a big sponsor, and they make Ironman PERFORM in 20-ounce bottles. That's what we'll be serving out on the course. We can bring in all the fluids well in advance.

LEE: What about the really perishable stuff?

STEVE: About two days before the race we receive hundreds case of oranges, bananas and apples. The bananas are local, but there aren't any oranges or apples grown here so those have to be brought in as well.

LEE: When do you start moving things out to the aid stations?

STEVE: Starting at midnight Friday, we send out two caravans of 40-foot tractor-trailers, each rig carrying a forklift. One caravan drops off pallets at the eleven bike aid stations, and the other does the same for the thirteen run stations.

LEE: What about ice?

STEVE: We get it from a local ice house. It's picked up starting about 6:00 race morning and caravanned out all day long. We have a schedule based on our estimates of usage, but the aid stations can call in when they get low, and we'll run special deliveries. The finish line alone gets about ten tons.

LEE: How much do you use altogether?

STEVE: A lot. About 25 tons of cube ice and 12 tons of block ice for the run course, and another twelve tons for the finish line and transition areas.

LEE: Wow. What about fluids?

STEVE: We go through nearly 100,000 bottles of water, soda and PERFORM on the race course, and another 47,000 at the various events.

LEE: That's a lot of plastic.

STEVE: The good news is, we recycle practically everything. About the only things we can't recycle are gel wrappers and sponges, although even the sponges are getting used by local artists. Don't ask me for what.

LEE: How much of a factor is weather in what's going to be consumed on race day? Do you have to make adjustments?

Stumbling Towards the Finish Line

STEVE: Not really. Look, it's always going to be hot and humid, and the only big variable is the wind, which we can't predict. If it's a really windy day, people are going to be working harder out there and longer and drinking more fluids. What we do is use past experience to predict consumption, and then we add ten percent when we stock the aid stations. That generally covers us, but even if it doesn't, the warehouse has plenty of extra stock. If an aid station sees things getting used up more quickly than we'd anticipated, they call in and we shoot more right up to them.

LEE: I took a look at your supplies list. I'm amazed at how many things on there I never would have thought of: alligator clips, dust pans, knives for cutting fruit at the aid stations, work aprons, eleven kinds of duct tape...

STEVE: And finishers medals, massage tables, 10,000 volunteer T-shirts, 2,000 finisher shirts, 4,000 trash bags, 55,000 sponges, 16,000 cable ties, 8,000 posters, quarter of a million paper cups...

LEE: And one gallon of something called "Goof Off." I don't even want to know.

STEVE: It's remove-everything-yucky goop in a bottle.

LEE: And you have to move all of this stuff around, too. Who handles that?

STEVE: I do, except for aid station deliveries, which aid station director Joe Loschiavo handles.

LEE: I saw the transportation schedule. Reads like an invasion plan, only more complicated.

STEVE: We'll start shipping things out on September 27, and there'll be multiple deliveries to the retail stores, expo, media, hospitality. Then we start delivering things for all the construction sites, starting with the pier area and Ali'i Drive.

LEE: Seems like a pretty intense effort to get everything at the pier area built in time. Why is it such a mad scramble?

STEVE: We don't officially take over the pier area until Thursday, so we can't start construction until then. On Wednesday we'll run four 40-foot tractor trailers out there with what's needed for the transitions and medical areas, then four more on Thursday and another four on Friday full of consumables for the finish area.

LEE: I asked Diana this question about the race in general and imagine I'll get the same answer from you: After all these years, do things pretty much run autopilot?

STEVE: [insert snort of derision here] Hardly. We get familiar with things year after year, but there are several sources of changes. As an example, we're always trying to reduce costs without reducing service. That means scouting around for better deals, ways of moving things around, estimating what's needed so we don't over order, especially regarding consumables. After each event, we go over every line item with the directors and talk about whether we can order less or do it a different way.

LEE: Any fundamental changes?

STEVE: Always, especially if there's a change in sponsorship or provider. This year we have a big change because PowerBar is a new sponsor. So there's product that's new to us, vendor booths that are completely different, and new ways of communicating and ordering.

LEE: And of course they're new to the event, too, so nobody has much precedent to go on.

STEVE: Exactly, and it's the same on the retail side. There's been a third-party retailer handling all the Ironman stores in Kona for thirty years, but this year WTC is going to be its own retailer. We used to store all the supplies in the warehouse, but WTC is bringing over its own stuff.

LEE: They already have stuff?

STEVE: Sure. They've been doing retail for most of the North American events, so they have a good handle on things, but we have to work out procedures for getting it done here.

LEE: So the warehouse crew gets paid a fortune, right?

STEVE: Right. Free sushi and beer during race week.

LEE: Why do you do it?

STEVE: Good question, and on certain days I try not to ask myself that. I think it's mostly the enjoyment of working with a team on a tough job and the personal satisfaction that comes from helping to put on a world championship event. How many other people can say they play a significant role in staging a sporting event that people want to come to from all over the world? I love the event, I'm in awe of the athletes, and sitting at the finish line watching them come in and knowing I played a part in allowing them to get there...hard to put into words.

LEE: You actually get to sit around at the finish?

STEVE: Believe it or not, race day is my easiest day. By Friday late afternoon the warehouse is empty, so the rocket's been launched and you just hope you did everything right to make sure it gets to orbit. Vickie and I have a traditional celebratory shot of Tequila at 6:00, and from then until Saturday night, my job is just to be available to troubleshoot.

LEE: You mentioned "certain days" when you don't ask yourself why you do it. When are those?

STEVE: Well, as much fun as race day Saturday is, it all comes crashing down on Sunday, which is the worst day of the year for me.

LEE: Because it's a letdown?

STEVE: There's not even any time to feel a letdown. Sunday is more hectic than any day was in getting ready. We have a contractual obligation to restore Kailua-Kona to its sleepy little self by noon, which means returning the pier and the streets to the town in the same condition as we found them.

LEE: So when does the cleanup whirlwind start?

STEVE: Two am Sunday, all hell breaks loose There's a continuous stream of tractor-trailers shuttling between the pier and the warehouse from 5:00 am through noon, carrying everything we'd put out there: consumable, banners, construction materials, fencing, carpeting, tents, racks...everything you see and a lot you don't has to be packed up, picked up and returned to the warehouse.

LEE: What about out on the race course?

STEVE: The same crew that delivered everything to the aid stations goes back out to bring it all back. We start caravanning from Hawi at about 2:00 in the afternoon Saturday and slowly work our way down along the course. Aid station volunteers are responsible for their own cleanup. They separate everything out, because we recycle everything possible, then they pile stuff onto the pallets it was delivered on and the sweep crews pick it all up. They haul 40-foot containers to pick up all the recyclable bags and dump trucks for the trash. We also pick up tables, tents, leftover consumables to go back into the warehouse.

LEE: Is there someone who handles the recyclables end?

STEVE: Matter of fact, there is. My wife, Rosalind, is the recycling team coordinator. By the way, the sweep teams also carefully inventory everything they pick up, including leftover consumables. That way we have a record of exactly what was used by every aid station and that helps us figure out how to distribute stuff the next year. On a "normal" day we'll get about ten percent back if we planned right, but if it's a tough, windy day, it'll be less.

LEE: So what's it like at the warehouse when all this stuff is flowing back in?

STEVE: Trust me on this: It's the last place on earth you want to be on Sunday morning.

LEE: And you?

STEVE: I'm the last person you want to be around. By mid-afternoon I start to seriously question what I'm doing here, and by 5:00 I can barely drag myself home to take a shower and get to the awards banquet.

LEE: How long does it take to stop swearing and get re-born in the spirit?

STEVE: Just a few hours. Once Peter's [Henning] race wrap-up video comes on the big screen, I'm inspired all over again.

Q&A with

Rocky Campbell
– Ironman Construction Director

There was a new stop sign installed near our house in Palm Springs last year. It took six months to get approvals and per-mits, three months to survey the site and take soil samples, two weeks to prep the area, and then a crew of six worked for two days to get the sign up.

JUMP CUT to Kailua-Kona: Twenty years ago I looked out at the corner of Ali'i and Palani and saw a sleepy street casually idling next to the ocean, minding its own business. The next time I saw it, that same corner looked as though it was ready to host the final leg of the Tour de France, complete with bleachers, a finishing arch, barrier fences, a media grandstand, massage and medical tents, and enough food, water and ice to service a cruise ship. What makes this interesting is that the time between my first and second looks was less than 36 hours.

So the first thing I knew was that the City of Palm Springs wasn't responsible for it. Then I wondered who was. Turned out to be a guy named Rocky Campbell.

LEE: Your responsibility is the start-finish area, right?

ROCKY: Yes.

LEE: You're called the construction director, but it doesn't look there's much actual construction going on.

ROCKY: There really isn't, although there used to be. In the early days there was a lot of physical labor building stuff and tearing it down. Now it's mostly about assembly and logistics, although we do build the finish line, the medal stand where athletes get their post-race photos taken, and some special-order structures for NBC and the like.

LEE: I did a piece on warehouse director Steve Butterfield last year. How does your job dovetail with his?

ROCKY: During race week, Butter's job is to get everything from the warehouse to the pier. Once his trucks get here, my crews take over and unload them. We distribute all the stuff and get the whole area set up.

LEE: What does that include?

ROCKY: The massage area, medical tent, bike racks, all the barricade fencing – oh, yeah: all the supplies, too.

Stumbling Towards the Finish Line

LEE: I've watched you guys work many times. Looks like utter chaos, and then all of a sudden everything's ready, like a snow globe in reverse.

ROCKY: It takes an awful lot of work and preparation to make it look easy. Thing is, there are no second chances. We've got agreements that dictate what we can and cannot do, and when, and this race starts on time on Saturday morning whether we're ready or not.

LEE: So failure is not an option.

ROCKY: If we fail, it's going to affect the athletes, and that's an unforgiveable sin.

LEE: How long have you been doing this?

ROCKY: I've been with the race about 30 years, director for 25.

LEE: Starting to get the hang of it, are you?

ROCKY: Somewhat. But every time I think we have it down pat, something changes or we figure out a better way.

LEE: Give me an example.

ROCKY: We used to rent those bleachers. It was a royal pain getting them here, then unloading and assembling them. Just a big headache every year. We wanted to buy our own, but where do you keep something like that? Turns out that there are these baseball diamonds just north of town near the old airport. So what we did was buy the bleachers and donate them for use at the baseball fields, with the proviso that we get to use them for a few days ever year. Worked out beautifully for everybody.

LEE: What a great idea.

ROCKY: The biggest example of things changing is when the course itself changes. One year they decided to put T1 out at the old airport, another year it was behind the King K...

LEE: Wasn't that to accommodate more bikes?

ROCKY: Yes, but we figured out how to get more on the pier so we didn't need to do that anymore. Those kinds of major venue changes require a lot planning, and there's no way to test things out in advance. You have to rely on your experience and instinct. Another example: A couple years ago Diana [Bertsch, race director] had this idea for putting in a set of stairs that the swimmers could use to exit the water and get onto the pier.

LEE: I remember when that happened. What was the reason?

ROCKY: Spectators couldn't see the swimmers exiting over on the boat launch ramp and she thought they were missing out on an exciting part of the race. So one of my guys designed it, our crew built it, then we kept our fingers crossed that it would work.

LEE: It was a great touch. I've gotten some of my best race photos at that spot and spectators love it.

ROCKY: Not all the ideas work out, but that one was a winner.

LEE: Do you also work Honu [Ironman 70.3 Hawai'i]?

ROCKY: Sure do.

LEE: And for all this you get paid, what...?

ROCKY: Fame and glory.

LEE: At least they're not taxable. So why do you do it?

ROCKY: A lot of reasons. It's fun, I love working with Diana and the other directors, I've got great guys who work with me year after year, and I get to be a part of the best sporting event in the world.

LEE: You have an assistant director, don't you?

ROCKY: Yes, Gwen Hobbs. She worked for me for about five or six years, then one year bike director Dave Huerta go sick so she did that for one race, then she came back as my assistant. But I figured out how to stop her from leaving again.

LEE: How?

ROCKY: I married her last month.

LEE: Seriously?

ROCKY: Yeah. She was my kind of woman.

LEE: How so?

ROCKY: Only girl I ever dated who had her own cement mixer.

LEE: She's also the only one in the family who's an Ironman finisher.

ROCKY: True. Last time was about ten years ago. She'd been hit by cars three times, but was still the top Big Islander and even beat the island men one year. And her son is the assistant bike director.

LEE: So how'd you get to Hawai'i? Didn't you own a lumber yard on the island?

ROCKY: I did. I served as communications officer aboard a Navy destroyer in Viet Nam during the height of that war. When I got out in 1970 my parents and grandparents were living in Hilo. A few people in the family were working at my grandfather's koa [an exotic wood often called "Hawaiian mahogany"] mill there, but eventually my father went out on his own and opened a mom 'n' pop kind of lumber yard there. In 1972 I moved over to Kona and opened a branch.

LEE: Is it still operating?

ROCKY: No, I retired. I still do some hauling, but that comes to a halt every year when the race rolls around.

LEE: How'd you get involved in the race?

ROCKY: The first or second time the race was held on the Big Island a friend of mine named Walt Stack, a teamster from Oakland, was in it. I manned an aid station from midnight to four a.m. and –

LEE: Hold it. Doesn't the race end at midnight?

ROCKY: It does now, but there were no cutoffs back then. Anyway, Walt usually came in around 7:00 am the next day and, since he was about the only racer I ever saw, my job pretty much consisted of waiting for Walt.

LEE: Not much of a job.

ROCKY: Not especially demanding, no. So one year I went down to help Mo Matthews, who was the swim director. I held a rope to help herd the swimmers through, then I brought down a couple of forklifts to help move things around. There was a construction director at the time and when she retired in 1988, I took over. Been at it ever since.

LEE: So when do you go into action?

ROCKY: The week before the race I prep the area behind the King K for all the support trailers that are going to be stationed there, but I really don't start hopping until the Sunday before the race. That's when we pick up the bleachers because those have to be in place for the parade on Tuesday night. By sunup that morning they're assembled and ready. Then, the morning after the parade, the first of several 40-foot trailers arrives at the pier. We offload them and assist the pier director but we're somewhat restricted because there's usually a cruise ship in and we can't use the pier until the last tender leaves at 6:00 that evening.

LEE: You're just down tools for the day?

ROCKY: No, we can do some things to get ready. We get the fencing up on the rock walls around the medical area and lay their carpeting out, get some fencing up around the pier, things like that.

LEE: Ali'i Drive is still open, isn't it?

ROCKY: Yes. Thursday morning we help Dave on the pier and then at 10:00 am Ali'i closes and we can really go to work. One of the 40-foot trailers comes down loaded up with the finish line and we get right to work putting that up. We used to let it go until Friday, but it was always a mad scramble to get it done on time so starting on Thursday gives us some breathing room. I've got a crew that does that every year and they've got it down to an art.

LEE: You're working around a lot of activity.

ROCKY: Bike check-in is on Friday so we like to be pretty much done by then, but we're still adjusting barricades, building platforms for the medical and timing sites, etc. By this time we've got 40-footers coming in with bananas and oranges, tables from the expo after that closes, water and so on. There's also an ice truck that comes onto the pier and stays there.

LEE: What do you do on race day?

ROCKY: Unless something goes wrong, nothing. I go to bed early, around eight, because I'm back on the pier at 3:00 or 4:00 a.m. A great bunch of guys from Cleveland who've been with me for years start gathering stuff up at midnight, wrapping it and getting it onto pallets. By the time I get there they've got two truckloads ready to be hauled out. We go nonstop because we're obligated to give the whole area back to the town by noon without any sign that a race even took place.

LEE: And you do all of that as a volunteer?

ROCKY: What can I tell you? I love it. Made a lot of friends, too. I've helped out at Ironman events in Switzerland and Austria and those were great experiences. I was at the inaugural Ironman Austria, and that was wonderful. Two years later we went back and stayed at the race director's mother's house. Ironman is that kind of community.

LEE: So when are you going to step up and race in one?

ROCKY: When you do. So I figure I'm pretty safe.

GREG WELCH:
Alive and Well

In October of 1994, I sat across the aisle from Greg Welch on a flight from Kona to the mainland, grimacing as I watched a steady stream of well-wishers violate entire chapters of FAA safety regulations in their eagerness to unbuckle seat belts and run down the aisles to offer congratulations. With every hearty handshake and back thump, I winced harder, until my wife Cherie nudged me in the ribs and said, "Go do something!" As I stood up and began traffic-copping the enthusiastic fans, Greg heaved a sigh of relief and whispered "Thanks, mate" as he sank back into his seat with a fresh grimace of his own.

Greg and I barely knew each other's names at the time. I was dimly aware of him as the happy-go-lucky Aussie constantly chided for wasting his considerable athletic talent on too much partying and not enough training, too much affability and not enough seriousness. The reason for all the congratulations on the fully-loaded 747 was that Party Boy had just clobbered a hugely talented field of star triathletes on his way to becoming the Ironman champion.

The reason for all the wincing and grimacing was that, unbeknownst to the well-intended conga line of admirers, Greg had fallen in the shower the night before and snapped his collarbone. Every handshake, shoulder punch and back slap was sending bolts of pain shooting through his shoulder.

Sir Plucky swallowed it and kept smiling. You had to look hard to notice that sweat was breaking out on his brow and his legs were weakening because he insisted on getting up to greet each well-wisher and each rise was getting shakier and shakier as the pain got worse and worse. But he was determined not to let on that he was hurting. "They shouldn't have to hold back," he said to me of the people wanting to shake his hand.

Greg was no stranger to pain. Two years earlier he'd managed sixth place while running with a flaring hemorrhoid that felt like he was being stabbed with a red-hot knife with every step. And only the year before he'd missed the 1993 Ironman because of a last-minute bike accident. He'd licked his wounds for about ten seconds before hunkering down to focus on the 1994 event, which he won with a time of 8:20:27. (Two years later he went a minute and a half faster and came in third.)

I won't belabor all of the achievements and accolades this celebrated Hall-of-Famer has racked up, including four different triathlon world championships at distances ranging from sprint to Ironman, half a dozen national titles, and Lord only knows how many something-of-the-year honors. Those have all been written about before, and you can look them up.

What I'm interested in is what life has been like for someone who, at the exact moment that he was the number one triathlete in the world and the odds-on gold medal favorite at the Sydney Olympic Games, was told that his racing days were over and he should be thankful that he was even alive.

* * *

Somewhere during the last quarter mile of the swim in the 1999 Ironman World Championship here in Kailua-Kona, Greg thought he was having an asthma attack. He had difficulty breathing and felt a painful, fluttering sensation in his chest. He stopped swimming for about five minutes and, when it didn't clear up but at least didn't get any worse, he started swimming again. After exiting the water he thought of quitting—something definitely didn't feel right—but the thought was fleeting, because Greg's decision flowchart for quitting only had two question boxes on it: "Am I still breathing?" and "Can I walk?" (There used to be a third—"Do I know what day it is?"—but after winning the world championship on the hottest day on record, he scratched that one off the list.)

He felt better in T1, but out on the bike he got hit again. Lightheadedness, shortness of breath, pain everywhere but all of it emanating from his chest. It went away, came back, went away...twelve times, plus another three on the run. Each time he emerged from the episode weaker and more shaken, but still he kept on.

Only after he finished the race did he discover that he'd been competing while in the throes of a frightening and often fatal condition known as ventricular tachycardia. Riders of the Lightspeed Tachyon racing bicycle know that "tach-" means "fast" and we all know what "cardia-" is. The regulatory mechanism in Greg's heart had gone completely haywire, turning that critical muscle into a runaway freight train. It was periodically pounding away at rates as high as 320 beats per minute, which was like holding the accelerator down with the car in park and the engine on. There's only so long that can continue without severe and potentially irreversible damage.

That Greg survived the race was remarkable. That he finished in eleventh place was the stuff of legends.

In early 2001, surgeons implanted a combination pacemaker/defibrillator in his chest. The former tries to maintain steady rhythm in his heart. The latter is another story. An on-demand device that only kicks in when needed, the defibrillator is a modern marvel of electronic brains and miniaturization, a cardiologist-in-a-box whose only job is to detect when the heart's normal ballet of electrical signals descends into a break dance of chaotic impulses that threaten to kill its host. When that happens, state-of-the-art circuitry jumps into action and counterpunches with stronger signals that overwhelm, and thereby tame, the heart's errant ones.

A miracle, right? A source of comfort to the wearer, who is keenly aware that the gizmo is ever-vigilant and will jump to the ready and so there's little to worry about, right?

Stumbling Towards the Finish Line

Okay, picture this: Greg goes out for a walk, blithely minding his own business, and gets about a hundred yards from the house when an invisible, malevolent gnome swings a sledgehammer in a wide arc and slams it into the middle of his chest. Stunned and breathless, Greg goes down. About two minutes later, when he's able to breathe again, he looks around, sees no one there and realizes what just happened. As he tries to get to his feet, the hammer hits him again. As he did during his last Ironman, Greg refuses to stay down and forces himself to try once again. This time he gets halfway home when *WHAM!* It happens again.

By the time he staggers back to the house and drops onto a couch, he's in too much shock to dial 911. The reason is that the gizmo in his chest does its thing by slamming an 800-volt lightning bolt into his heart, which feels a lot like, well, getting an 800-volt lightning bolt slammed into your heart. Every defib episode is supposed to result in a hospital visit, but he's had six of them in the space of twenty minutes, and it lands him in intensive care for three days, where the miracle gizmo kept hitting him anyway.

So, yes, the thing was keeping him alive, but having a bomb in your chest with the timer set on "random" is not quite the same as chicken soup and a hug from Mom and, all in all, a far cry from how the world's greatest triathlete envisioned his future.

That was in 2003, the worst year of his life, but it ended with a turnaround. Surgeons cut into the femoral artery in his leg, threaded a catheter into it and pushed it clear up to his heart, where a miniature camera identified spots of ventricular damage and a second device fried them into quiescence. A little adjustment in medication, three months of recovery, and the awful shocks stopped.

But...the runaway v-tach episodes didn't. When his heart spontaneously decides to run a marathon at sprint speed, his pacemaker goes into a special mode in which it tries to pace the heart faster than its intrinsic rate in an effort to break the tachycardia before it progresses to ventricular fibrillation. It will try this "antitachycardia pacing" trick half a dozen times or so and, if it doesn't work, the device surrenders by delivering that 800-volt uppercut. So far it's worked every time, but each episode is a Psycho-class nail biter that's keeping Greg off his surfboard and off the golf course. There's hope, though: A new procedure he's investigating might finally rid him of his membership in the cardiac Russian roulette club.

What keeps him going under circumstances that routinely crush people into clinical depression?

"His wife and kids," offers Paula Newby-Fraser, longtime friend and many-time Ironman champion. "He adores those girls and wrapped his life around them."

During Ironman Japan in 1993, Greg got hit head-on by a car and broke both his clavicle and a wheel on his bike. There wasn't much he could do about the collarbone, but as for the wheel? Sian Welch, who was also competing, gave hers up so he could finish the race, which he did, coming back from 60th place and winning it. (He went straight from the finish line to the hospital, where he was visited by race officials who informed him that he'd been DQ'd for receiving outside assistance. He didn't argue, even though Sian wasn't an outsider but a competitor, because none of the officials spoke a word of English and it wasn't until the next day that he finally learned what they were trying to tell him.)

Years later, Sian threw Greg another lifeline, this time in the form of Emma, little sister to first daughter Annie. At the very nadir of his medical odyssey, Greg got the message loud and clear: *This is why you fight. This is why you need to stay alive.*

It worked. They're why he gave up stand-up paddling and other beloved sports that, while benign for most of us, were potentially lethal to him. They're why, when he occasionally and inevitably feels himself slipping into the abyss, he only has to think about his girls to pull himself out and shake it off.

Close friends can tell when it happens. "He disappears for a few days," Newby-Fraser says, "and that's how we know he's had an episode. He's not interested in sympathy, so he slinks off, gets over it, and comes back."

Sir Plucky doesn't complain, he isn't bitter, and he's damned if anyone is going to see him give even the appearance of being down or feeling sorry for himself.

"I was dealt those cards and I played them right from the get go," Greg says. "When I got the word that my athletic career was over, I was stunned for about ten seconds, and then I started thinking about two things: staying alive and what's next."

Staying alive is something the rest of us rarely think about as a deliberate activity, but for Greg it became as routine as brushing his teeth. The Olympic-caliber frat boy gave up alcohol, caffeine and anything else that could be remotely classified as a stimulant and threaten his heart.

He shrugs it off lightly. "They said they were dangerous, so that was it. No way do I deprive my kids of a Daddy because I feel like having a beer."

As for what he would do next, that turned out to be easier than giving up pub-crawling with his mates. How do you parlay charm, radiant affability, the gift of gab and uncanny athletic insight into a new career?

You go on television. Greg became a WTC employee, the go-to guy for expert on-air commentary who also hosts webcasts, acts as technical advisor and is deeply involved in anti-doping. For the past few years, he's also been Oakley's global sports manager for multi-sports, outdoors and track and field.

"I bloody love it!" he exclaims. "I get to see all the guys I used to compete against!" And they get to see Greg without having to compete against him, so it's a win-win all the way.

To say that nothing teaches you more about life than a brush with death is a cliché, but, like all clichés, it's grounded in truth. "Life is so fragile," Greg muses in a contemplative moment, "and so worth protecting." He's talking about his daughters and he realizes that, while he can't wrap his arms around them forever, he can take care of himself both physically and spiritually and thereby afford them the benefit of not just his presence but his outlook. To grow up around someone who doesn't take life for granted is a gift.

To be that someone is a blessing.

RUDY GARCIA-TOLSON:
Part I: ATHLETE

About seventeen years ago, my bride Cherie was swimming laps in a pool in Rialto, California, minding her own business, when she was suddenly struck by a torpedo. She turned around and was only able to glimpse the offending bit of waterborne ordnance long enough for it to pop its little head up and mumble "Sorry!" before it shot off toward the far wall. Luckily, she was able to scramble into an adjacent lane and thereby avoid a second attack.

But, as she watched the missile fly by on its return path, she noticed that it was all bow and no stern, its propulsive power deriving exclusively from a set of churning arms with no secondary wake where the legs should have been. Conversing with the torpedo's mother after the workout, she learned that she'd been rammed by a seven-year-old boy named Rudy who didn't have legs but did have about eleven different ways of overcompensating for their absence. Barreling heedlessly past 50-year-old women lollygagging in his lane made it an even dozen. (The "lollygagger," by the way, had just won her age division at the Ironman World Championship in Kona, clearly impressing the hell out of young Rudy.)

Six months after that chance encounter, Rudy competed in a triathlon with his brother Richard doing the bike and Cherie doing the run as relay partners. For Rudy, that event wasn't some "I'm just happy to be competing" assertion of his independence accompanied by soaring violins and teary-eyed onlookers. When I stuck a video camera in his face and asked him what his goal was, he homed right in on the lens and said, "We're gonna kick butt!" Ninety minutes later he was on the medal stand.

Seventeen years later, he's here in Kona trying to become the first double above-the-knee amputee to compete in, and complete, a full Ironman. And, no surprise, he's chosen the toughest course in the world to do it.

* * *

Rudy was born with enough physical calamities to challenge half a dozen lives. The worst of it was in his legs, which were sufficiently afflicted to require fifteen surgeries by the time he was five. After fifteen surgeries, you kind of start to get the feeling that maybe doing the same thing over and over and not getting a different result isn't the best way to spend your life. The surgeons apparently thought so, too, but how do you get a seven-year-old to understand that?

"Am I ever going to run around with other kids on these?" Rudy asked, pointing to his scarred, twisted limbs.

"Doubtful," the surgeons replied. "Your best bet is a set of prosthetic legs."

Rudy thought it over for a good three seconds. "Fine," he announced, in a tone indicating that there was no need to phone up the pre-amputation psych counselor. "Get rid of 'em."

They got rid of 'em and thus created the torpedo. Six years later he became the youngest challenged athlete to earn a medal at the USA Swimming National Disability Championships, setting the U.S. record in the 200m breaststroke. The following year he set a national record in a half marathon, then broke it himself the year after that.

In 2002 he was an opening day speaker at the Paralympics in Salt Lake City, where he also carried the torch. Two years later, at the Paralympics in Athens, he won his first international gold medal and set a new world record in the 200m individual medley. There would be more of those—gold medals and world records both—in the years following, including in Beijing in 2008.

Then he decided to get serious. Ironman had been in the back of his mind ever since his first tri, but it wasn't until he saw the magnificent Sarah Reinertsen do it that he made up his mind. Sarah is a "single above" (one leg, above-the-knee amputee) who first attempted the Kona course in 2004 but missed the bike cutoff by fifteen minutes. She came back the following year (a simple phrase, that, but it tells you most of what you need to know about these kinds of people) and this time blasted across the finish line with nearly two hours to spare.

That's all Rudy needed. He started training in 2007 and moved to the Olympic Training Center, but he got a little distracted while breaking those world swimming records and didn't really crank up the Ironman training until he got back from Beijing in 2008.

He's had help, from a wide variety of sources. First among them is Ironman Hall-of-Famer Bob Babbitt, co-founder of the Challenged Athletes Foundation and one of the planet's staunchest and most tireless advocates for the idea that the label "athlete" applies to a lot more people than we'd think. Paul Huddle has provided training plans, the Össur company provides "prosthetic legs for every occasion," Cherie has taken him for long bike rides in 115-degree desert heat, there's veteran Ironman wheelchair racer David Bailey, the PowerBar people...the list goes on.

Stumbling Towards the Finish Line

On race day, however, despite the crowds who will be cheering him on at several widely separated points on the course, Rudy will be alone, like a boxer accustomed to a 50-man entourage who steps into the ring and suddenly realizes that everyone else is outside the ropes.

* * *

Triathlon is tough enough on two good legs. The challenges facing Rudy at the Ironman are formidable.

His strength is in the swim. It's where he least misses not having lower legs. While he doesn't get the benefit of roll stabilization or the extra bit of propulsion from kicking, he also doesn't suffer the drag that afflicts two-legged swimmers. (Ever notice that the best swimmers in the world have long torsos and short legs?)

He's also got the run under control. He uses a special pair of legs that makes him look like he's standing atop two letter C's. The little bit of spring action in those half-circles of fiberglass substitute for the natural springiness of ankles and calves under a hinge-like knee. What they don't do is retract the trailing foot upward as it's brought forward so that it clears the ground before being planted in front again. So instead of bringing the back foot straight forward under him, he has to swing it outward in a wide arc. (A word to athletes who think it'd be neat to run next to him this Saturday: Treat him like you would one of those chariots with the spiked wheels in *Ben Hur* and give him a wide berth.)

He's also about two feet shorter than usual when he runs, having figured out that being close to the ground is a lot more stable than being high in the air. Choosing your own height is one of the few really cool advantages of having prosthetic legs.

The bike is where things really get squirrelly. Rudy doesn't have quads or hamstrings to call on and has to push through 112 miles relying solely on his glutes. He also can't stand up on the pedals, which means that he has to ascend steep hills sitting down. Other triathletes do that, but not being able to stand up has another nasty implication, and that is that he's got no way to give his butt a break once in a while. It's planted on that seat for the duration. And if he feels himself getting blown over by a side wind? Snapping his shoes out of the pedals quickly is quite a trick.

When he was ten years old, Rudy became the youngest bilateral amputee to complete a triathlon on his own. In 2007, he became the first "double above" to complete a half Ironman. Last year, he conquered the Wildflower long course, proving that he could handle towering hills on the bike, and a few weeks later he threw in the Honu half Ironman, laying to rest any doubts that he could tolerate debilitating heat and miles of running on grass.

Saturday will be different. Not just linearly longer, but exponentially harder. Rudy is one of the toughest guys I've ever met, but finishing this course is far from a Disney-esque, cue-the-swelling violins certainty. Two years ago I was at the finish line when Scott Rigsby, another tough-as-nails son-of-a-gun, became the first double amputee to finish the Ironman on prosthetic legs. Scott is a below-the-knee amputee who still has his own knees and a good set of quads, and yet there were fewer than seventeen minutes left against the 17-hour cutoff when he triumphantly broke the tape.

Here's what Rudy's up against:

The swim: "I can do it in under an hour," he told me yesterday. Yes, he can. And he doesn't plan to be lifted out of the water, as is the custom with challenged athletes. He's going to run out of the water on his bare stumps and put on a pair of walking legs. When he gets to his bike, he'll exchange those for biking legs and take off.

"One thing I learned at Honu," he said, "is to take the time to get all the sand off my shorts." At the Honu 70.3, he didn't do that and suffered for it mightily when sand got between his stumps and the sockets in his prosthetics and ground into his skin with every pedal stroke.

The bike: I would have thought the bike would give him the most trouble, because of the hills, but he's not worried about it. "I rode the hardest part of the course at Honu," he says, "and got through it all right. So I know that if I take it easy, I can handle twice the distance." He's also got updated biking legs that he and his prosthetist came up with.

What about the infamously fierce side winds, the same ones that blew Madonna Buder clear off her bike three years ago and resulted in a broken clavicle?

"If they come, they come," he says with smile and a shrug. "I'll deal with them."

Target time: 8 hours

The run: Despite his prowess as a runner, this is the piece that concerns him the most.

"I have the strength and the endurance," he asserts. "The problem is the effect on my stumps."

Rudy's never run more than twenty miles and, even at that distance, which is a full 10K shorter than the full marathon that comprises the last leg of Ironman, the pain was significant...and it didn't come after a 112-mile bike ride. No configuration of his prosthetics can completely avoid the constant rubbing against his skin, and he has no idea how much worse it's going to be not only at the longer distance, but after the trauma of (at least) eight hours of cycling.

"If I'm ahead of the clock and there's time," he told me, "I'm fully prepared to sit down right on the road and take the occasional breather."

He did it at Wildflower, removing both legs and letting them breathe. "The only problem," he said with a laugh, "is that people running by kept stopping to offer help! I had to keep explaining that I was just taking a break."

Rudy knows a thing or two about pain, especially the distinction between when he should muscle his way past it or listen to the signs and ease up before too much damage is done. It's a virtual certainty that he's going to bang right up against that decision point this Saturday, not only because he's putting himself where he's never been before but he's doing it with a new challenge he hadn't anticipated. Two weeks ago, one of his stumps became inflamed and warm to the touch. When it swelled up alarmingly he was put on antibiotics. He hasn't run since, and won't until race day, which is not the best way to handle the run-up to an Ironman.

When I asked him about all of this, he waved the question away. "There's no decision to be made," he said. "I'm finishing this race."

What about potential damage?

"Doesn't matter. I know it's not smart but if I can move forward, I will, no matter what."

Which brings us to the question of why he's doing this race in the first place.

* * *

Rudy had never planned to be the poster child for overcoming adversity. I mean that literally: He's on posters about overcoming adversity. In retrospect, however, it was inevitable.

My own take on his life is that it's not about achieving but striving. His mantra is "What's next?" because what's past isn't worth dwelling on, and winning medals and setting world records aren't the answers; they're the questions: *If I did that, what's to say I can't do something more?*

Rudy's odyssey began as a self-oriented one but gradually morphed as his world-view expanded. He's been a source of wonder and admiration for a long time, but it took a while for him to realize that he was a source of inspiration as well, not just indirectly as a model for rising above one's circumstances in general, but directly. There are kids out there with missing limbs and other infirmities who believe that leading limited lives is their lot and the sooner they accept it and stop fighting it, the better off they're going to be.

Imagine a legless kid in a wheelchair thinking he's going be there for life accidentally channel-surfing his way to a certain television show in December and finding some other kid who looks just like him *doing a freaking Ironman.*

Primarily as a result of his involvement with the Challenged Athletes Foundation, Rudy is keenly aware of that kid and his own effect on him. His impact on that community has already been profound. "But if I finish an Ironman?" he muses aloud. Then he shakes his head, answering his own question. "Those kids are going to believe there's nothing they can't do."

My own feeling is that that's what they're going to think as soon as Rudy steps up to the starting line, whether he finishes or not.

Fortunately for the people all over the world who are going to be following him on race day, that's not the way Rudy thinks.

Part II, The Rudy Projectile:
IRONMAN ARIZONA

I'm not normally a sentimental human being, unless by "sentimental" you mean cynical, sarcastic, skeptical and curmudgeonly. When I hear the moniker "hero" conferred on a six-year-old who dialed 911 after he smelled smoke, my gag reflex kicks in. People and events worthy of our collective admiration are scarce in real life, and it doesn't do us proud to keep inventing headlines out of thin air just because we're hungry for some positive news.

All of which makes me treasure those rare moments when something genuinely inspiring occurs, one that doesn't need all the machinery of a multi-billion dollar news manufacturing organization to "help us see" that it's important. Such an event took place last Sunday [Nov. 25, 2009] when a man named Rudy Garcia-Tolson crossed the finish line of Ironman Arizona with over 50 minutes left on the cutoff clock.

Rudy doesn't exist from the mid-thigh down. He ends at the same place Bermuda shorts do. He doesn't have most of the leg muscles that you and I use to walk, and he has virtually none of the ones we use to pedal a bicycle. And yet this double above-the-knee amputee managed to do something only a very small number of able-bodied people in the world can do. Following in the prosthetic footsteps of pioneers like Sarah Reinertsen and Scott Rigsby, he leaped (pun intended) over a chasm of impossibility, failed, leaped again, and this time landed upright and triumphant on the other side, marking his place in history with all the thunder and consequence of a Lindbergh, Hillary or Yeager. From then on, the rules governing the limits of challenged athleticism had to be rewritten.

It wasn't easy, and very few among the frenzied crowd gathered at the finished line had any idea what Rudy had gone through to get there.

"UNFINISHED BUSINESS"

That's what Reinertsen, with one leg gone above the knee, called her first Ironman attempt at the Ironman World Championship in Kailua-Kona, Hawai'i in 2004. She never got to the run because she missed the bike cutoff, and her race was cut short. A year later, she came back and tried again, this time leaving nearly two hours remaining on the clock when she arrived at the finish.

Scott Rigsby, the first double below-the-knee amputee to finish Ironman, also needed two tries to do it. When Rudy didn't make the bike cutoff in Kona this past October, he realized that maybe there were some things in life his iron will couldn't push him through. He got smart in a hurry, but he didn't get any more patient: He signed up for Arizona, which was to take place a scant six weeks later, then went into training overdrive. The philosophical foundation of his workout regimen was simple: If he could just complete the bike segment under the cutoff, he'd have a lock on finishing the whole race. After all, he's a two-time Paralympic swimming gold medalist and a great runner to boot. So the primary emphasis in his training was to get him through the bike.

Turns out it wasn't quite that simple, but nobody would know until about fourteen hours into the race.

Less than a minute before the starting cannon went off, the strap on Rudy's goggles broke. There was no time to replace them so he tossed them away and did the whole swim without them. He had a little trouble navigating at first, but it was a lot less chaotic than Kona, and he handled it well. His goal had been 59 minutes, and he finished in 1:01, in 141st place out of over 2,400.

He gave back fifteen minutes, though, because the cold was worse than swimming without eye protection, and it took him nearly that long to warm up enough to leave T1.

The bike was as he expected it to be: awful. Rudy can't stand up on the pedals and doesn't have a good way to relieve the inevitable strain on his lower back. Before he'd made the turnaround on the first of three loops, the pain had settled in and wouldn't quit. While he was dealing with that, he got a flat tire, with no tech support people anywhere in the vicinity. It turned out to be a good thing: Getting off the bike to change the tire himself took a while, but all that moving around worked out the kinks in his back and the next half hour of pedaling felt better.

The second loop was much worse. The ache in his back kept increasing. Negative thoughts began to intrude, and he started to worry about how much time he was taking. A headwind out on the Bee Line didn't help, but a breeze at his back on the way down did. The third and final loop was smoother. Rudy hammered the last 90 minutes, and things looked pretty rosy when he finally finished. It may not have been an especially pleasant eight hours and forty-five minutes, but he came into T2 with half an hour to spare and, as one observer put it, "looking like the weight of the world had just been lifted off his shoulders." The long-dreaded bike that had bested him in Kona was finally out of the way.

BACK TO BATAAN

With a comfortable seven hours available to complete the 26.2-mile marathon, Rudy took his time in the changing tent, knocking down a sandwich and some chips. He emerged at around 5:10 pm, ready to attack the run like it was a mortal enemy, and passed over a dozen startled runners before he'd gotten even 200 meters into the course. For the first short loop of 3.5 miles he averaged 9:15 per mile—a great pace for an Ironman amateur, a blistering one for a double amputee. Uncertainty among spectators regarding his ability to finish began to give way to wild speculation about his likely time across the line.

The second segment of 8.6 miles didn't go as well. He slowed toward the end, began walking periodically, took the occasional stretch, but, after all, he'd known it was going to be long and painful, so there wasn't anything surprising going on. The guy had practically killed himself getting through the bike and a toll was taken. Besides, he had well over five hours remaining to the 17-hour cutoff and, as he himself had put it, "Once off the bike I could probably walk 26 miles and still get there in time." Average pace for that segment: 13:24

By segment three, the wheels were coming off. It was more walking than running now, and neither looked good. While Rudy can vary his stride length, his tempo tends to remain constant because he needs to swing his legs in a wide arc in order to bring his back foot forward. If he can't maintain that tempo, he can't run, and transitioning from walk to run involves a serious decision about whether he has the strength to get his legs swinging. If his form breaks down, one leg or the other doesn't go wide enough, and he has to lean to compensate. All that leaning strains his back, which saps his strength, which compromises his form, which strains his back...the vicious cycle is hard to break.

At mile 18.5 he got his second massage of the night from the "Cramp 911" guys at the Priest Avenue aid station. After removing his legs, he had his lower back worked on and his stumps rubbed down. Ten minutes later he hit the street like a man reborn, jaunty and rejuvenated.

It lasted about a quarter of a mile. He began stopping completely, lying down on the ground, sometimes trying to bend his torso to relieve the strain in his back, sometimes just staring up at the sky and not moving at all. He'd gone glassy-eyed and uncommunicative; where earlier he had flashed smiles and engaged in bits of banter with fellow competitors, he now seemed enclosed in a shell, lost in himself and unwilling or uninterested in engaging with the rest of the world. His average pace for the segment was 16:25 and, at one point, it had taken him over half an hour to cover a mile. By mile 22 he was in a deep hole, a strange and alien place he'd never experienced before, and nobody who saw him thought he had a prayer of even taking himself off the course under his own power, much less finishing the race.

He felt himself slipping, the urge to stay down and fall asleep almost overwhelming. He couldn't even have told you where it hurt, because the pain was everywhere, but even that wasn't as bad as the doubt. Rudy had never run a marathon before and, while he'd had every confidence that he could, he really didn't know for sure. Maybe trying his first one at the tail end of a 2.4-mile swim and a 112-mile bike ride hadn't been the smartest idea. What if it was flat-out impossible and he just didn't know it? How much was he going to hurt himself only to discover it had all been for nothing?

He pulled off his legs and then yanked the liners off his stumps to let them air out. He massaged what remained of his legs, hard, trying to work out the knots and soreness. Negativity assaulted him, but there was one thought he kept pushing aside, and that was the thought of quitting. It was literally unthinkable. His mind skipped around to the thousands of people who'd shouted "Go, Rudy!" over the past fifteen hours. There hadn't been a spectator or fellow competitor who didn't know who he was and hadn't done something—a shout, a wave, an extended hand hoping for a high five—to let him know they were on his side and pulling for him. Exhausted athletes on the third loop of the run had expended precious and dwindling breath to call out encouragement. Each had been a jolt of adrenaline for him, and the idea of wasting those expressions of good will and hope was more than he could bear.

Now, down on the ground, even through the haze enveloping his mind, he could sense the uncertainty in their voices as they passed in the dark. Were they wondering if he'd already quit?

He hadn't. Not even close. That he was going to make the cutoff wasn't up for negotiation; the only issue was how.

He looked at his watch: 10:30. He had 90 minutes to cover four miles. It was going to hurt like hell no matter what, but if he could run the entire distance instead of periodically walking or dropping to the ground, he could get it done sooner.

A call came in from the cast of coaches waiting at the finish to the cyclists hovering behind and in front of Rudy. "At the next aid station, make him drink two cups of broth, and two at every aid station after that." *If he makes it to the next aid station* was the thought out on the course.

Rudy was unaware any of that was going on. Something had just occurred to him. After all he'd been through and accomplished, after all the testing and triumph, he'd never really answered one question that lay at the heart of his lifelong odyssey: *What am I really made of?*

He decided it was time to find out. He pulled on his liners and legs, picked himself off the ground and began running. To those who had been following him, it looked like just another in a series of seemingly futile attempts to regain his rhythm and try to get something going. There was no way he could last even 50 meters at that pace.

Fifty meters later he sped up, and only slowed down to knock back the prescribed two cups of broth at the mile 23 aid station. As soon as he tossed the empty cups, he began running again, just in time to confront a long uphill—a vicious pull that was sure to dispirit him and send him back to the pavement.

As soon as he hit the hill, he sped up again. Surely he was going to burn himself out, maybe even put himself into a coma. He stopped at Station 24 for some more broth and a little food then hit the path along the river. The thwk-thwk of his carbon-fiber feet on the sandy cement had the same metronomic steadiness of his earlier running, but now his stride length was the same as when he'd exited the changing tent over 5-1/2 hours earlier. He was hurtling along the river, his eyes gone from glassy to glistening, heedless of the disaster that would occur if one of those feet hit an errant rock or a crack in the pavement at that speed.

He didn't care. He was determined not to come stumbling across the finish line at the last possible second. He wasn't just out to make history, he was out to *represent*, and finishing strong didn't mean a 50-meter burst at the end, it meant three more miles of serious, nonstop, high-speed running. He had a statement to make, and there was only one way to do it.

Having made up his mind, the fog began to clear, and he settled into the groove that had been eluding him. At the short but very steep uphill leading to the Rural Street Bridge, Rudy powered up as though riding a T-bar on a ski mountain. By the time he got onto the bridge he was hitting sub-9-minute miles and shot past the last aid station without grabbing so much as a cup of water. He didn't slow down until he'd run into the solid wall of photographers waiting on the other side of the finish line, 16 hours, 6 minutes and 27 seconds after he'd begun the race.

It was a performance that was as puzzling as it was stunning. Rudy had a lot at stake, and his courage and fierce determination are undeniable, so it wouldn't have surprised anyone had he roused himself past the pain in his stumps, the ache in his back and the fatigue clouding his mind and dragged himself those last few miles toward a final stagger across the line. That would have been historic and heartwarming. It would have been understandable. Even a last minute, all-out effort to run the last forty or fifty meters, adrenalized by the cheering crowd, would have been well within athletic precedent.

But where did over three miles of power and speed come from? He'd spent a good chunk of the final run segment flat on his back yet still managed to *average* 13:45 per mile.

It didn't make any sense, and Rudy wasn't saying. He might have ascended from the abyss, but during those last few miles he hadn't spoken to anybody. He'd found a zone and maybe it was so delicate and tenuous he wasn't willing to risk breaking its spell, so he tuned out everything and just kept going.

It's a certainty his mind was clear. A block before the finish he peeled off two layers of pullovers so that the Challenged Athletes Foundation logo on his shirt would be visible as he entered the finishing area. He smiled for the first time in hours as soon as he crossed and gave a lucid interview to race announcer Mike Reilly, who had no idea what Rudy had been through and found no evidence in his demeanor to indicate that the day had been anything but a lark, another in an inexorable series of towering and inspirational accomplishments.

By Tuesday, Rudy was still aching everywhere and had developed a case of pinkeye from the ungoggled swim. As he mentally replayed the experience, he found most of his thoughts centered around the support he'd received and the effect it had on letting him become the first "double above" to complete an Ironman. Coaches, family, friends, the Challenged Athletes Foundation, untold numbers of spectators and fellow competitors along the course...if there was a way for him to thank each of them personally, he would. But, at this moment he had to force himself to refocus. The next morning he was heading down to Rio de Janeiro to compete in the world short course swimming championships.

I don't know exactly what to make of what I witnessed, or how to sum it up, except for this: A man was born last Sunday, and I'm through referring to Rudy as a "kid."

Q & A with ELLEN HART
"You Can't Make This Stuff Up"

WRITER: I got this swell idea for a movie! You're gonna love it!

PRODUCER: I'm listening.

WRITER: It's about this girl. She's smart. She's athletic.

PRODUCER (rolling his eyes): Lemme guess: Drop-dead gorgeous?

WRITER: Absolutely! She goes to Harvard, just like four of her sisters and brothers. She's a star athlete, eight varsity letters in three different sports. Breaks records left and right.

PRODUCER (more eye-rolling): Uh-huh. Got it.

WRITER: Qualifies in the 10K for the 1980 Olympics, but the president decides we're gonna boycott the games. She runs the trials again in 1984, this time in the marathon. Meanwhile, she breaks the U.S. record in the 30K and the world record at 20K.

PRODUCER: Are you kidding me with this stuff?

WRITER: Oh, wait, I almost forgot: She goes to law school, see? And she gets hired by one of the best law firms in Denver!

PRODUCER: I think it's time for you to leave.

WRITER: No, no, there's more. She marries the mayor...

PRODUCER: I'm warning you...

WRITER: Listen'a me, will ya'? The guy goes on to be a cabinet secretary in the Clinton administration! Meanwhile, she's on the President's Council on Physical Fitness and Sports! She's on the U.S. Olympic Committee!

PRODUCER: That's it. (picks up phone) I'm calling security.

WRITER: It gets better! While all this is going on, she's got this horribly debilitating eating disorder that nobody knows about!

PRODUCER: Get out! (Drops phone and pulls Ninja sword from display case behind his desk) Now!

WRITER: (running for his life) Wait! You don't understand...it's all true! Get it? It's a true story!

CUT TO: Visual of Ninja sword flying through the air headed for writer's head

---

LEE: All makes perfect sense to me. You were beautiful, smart, athletic, in school at the most prestigious university in the world...no wonder you developed an eating disorder.

ELLEN: So we're done here?

LEE: Not quite. When did it start?

ELLEN: Senior year at Harvard. I played basketball and soccer, ran track and field, and did well in all of them. But I was packing around 135 pounds and my track coach decided to point that out to me. I lost about ten, but when I got back from Christmas break, he said it looked like I'd put some back on.

LEE: What was he doing...scouting you for Vogue?

ELLEN: He probably meant well. But right then and there I swore that I'd never put on another pound.

LEE: And, perfectionist that you are...

ELLEN: I did it in spades. The whole gory mess.

LEE: How did people not notice that you had a problem?

ELLEN: I was as driven about hiding it as I was about everything else in my life, and I managed to still excel athletically. But in some strange ways that sometimes made things worse.

LEE: Such as...?

ELLEN: I ran the 10K in the Olympics trials in 1980 and came in third.

LEE: And this was a bad thing?

ELLEN: It shouldn't have been. But the 10K for women was just an exhibition sport in the Olympics at that time, so it wasn't the real thing.

LEE: But you knew that in advance.

ELLEN: True, and I was fine with it, especially since I had a chance to go to the Games, except they were in Moscow, remember?

LEE: The ones we boycotted.

ELLEN: So I qualified in a sport that didn't exist for a team that wasn't going. I was used to participating and winning, and now I couldn't do either. I was already vulnerable and that just made things worse.

LEE: But you were still competing on the international scene, doing well and setting records.

ELLEN: Nothing that had happened reduced my drive. If anything, it intensified after the trials because it fueled the fire for the next time, which would be 1984. Look, I did everything to the max, including being a good athlete and messing myself up at the same time. And when I became a pure runner, losing all that weight was a tremendous advantage. Same engine, lighter chassis.

LEE: If that's true, here's a weird question: What was the downside to the eating disorder? At least from an athletic perspective.

ELLEN: A couple of things. The first is that I didn't stop when I hit the optimum weight. Another is that there was a lot of physical damage being done inside that took its toll. And then there was a psychological erosion that affected my confidence, my motivation, my ability to focus...it's a whole cascade of negative effects.

LEE: You married the mayor of Denver, Federico Pena, who went on to become a cabinet secretary. He had no idea what was going on with you?

ELLEN: He knew I had some problems, but no idea of the real extent.

LEE: A high-functioning bulimic.

ELLEN: That's what's so insidious about eating disorders. When you're not bingeing and purging, you can appear perfectly normal. I got through law school, worked at a prestigious firm, handled all of the "first lady of Denver" obligations just fine. Sure, there are periods of deep depression but it's easy to pass them off as unremarkable moodiness. Nobody knows you're dying inside.

LEE: How long did this "double life" go on?

ELLEN: About ten years.

LEE: Then what happened?

ELLEN: I was pregnant, and the baby was in trouble. I needed to be a hundred percent healthy and any risk to the baby, however slight, was simply unthinkable. I had to do something.

LEE: And that was...?

ELLEN: Well – and this is going to sound a little hokey, but it wasn't – I made a deal.

LEE: With whom?

ELLEN: Whatever higher power there was. I said I'll stop my self-destructive behaviors, all of them, for the rest of my pregnancy. And if I do, you give me a healthy baby.

LEE: You put a time limit on it?

ELLEN: I wanted to make a reasonable promise, something credible, without overdoing it. So that was the deal.

LEE: Did you hold up your end of the bargain?

ELLEN: It wasn't easy but I had the strongest motivation I'd ever had for anything. And I got a beautiful, perfect baby.

LEE: What happened after she was born?

ELLEN: I didn't go back to my old ways. I stayed healthy for eleven years.

LEE: I've got a background in psychology, but I was more into psychopaths (go figure), so all of this is news to me. Is an eating disorder like alcoholism or drug addiction? Are you never really "cured" and have to be careful and vigilant every second of the rest of your life?

ELLEN: Kind of. The same kind of predispositions that got you into trouble are still there waiting to trap you again. But it differs from a substance addiction in one important way: An addict can engineer his life to stay away from booze or drugs but there's no way to stay away from food. You have to eat, several times a day, so food is always there and there's no way around that.

LEE: So what's it like going to a restaurant with you? Are you like an obnoxious ex-smoker or drinker gone all righteous and ready to pounce with a lecture if I order a second crème brulee?

ELLEN: Nah. But I'm pretty careful about what I eat myself – dressing on the side, you know --

LEE: I do know. Some of the stuff my wife eats looks like it was grown in Chernobyl.

ELLEN: -- but it has a lot more to do with managing nutrition so I can compete better than it does with flashbacks to the bad old days.

LEE: Any relapses?

ELLEN: A couple. Getting divorced, which is traumatic enough for anyone, was a particularly rough blow that set me off again. Then, just last year, with a lot of stressful things bumping together all at once in my life, I did a big race and it didn't go well. Afterward, and at the worst possible moment, another athlete remarked that I might do better if I lost a few pounds.

LEE: Did he end up in the ER?

ELLEN: No, but I almost did. It's what we call a triggering event and that one was a beaut. I lost a good bit of weight but I got help and got control before anything serious happened.

LEE: Does it help that you've done so much work in this area, including a lot of public speaking? You even started a foundation.

ELLEN: Sure. I had some notoriety from the movie (*Dying to be Perfect: The Ellen Hart Pena Story*, 1996) and I used it to start the foundation. Doing that kind of work keeps my sensitivity and awareness heightened. And I'm so into endurance sports now that I wouldn't want to do anything that compromised my abilities in that area. I'm very healthy right now.

LEE: Do you think that there are women in triathlon with eating disorders?

ELLEN: I know there are, and so do the experts I work with. Think about the personality types that are attracted to a sport like this: driven, Type-A perfectionists who rarely feel like they've done enough. Surround them with high-performing athletes who look like they were carved out of marble and you've got the textbook setup for all kinds of obsession-centered problems. Even Chrissie Wellington ran into trouble. Thankfully, she came out of it okay.

LEE: Maybe there's some good you can do on that front.

ELLEN: I'm already working on it.

LEE: Let's back up a little. You were a world class runner, so how did you get into triathlon?

ELLEN: I ran the marathon in the '84 Olympic trials and really loved the feeling of long distance running. I started getting healthy again in the early 90s but then had plantar fasciitis, which took two years to heal. I got a bike for my 47th birthday and separated my shoulder on my very first ride, but I got past it and did some swimming and biking. In 2006 I did two sprint-distance triathlons and one international without intending to run the last leg, but I'd brought my shoes and did, limping the whole way. The next year things felt better, and I qualified for nationals. I'd intended to go back to running but had already paid for nationals, so I figured I might as well go.

LEE: That would have been Portland in 2007.

ELLEN: I qualified for two Team USA events there, which gave me the extraordinary opportunity to race on behalf of my country, so I was feeling pretty good about triathlon. My first 70.3 distance was Harvest Moon. I came across the line in 4:52 with absolutely nothing left in the tank, so when a friend suggested I try a full Ironman, I thought, Do this twice? Are you insane? And laughed it off. But next year I went to Lubbock and when I won a slot, I took it, and did my first Ironman in 2008.

LEE: So your very first Ironman was the world championship in Kona?

ELLEN: Yep. I'd never ridden 112 miles before, swum 2.4 only once...I was naïve, I was scared, and I felt unprepared.

LEE: You came in third, behind Laura Sophiea and less than a minute behind Donna Smyers. That's some debut.

ELLEN: It was going to be a bucket list check-off for me but was just too incredible. There's a spiritual place I get to in an Ironman that I don't get to any other way. I've done a lot of sports at a high level but Ironman is utterly unique. It's like getting right to the essence of things.

LEE: How many have you done altogether?

ELLEN: Three, all in Kona. I had a stress fracture in my foot in 2009 and had to skip that year, and in 2010 I won my age group and missed the course record by twenty seconds. I also had one of the greatest experiences of my life, which was seeing my son and not-yet-husband Rob popping up all over the place on the course and cheering me on. I started the run eighteen minutes behind and knew for certain I could make it up, and I did. It was a real team effort and, that December, Rob and I got married.

LEE: Last year you came in second to Theresa Rider.

ELLEN: I got into debt on the swim and never fully recovered. Theresa is an exceptional athlete and such a strong performer in all three disciplines. There's no room for error when you're competing against someone like that.

LEE: I saw you race the Ironman World Championship 70.3 in Las Vegas two months ago. It was a ridiculously tough day, and only one age grouper in the entire field managed to set a new course record. Wait, that was you.

ELLEN: I had an early wave and missed the worst of the heat.

LEE: So did everyone else who started early. You being modest?

ELLEN: I'm really not.

LEE: So let me go way out on a limb here: You're not in Kona just to finish, right?

ELLEN: Very funny. No, I'm out to win.

LEE: Not going to be easy.

ELLEN: It's never easy. If it was easy, you'd be doing it.

LEE: Point taken.

[Ed. note: Ellen finished second in her age group at the 2012 Ironman World Championship, just two minutes and 22 seconds behind Australia's June Ward. She won in Cozumel the following month.]

Q & A with
KAREN AYDELOTT

A veteran triathlete who lost a foot several years ago, Karen Aydelott handed me one of the best lines I've heard in a long time: When I asked her why she was racing in an able-bodied division at Kona, she replied, "Because it was too hard to qualify as physically challenged." I spent some time talking to Karen to try to get answers to the seventeen questions spawned by that one answer.

LEE: I'm still reeling from that, so let's start at the ending. First, are you really entered into an able-bodied age group?

KAREN: I am. Women 65-69.

LEE: Who do you think you are...Oscar Pistorius?

KAREN: No, but we share one thing in common. The only way we could get into the events we really wanted was to compete alongside able-bodied athletes.

LEE: Okay, but Oscar had no choice because there are no PC divisions at the Olympics. There are at the Ironman World Championship.

KAREN: Yes, but they're too hard to get into.

LEE: Let me guess: You have to give an arm and a—

KAREN: No, even that won't do it, nor will training your heart out. The problem is that the entry rules for challenged athletes were changed a few years ago so that it's now a lottery system. I tried twice to get in and didn't make it. By "trying" I mean that I entered the lottery and waited. There was nothing I could do to influence the process.

LEE: Not an ideal situation for a born competitor like you.

KAREN: It wasn't at all, and I was more and more eager to get back to Kona.

LEE: I've seen you race here. How many times altogether?

KAREN: An even dozen.

LEE: With plenty of top-five finishes, including a win.

KAREN: I love this event, and I realized that the highest probability way back was the standard qualifying route.

LEE: We'll get to how you did that in a second. How did you get into triathlons in the first place? Were you always athletic?

KAREN: Not really. I was in high school before Title IX and didn't have a lot of options, but was still on the swim team and took ballet lessons. That's when I got my first inkling that I was cut out for longer events.

LEE: You did endurance ballet?

KAREN: Very funny. No, on the swim team. The longer the race, the more I liked it. Of course, the longest event was the 400-meter individual medley because everyone was convinced that women would drop dead if they tried anything more strenuous.

LEE: What sports did you do in college?

KAREN: Synchronized swimming and modern dance. That was it until my two boys were born.

LEE: What happened then?

KAREN: I wanted to get fitter and also recover from two 9+ pound babies. I went to the Y, then started running in the gym and liked it. That was right at the beginning of the running boom, and Nike had just come out with a shoe made from a women's last. I was also in a difficult marriage and needed some escape, so all of those things sort of collided. I wasn't an especially good runner, but I did a bunch of marathons and enjoyed them.

LEE: And triathlon?

KAREN: I kind of stumbled into it. Someone was talking about a sprint event close to where I lived. I signed up, won my age group and thought, I'm probably going to get better at this than I am at running.

LEE: Were you any kind of cyclist?

KAREN: Not at all. I didn't get my first decent bike until I was 40. It was only $400 and I had to pay for it on time.

LEE: Really?

KAREN: Like I said, it was a difficult marriage. I thank the stars for John [Hubby 2.0, and a certified good guy] every day.

LEE: So you still liked the endurance stuff once you figured out you weren't going to drop dead?

KAREN: I like challenges, and I was pretty good at the long distances. Muncie was my first 70.3, and it was a wonderful experience. I actually qualified for Kona, but it seemed so over the top that I turned down the slot without a second thought.

Stumbling Towards the Finish Line

LEE: To most people in this sport that'd be like turning down a MacArthur Fellowship.

KAREN: No kidding! That's about when I started hearing a lot of buzz about Ironman, and ordinary mortals doing it. I gave myself two years to get ready, but the next year when I won a slot at Iron Horse in Springfield, I decided to go for it.

LEE: That would have been 1989, the year of the—

KAREN: Iron War, between Mark Allen and David Scott. And I saw it!

LEE: You did? How?

KAREN: They were coming in as I was heading out. I didn't learn the full significance until later, but I knew that two guys shoulder to shoulder toward the end of the race was a really big deal.

LEE: How'd you do?

KAREN: It was very tough. Hyponatremia and everything else you could imagine. I finished in around 13:30 and was very disappointed. Of course, I'd sell my soul for that time now.

LEE: But you weren't discouraged.

KAREN: Not in the slightest. I planned to stick with it until I ran the race I knew I had in me.

LEE: Surprisingly tough age groups you moved through. You must have come up against [11-time age group winner] Lesley Cens-MacDowell over and over.

KAREN: Not to mention your own lovely bride three out of every five years. But I improved steadily, started placing, then I had a great race in 1997 and won.

LEE: We're getting to the bad part. First tell me where you grew up.

KAREN: I was originally from Philadelphia. My father was an army doctor and we moved around a bit when I was very young, but after he got out we settled in Decatur, Illinois, where he opened a private practice. I lived there until I went to college at Wellesley.

LEE: What did you study?

KAREN: Art history.

LEE: Ah: So you had a real practical bent.

KAREN: It worked out pretty well. My first job out of school was with American Heritage Publishing, where I did research on pictures for [Pulitzer Prize-winning historian] David McCullough, who was with the Smithsonian Institution. I moved to Minneapolis after getting married and lived there for 25 years. I was executive director for two YMCAs there, and then one in San Luis Obispo when I decided to come to California in 1996. I then ran a Y in Pasadena for nine years and moved back to SLO when John retired.

LEE: The accident happened in Pasadena.

KAREN: I'd been riding for a few years with some pure cycling guys who challenged me to keep up. I got really great workouts, but one June morning in 2006, some driver who wasn't paying attention slammed into me from behind. I heard the noise before I felt anything and thought I could keep the bike up, but I fell and ended up under the car. The driver had been going so fast she couldn't stop right away. The force of being dragged along like that flipped me over and took my ankle out.

LEE: What does that mean, took it out?

KAREN: It's what they call an "explosive break." The lower couple of inches of the fibula were blown away. Pieces of it ended up on the road.

LEE: Did you know right away how bad it was?

KAREN: I knew it was bad. What I didn't know was that it wasn't fixable. Nobody did until much later.

LEE: But they tried.

KAREN: I had eleven surgeries, including on my back which was also injured in the accident. The pain was unbearable and a year later they fused four vertebrae. It was a risky procedure, but very successful.

LEE: And the ankle?

KAREN: A different story entirely. They first tried to fuse the bones. It didn't work, and an infection set in, which is very common with ankle injuries. They tried again, it didn't take, bones slipped and got misaligned. At one point they took my talus out – that's the second largest ankle bone and transmits the entire weight of the body to the foot – and my leg got two inches shorter. I also looked like I had a club foot, which didn't exactly elevate my spirits.

LEE: When did you figure out that this wasn't going to work?

KAREN: Two years after the accident. After all of those surgeries and setbacks it was clear to me that this was never going to work, that it was going to hurt all the time and I'd never walk right again.

LEE: How do you arrive at the decision to have it cut off?

KAREN: I was completely ready. I researched it, talked to people who'd been there, and I knew that the only way I'd ever be able to walk without a limp and ride a bike and wear normal shoes was to do it on an artificial lower leg that could be built to perfection, instead of my mangled ankle that couldn't be fixed at all. In other words, I needed to be me again and that was the only way.

Stumbling Towards the Finish Line

LEE: Looking back, are you happy with that decision?

KAREN: Absolutely. I've never looked back. That's not say there haven't been plenty of frustrations along the way, but I improved steadily, I had some real control over the situation, and I'm way ahead of where I could even hope to have been, both mentally and physically. Getting my first socket was like being reborn. I hadn't walked much in two years and now I could.

LEE: How long before you got back on a bike?

KAREN: The surgery was in July; I was riding by December. A year later I did Big Rock [an international distance triathlon], then the Desert Triathlon the following spring, then the Oceanside 70.3. I didn't have my running foot yet, but I did it anyway. I kind of trotted the whole way but I finished and it was thrilling.

LEE: I suspect we've skipped over a whole lot of pain and suffering in trying to summarize this odyssey.

KAREN: You have no idea. But there were some significant positives that far outweighed the negatives. And by positive I mean more than just getting my mobility back.

LEE: Such as?

KAREN: The extraordinary support I received. It was hard for me to ask for help; I wasn't used to being on the receiving end and it took a while to learn the importance of letting people be helpful.

LEE: Are you talking about moral support, physical assistance...?

KAREN: Both. The prosthetists who worked with me were extraordinary people, the Challenged Athletes Foundation helped in very substantive ways, I had experts like Peter Harsh, my coach, Mark Sortino, my faithful "handler," Ray Barrios, and the entire Fortius racing team. There was also Alisa Benson, a former triathlete who had to give it up because of her own health problems, and your own wife, Cherie, who stuck by me from the very beginning. As determined as I was, I simply couldn't have made it alone. Having the support of all of these people made me believe I could do this.

LEE: Any of them here in Kona now?

KAREN: Mark is here, Ray and his brother, Alisa and her husband.

LEE: After all your years of racing, you had to get injured to finally get your own entourage.

KAREN: And you know the funny thing?

LEE: There was a funny thing?

KAREN: Yes. Some of the more severely injured military guys I met through CAF dismissed my little problem as a "flesh wound!"

LEE: You gotta love those guys.

KAREN: It's all relative: I still had a knee on the injured side and one entirely good leg.

LEE: So how'd you qualify for the world championship?

KAREN: I'd done Arizona and St. George and didn't finish either of them.

LEE: Must have been pretty discouraging.

KAREN: Exactly the opposite. I was greatly encouraged by both. I'd gotten really far into the run and only missed finishing because the clock ran out, not because I quit. That told me for sure that I could do it. When I went back and raced Arizona again, I finished and I qualified.

LEE: And you raced that as able-bodied?

KAREN: I did all of them that way. What did I have to lose? Turns out there was only one other competitor in my division, she didn't finish, so here I am in Kona.

LEE: Women 65-69 is much bigger this year: 17 athletes. What's your goal?

KAREN: If I finish, I'll be the happiest person on the island, and I'll also be surprised. It's a huge challenge for me.

Stumbling Towards the Finish Line

LEE: What's the biggest component of that challenge?

KAREN: Probably the weather. I have to get it done on the swim and bike and then survive the run, and I don't have a lot of experience with humidity. St. George was also hot, but it was dry.

LEE: I did a couple of articles on challenged athletes during race week last year, and Scott Rigsby told me about this vacuum system on his prostheses that pumps perspiration out.

KAREN: Unfortunately, that design won't work for me. I'm prepared to stop and take the leg off to dry it if I have to, or if it's putting so much pressure on a nerve that the pain gets overwhelming.

LEE: You did Arizona on your walking foot, right? Will you do that here in Kona?

KAREN: No. In Arizona I had an ulcerated sore and the running foot was so agonizing I put on my walking foot after three miles.

LEE: Are you allowed outside assistance for changes like that?

KAREN: No, so I was lucky to be on that course because it loops back right past the transition area. I was able to get the walking foot myself and not break the rules.

LEE: No such luck in Kona.

KAREN: All part of the challenge. I may have won this race once, but if I get across the finish line by midnight this year, this is the one I'll be looking back on for the rest of my life.

[Ed. note: Karen didn't make it to the finish line by the midnight cutoff, but she did manage to get through most of the run, an incredible accomplishment considering the 2012 event featured some of the toughest race conditions seen in years.]

CHERIE GRUENFELD:
One From the Heart

[Ed. note: This feature article, which appeared in the August 2010 issue of Inside Triathlon magazine, was the winner of Triathlon USA's "Article of the Year" award.]

Asking me to write a story about my wife is like asking one of Donald Trump's assistants to write one about him: It's bound to come off as fawning, sycophantic and blitheringly mawkish. Given that Cherie is also my unofficial editor, there's considerable personal liability attendant to the assignment as well. Cautionary instructions provided to professional bomb defusers come to mind.

Nevertheless, I soldier on, because it's a story worth telling, not so much in the chronological detailing of the evolution of a champion age grouper, but because of the opportunity to ponder the nature of seemingly contradictory tendencies within a single person.

I'll explain.

* * *

I co-wrote Evander Holyfield's autobiography two years ago. I think that his camp was expecting me to be bowled over by his work ethic, ability to absorb pain, his dedication and his mental strength. There were more than a few puzzled looks when I seemed to take it all in stride, like I see this kind of thing everyday.

That's because I do. I live with a triathlete who's competed in twenty-two Ironman events and won her age group in thirteen, nine of them in Kona, and is the owner of a handful of world and U.S. records. She may not have gotten $34 million for going three rounds with Tyson, but it was pretty obvious to Evander from the get-go that she had a lot more in common with him than I did.

But my intent here isn't to belabor the givens. Yes, she spent winters arising at 4:30 five mornings a week to make her way down a treacherous mountain road through various combinations of fog, snow and ice to a pool an hour away, but there are thousands of stories like that, all better left to the likes of mountain climbers who like to talk about who lost the most toes on K-2.

Inconsistencies are what fascinate me. Years ago I asked Cherie to call a client of mine and tell him I'd broken down on the road and would be late for a meeting, when the fact was I'd overslept. She stared at the phone for a while, picked it up, set it down, picked it up again, dialed and hung up, then stared at it some more and finally froze altogether. That's when I made the discovery that she's genetically incapable of lying. At all, to anyone. Not to traffic cops, used car salesmen, loan officers, potential employers, warranty adjusters, customer service agent, children...not to anyone to whom the rest of us dissemble as easily as we sip coffee or diddle our tax returns.

So what's inconsistent about that? Before becoming a triathlete, Cherie was one of the best software salespeople in the business. She'd risen to executive marketing positions in two highly advanced technology companies, including the Artificial Intelligence Corporation. It was said of her that she could sell you your own desk, and she was especially famous for having been named Salesman of the Year at database pioneer Cullinet by selling $2.4 million worth of software that hadn't even been written yet.

That ain't natural. How the hell can anybody sell like that without lying?

* * *

Speaking of natural, is there such a thing as a natural athlete? Of course there is. I know this for a fact because I'm not one, but I can spot someone who is at a thousand paces. As it happens, that's how I spotted Cherie, walking into a crowded room at a corporate conference thirty-three years ago. While the majority of the throng traipsed through the doors in various degrees of stagger, lurch and droop, this one wafted in like the puck on an air-hockey table. Watching her walk was like watching a bolt of silk unfurl. "Bring me that one!" I said (out loud, as it turned out, much to my chagrin). Later that evening someone did, during an award ceremony for the various athletic contests that had gone on that afternoon for conference participants. Seems Cherie had entered the men's tennis tournament...and won it. The organizers tied two tennis balls together with a length of string and dangled them as they called Cherie to the podium, where they awarded her an "honorary pair of balls" along with the first place trophy.

The next morning I played tennis with her myself.

Oh. My. God.

* * *

The competitive spirit is traditionally spoken of in warrior terms. After all, competition is a zero sum game. One wins, many lose, and the victory is as much about the vanquishing of the foe as it is about the ascension of the winner.

But there is an important distinction between "I won" and "I beat everybody."

For some, including Cherie, the point of competing isn't to trounce the opposition; it's to elevate yourself. Podium position isn't the goal; it's the scorecard.

Some years ago, Cherie badly twisted an ankle about two miles before the finish of the Wildflower Long Course Triathlon in central California. While still on the ground she was passed by Barbara Warren, a good friend who would go on to win the race. Cherie got up and managed to finish second. At the award ceremony she put on a pair of socks to hide the blue-tinged swelling and forced herself to walk to the podium without limping. All the crowd was to know was that Barbara was the better athlete that day.

In sports like golf and bowling, you can compete without competitors. The sport comes with built-in quantification. Shoot 79 when you've never broken 80 before or bowl 12 above your average and you're getting better. I used to make a lot of friendly golf bets with Cherie's brother, Larry. Sometimes we played against each other two or three times a week. Thing is, I only actually see the guy once or twice a year because he lives in Washington and I live in Palm Springs. Doesn't matter that we play 1,500 miles apart because, later in the day, we just compare score cards by email.

Triathlon isn't like that. The conditions aren't repeatable and absolute numbers are largely meaningless. That's why some years will see a dozen age group records broken in a race and others might see one or two. Your only measure is how you stacked up against everyone else undertaking the same race.

This is especially true of older athletes. The difference between them and younger ones is that the older ones are getting older. The younger ones aren't. They're still getting better.

Cherie is graceful about many things in life, but aging isn't one of them. The decline in her abilities was sudden and, despite her considerable intellect, she truly doesn't understand why that should be so. It just didn't seem to be a given that, even at 65 years of age, she should have fallen that far.

In a way, she's right. It started with a senseless accident at the 2002 Ironman Utah that shattered her clavicle, broke five ribs and tore up her hamstring. It continued with another bike crash a few years later that wrecked her shoulder. Both involved questionable diagnoses, delayed and unorthodox surgeries, and difficult recoveries. A third incident that was "solved" with cortisone in her knee may have been the cause of her current inability to lift her right foot high enough off the ground when running, to the point where the rubber on the sole of her right shoe literally disappears after twenty-five miles. To any dispassionate outside observer these are all obvious proximate causes of her compromised performance.

Except to Cherie. She doesn't believe any of those should have brought her down that fast. Aging shouldn't have, either.

So what did?

"I don't know," she'll tell you. "But I should be doing better than I am."

This from a woman with three college degrees.

I should have known better. Once when we were in Panama, we rented a couple of surfboards and headed for the beach. I'd surfed for years as a teenager and was having a blast riding the near-perfect waves, but Cherie couldn't manage to stand up for more than a second or two without falling over. This was kind of strange from someone that coordinated. A few months before that we were visiting a friend who'd just gotten one of those training golf clubs with a shaft consisting of three hinged sections that flopped around independently. The idea was that if you made a perfect swing, all three sections would stay aligned and look like one solid shaft. My buddy and I had been struggling with the thing for half an hour, and it was like trying to shoot pool with a rope. Cherie picked it up, took her stance and swung it just once. It looked as though all three sections had been welded together into a solid steel beam.

So here she was, flopping around helplessly in the Pacific while her clumsy husband was doing the *Endless Summer* thing a few yards away. After about half an hour of this she was pounding her fist on the board in howling frustration. Clearly she'd had about enough, so I came over to grab her board just as a wave came in and flipped it over. Sure enough, all three fins on the triple-skeg design board were missing. Duke Kahanamoku himself couldn't have ridden that useless piece of junk.

When I explained that, she wasn't a bit mollified. "Should have been able to ride it anyway," she muttered.

There was no convincing her. Then I gave her the board I'd been riding.

Oh. My. God.

* * *

So what's it like to live with her on a day-to-day basis?

If she's not injured, fine.

Cherie has a thriving coaching business consisting of both private clients and others via Ian Murray and Jamie Silber's Triathlon Training Systems (TTS). When one of those clients gets injured, Cherie counsels patience and a rational, careful approach to recovering and getting back in the game.

If I were to tell you what Cherie is like when injured and how she approaches getting back into the game, it would not only put the zonk on everything I've been telling you about her but would also wreck her entire coaching business.

So the only thing I'll tell you is this: When she's been hurt and unable to train or compete, rabid Rottweilers have been known to skitter fearfully to the other side of the street when they see her coming.

* * *

If there's one common trait that characterizes champions, it's unapologetic self-absorption. It's necessarily that way. After all, there are hundreds of thousands of people who are genetically wired to be great runners, boxers, swimmers or triathletes. What turns some of them into champions are discipline, unrelenting drive, off-the-scale work ethic and a willingness to sacrifice others to their own cause.

How does that square with an expansive generosity of spirit toward those less fortunate?

Usually, it doesn't, which is why celebrities fork over millions to public relations agencies who make a living by painting their clients as something they're not, because if they were, they wouldn't need a public relations agency in the first place.

It's a question that plagued Cherie not long after she discovered her long-distance running abilities and began winning medals. The more she won, the harder she worked, placing the kinds of demands on herself that anyone who reads *Inside Triathlon* is already well aware of. Things that didn't fit in the training schedule didn't get scheduled. Even things that did were often amended, sometimes inconveniently, to accommodate.

It was a conscious choice, and I was all for it. But it bothered her. She wasn't used to it. And something was missing.

About nine years ago, she was invited to speak at an elementary school in a troubled part of the troubled city of San Bernardino. It was in connection with an underfunded, essentially desperate program to try to bring some light to young lives that had seen very little of it. Cherie, an avid proselytizer for her sport, talked about triathlon and then asked who among the listeners would like to try one. Several hundred hands shot up, and at a tryout a few days later, she chose a small group to see who among them might take it seriously.

Out of that humble beginning grew the *Exceeding Expectations* program. Much has been written about this extraordinarily effective effort to turn around lives given up for dead, so I won't belabor the details here. Suffice it to say that she brought the same zeal and dedication to that endeavor that she had to everything else she'd done in her life and career.

But let me be clear, lest you think I'm trying to draw a parallel with Mother Theresa or Albert Schweitzer: Cherie isn't out to change the world or start a movement, and she's not on a special mission at the behest of some inner voice. She simply fell in love with these kids. She saw lives that had essentially been discarded, not out of conscious malevolence on anybody's part, but out of the same despair that afflicted their families, their neighborhoods and, depressingly often, their schools. Experts, armed with statistics and experience, took Cherie aside and warned her that she was not only wasting her time but risked giving false hope to the hopeless. "A third of these kids," she was told repeatedly, "are going to be dead or in jail by the time they're eighteen. More than half will never make it to their senior year in high school, the girls mostly because they'll get pregnant."

Stumbling Towards the Finish Line

Cherie, as usual, cut to the heart of the mater. "If their lives are hopeless anyway, what's the harm in trying?"

"Oh, I'm not worried about them," one counselor replied, waving dismissively at the school building as though writing off every kid in it. "I'm worried about you. You're going to get your heart broken. I guarantee it."

After nine years and eighty-some-odd kids, two dropped out of school, two got in trouble with the law and one got pregnant. One was killed by a hit-and-run driver and another was killed in a drive-by shooting.

But: Edgar is in the U.S. Marines, Jose is in the army stationed in South Korea, and Marvin is in the navy. Nik, Carlos and Mikey are in college—Nik at UC San Diego. Marlene is finishing her last three years of high school in college, with two full years of college credit, as part of a special program for highly motivated students. Vianey has been chosen to participate in an exclusive summer camp for future leaders of California. Josh and Damien—both adopted by the teacher who co-founded Exceeding Expectations with Cherie—are in the San Bernardino County Schools Honor Orchestra, and Josh is in a special school for gifted children. Those are the highlights. Across the board, grades are up, behavioral problems are virtually non-existent, and the kids are learning how to set goals and work to achieve them.

Why? For the same reason that the program hasn't been successfully duplicated by any of the hundreds of people who have called Cherie over the years and asked how to start one in their own communities. "There's no magic," she explains patiently. "Talk to every kid every few days. Every single one, and if you don't see them, call them. If they don't have phones in the house, buy them cell phones. You have to get their report cards and crash down on them if they're sub-par. You have to be in their faces constantly, one on one, and be willing to go into their homes and negotiate with their parents if you see things going south. You have to make them understand that there's at least one person in the world who isn't going to let them get away with doing less than they're capable of and make it your business to know exactly where that line is. You have to take them out for training, get them to races, bargain with race directors to get entry fees waived or discounted, round up volunteers who will be in it for the long haul instead of once in a while, arrange for transportation for every event and, when you have all of that covered, you have to beg for money from your friends, your family and just about everyone you come into contact with. You have to do it constantly, and shamelessly, because no matter how humiliating it is for you and how annoying it is for them, the alternative is to do less for the kids, and that's simply unacceptable. Oh, and one other thing: You never, ever give up on a kid, no matter what he does. Ever."

In nine years, she has yet to get all the way through that speech without losing the listener. *Exceeding Expectations* isn't about supplying money and building athletes; it's about supplying yourself and building people. If you're a kid on the EE team, you show up for training and races on time and prepared. At races, you'd best be looking people straight in the eye when you tell them your name. You say thank-you to the race director who comp'd your entry and to the volunteers who showed up to run or swim with you. At the annual EE Swimathon, you make the fundraising calls yourself. Cherie doesn't care how much you raise. She cares that you picked up the phone, made a call, stated your case and then followed up with a letter. Medaling in a local triathlon isn't going to get you through life; having a basic set of social skills will.

Interestingly, when it comes to certain life skills, EE kids have it all over their more fortunate counterparts in mainstream society. They've learned that complaining doesn't work; taking matters into your own hands does. At the Desert Triathlon a few years ago, we saw a fourteen-year-old from Brentwood throw a temper tantrum when his bike computer didn't work that ended with him throwing the bike at his mother's feet and storming off without finishing the race.

About an hour after that, when Cherie went to retrieve twelve-year-old EE team member Brandon's bike from transition, she discovered that it wouldn't shift.

"How'd you change gears?" she asked him back at the EE equipment trailer.

"I didn't," he replied nonchalantly. When he couldn't get it to work, he simply hunkered down and did the entire bike course in one gear, playing the hand he was dealt as best he could because it never occurred to him that it could be improved.

Cherie's own education has been interesting. There was the time young Julio heard her lamenting that we didn't have a bike for one of the kids. (All the bikes are donated by friends of the program and are kept in a trailer we haul to races and workouts. If the kids took them home, we'd never see them again.) He went up to her and said, "What kinda bike you need?"

"Why?" Cherie asked. "Do you know somebody who has one we can use?"

 "Didn't say that," Julio replied. "What I'm asking, what kinda bike you need?" I stifled a giggle. "And how many?" Julio threw in.

Cherie was still all wide-eyed innocence. "But..."

I grabbed her away and explained. Then she turned around and explained a few things to Julio. It was a pretty funny scene.

Julio was the boy killed in a drive-by a year later.

* * *

The other big preoccupation of Cherie's life is Kona. It's the preoccupation of a lot of triathletes, and all the reasons have been well documented by far better scribes than I, so I won't attempt to go them one better. If you've been here during race week, you already know why. If you haven't, you can't possibly know. But, in addition to the usual, there's one added attraction for Cherie, and that is that she's hopelessly, head

Stumbling Towards the Finish Line

over heels in love with athletes. Any athlete, no matter the sport. It's why she's the one who has the *Sports Illustrated* subscription and the one who devours the *Los Angeles* and *New York Times* sports sections each morning before they even make it upstairs. She's fascinated by people who excel at anything, but athletes in particular, and she's remarkably tolerant of eccentricities that drive me nuts so long as the eccentric is dedicated to something and cares deeply enough to pursue it diligently.

In Kona, she doesn't have to admire them from afar. She gets to rub elbows with pros and age groupers, hear their stories, watch them compete. On race day the ritual is always the same: finish her race, get a quick massage, run up to the condo (she insists that we stay within a seven iron of the start-finish line so we've been ensconced next to the stone church on Ali'i for about twelve years), shower and change, then get back down to the finish area and marvel at the rest of the finishers until midnight.

In her book *Become an Ironman*, Cherie tells the story of someone standing invisibly in the shadows of some bushes on the last corner of the race before the turn onto Ali'i. As each exhausted runner went past he'd softly call out, "Welcome home." He did that for years, then suddenly disappeared. She was always sorry she never got a chance to find him and thank him.

I'm starting to wonder if he was ever really there.

* * *

Cherie's is a life filled with wonder and accomplishment, all of it informed by purpose. She's convinced that life has to have some meaning, that one's existence can't possibly be an accident of molecules, lightning and chance. That deep conviction doesn't spring from religion or any special inclination toward esoteric philosophy, but from her ability to cut directly and logically to the heart of things without discursions into self-indulgent navel-gazing. *"If life has no purpose,"* she concludes simply, *"then there would be no purpose to life."*

In other words, the fact that we're here is all the rationale we need for assuming that there's a reason.

A lot of the kids in Cherie's program are Hispanic. Despite the close proximity to the ocean of many in that community, there's an odd but deep-seated fear of water, which presents a bit of a challenge when you're using triathlon as the vehicle for trying to transform their lives.

They didn't trust the water, but they trusted Cherie, so what she did to get them accustomed to being in a pool was to put the littler ones on her back and carry them, one by one, through the swim leg of a race. At the Highland YMCA Sprint triathlon a few years ago, a buddy of mine snapped a shot of her carrying Brandon, the kid who did an entire bike race in one gear, just as they both glanced up prior to making a turn.

Of the thousands of photos taken of her, it's by far my favorite. It's hard to tell which of the two, Cherie or Brandon, was radiating the purest joy in that captured instant, or if the joy was in the sharing and therefore inseparable.

Either way, it's impossible for me to look at that picture and not be profoundly thankful for having her in my life.

THE SECOND PART:

NOT SO FUNNY STUFF

Things you might want to know

Barbara Warren: A reminiscence

[Ed. note: Barbara Warren died on August 26, 2008, three days after being paralyzed as the result of a bike crash at the Santa Barbara Triathlon. Her identical twin, Angelika Castaneda, turned off her ventilator at Barbara's request. This piece was Lee's tribute to his and Cherie's old friend.]

I'm not going to tick down a list of Barbara Warren's accomplishments or virtues. First of all there's not enough room, and many other people who knew her much better than Cherie or I did will see that it gets done properly. So just a little story.

We first met Barbara and her sister Angelika at Mike & Rob's "Most Excellent Triathlon" in 1992. They finished first and second, but both had already qualified for Kona so the slot rolled down to Cherie, leading to her very first Ironman. You couldn't miss Barbara and Angelika: From half a mile away either one of those strikingly beautiful ladies, their athletic physiques as trim as their haircuts, could turn heads, but the two of them in combination made you blink hard and look again.

We ran into them many times at races but it wasn't until 1995 that we really got to know them well, and not in a way that was fully planned. Cherie and the twins, along with Mary Ann Buxton, got together to compete as the first all-female masters relay team in the Furnace Creek 508, a 508-mile bicycle race across Death Valley. The plan was for four men, including Mary Ann's husband Bart and me, to provide support using two vehicles: our Ford Explorer and a motor home provided by the twins. Two women at a time would trade 20-minute bike sprints while the other two slept in the RV, and every four hours the teams would trade places. It was a great plan.

Two hours into the race the motor home broke down.

End of race, right? Not as far as Barbara was concerned. Matter of fact, I don't even remember any decision process taking place. We were all kind of standing around scratching ourselves, and after about three minutes of that Barbara jumped on her bike and began pedaling away. "You guys figure it out," she called back over her shoulder with a wave. "We have a race to ride."

Just like that, the question was no longer "Do we continue?" but "How?" While Bart and I strapped two bikes to the roof of the Explorer, the other two guys hauled as much food and water out of the RV as they could stuff into the cargo area and still leave room to throw one more bike on top. Then Cherie, Angelika and Mary Ann piled into the back seat and tried to get comfortable while Bart, the team coach and navigator, took the right front seat and I got behind the wheel. We said a quick goodbye to the remaining two guys who were tasked with getting the RV back in the game, and took off after Barbara.

Owing to very steep hills, stiff winds and a noon start, the race took us through the night, the next day, and on until the wee hours of the second night. Five of us at a time were crammed into a small and uncomfortable space overflowing with coolers, clothes for both hot and cold conditions, cycling shoes, maps, spare parts and Lord knows what else. We didn't see a bathroom the entire time, sleep was fitful and short if it happened at all, there was no way to cook or even do simple food prep, and we had to follow close behind the cyclist-of-the-moment, a nerve-wracking task even in daylight when you're fresh, and all the time trying to remember that this was a competitive event, not a training ride.

As it happened, we had a blast. The tougher it got (like when the two-way radio system went on the fritz), the more fun we had. And a large part of the reason for that was Barbara, whose unrelenting optimism and sunny disposition made it virtually impossible to let a negative thought intrude on the experience. There was nothing conscious or artificial about it, either, no speeches about overcoming obstacles or giving it the old college try or character building. Stuff came up; she handled it quietly and moved on. So the rest of us did, too.

Once, when were wrestling with some balky bicycle brakes during a changeover and trying to stretch our aching backs at the same time, Barbara slapped on a pair of running shoes and headed off into the inky night. We finally picked her up about five miles down the road. Even when she stood up from behind the car during a roadside potty break to find me standing there with a video camera pointed at her, her immediate reaction was to laugh.

There was one episode that was ironic, in retrospect. Coming out of Death Valley toward the town of Baker at about 3:00 am, Angelika was on the bike during a steep descent. The more daring of the twins, she was not only down on her aerobars but pedaling furiously. When I had her speed matched at a safe following distance I glanced at the speedometer. It read 55 mph. That's when I noticed Barbara leaning forward in the back seat, hands clasped tightly together in front of her face, anxious eyes glued on her sister. "I can't stand it when she does that," she said softly. "I don't know what I'd do if I lost her." I don't think she breathed again until Angelika was safely off the mountain.

We never got the motor home back. About two hours before the four girls rode side-by-side across the finish line, the radio crackled and the two other support guys finally showed up ... in a rented, two-door Honda. It was Barbara who laughed the loudest at the sight and suggested that we finish the race using only the Explorer, which is just what we did.

I never would have believed that I could have enjoyed that experience. I'm ready to open a vein if the line at the grocery store is too long. But there was something about Barbara, as well as her sister, that would have made any sort of complaint wildly out of place and inappropriate. Once I figured that out and settled into just handling the situation, two things happened. The first is that I had an experience I'll never forget while learning some very important lessons about life. And the second is that I fell in love with both of those amazing women.

Thank you, Barbara.

A Word to the Triathlon Widow

[Ed. note: This article, originally published in Competitor Magazine in 1999, remains the most popular of all Lee's pieces in terms of requests for permission to reprint, mostly by endurance sports coaches wanting copies for their clients.]

A question that seems to pop up with depressing frequency is whether there are any support groups for triathlon widows. Tongue-in-cheek, to be sure, but beneath the glib sarcasm lurks a very real set of issues.

I would venture that, for the vast majority of married or POSSLQ'd ("Persons of Opposite Sex Sharing Living Quarters") participants in this sport, the union preceded the triathloning, thereby rendering the latter somewhat of a surprise, undoubtedly one of slightly greater weight than the greeting-him-in-your-underwear-after-a-tough-day-at-the-office variety. Meals together on the run or not at all, alarms at 4:45, the sudden disappearance of red meat, and a new Lightspeed instead of new carpeting are only a few of the tribulations attendant to a strange activity that is, in statistically demonstrable terms, at least three times as demanding as the kinds of obsessions normal folks in your neighborhood get into on weekends.

You may feel, as many others do, that these are "tri-ing" times indeed, and, as supportive as you'd like to be, something doesn't feel quite fair about it.

Well.

* * *

About fourteen years ago [1985] my bride, Cherie, decided to try running a marathon, this at a time when we both had high-pressure positions, putting in 80-hour weeks and traveling some 200,000 miles a year between us. It wasn't easy on her: She'd get up at four in the morning to run in places like Denver in February and would lace up in the evenings when home to hit the Pacific Coast Highway. We saw even less of each other than we had before, and sometimes the only chance we had to talk was when I'd ride along with her on long weekend runs and periodically hand her water.

Her first marathon was a wonderful experience, and the bug bit her badly. She decided to do more of them, qualifying for Boston a year later. By that time the novelty had somewhat worn off for me, and I confess that there were times when I myself might have been just another problem to be handled as she gamely tried to cope with the new demands she'd added to her life. I know that I rolled my eyes a time or two when training interfered with something I'd planned and passed the occasional tart comment in response to yet another disruption.

The weather on the morning of the Boston Marathon was dismal. We huddled together miserably against a freezing rain, hoping in vain for some relief prior to the start. When the announcer called for the participants to begin lining up, I stared in wonder and with a small measure of guilt as Cherie stood up, tossed away her warm-up suit and stepped bravely into the teeth of that stinging drizzle clad only in shorts and a singlet while I remained covered. In the fifteen minutes before the gun went off, she began shivering uncontrollably while I watched from the sidelines.

I managed to see her at about a dozen spots along the course. As an increasing proportion of the field struggled, pain etched on their faces, my wife ran steadily. If she felt any pain, it didn't show, and every time I saw her, the smile would be wider than before. The strength of her upright posture, the elegance of her stride, even the oh-so-into-it attitude that seemed to shoot off her body were clearly evident to even the most unknowledgeable onlooker. Her last six miles were faster than the first six.

I saw her cross the finish line from high in the bleachers. A volunteer quickly wrapped her in a space blanket and just as quickly left her. Alone in that crowd, Cherie's eyes were closed as she walked slowly forward, her face a picture of the purest serenity, the most radiant inwardness I'd ever seen. In that moment, all of the work, sacrifice and determination of the previous eighteen months were telescoped to a pinpoint, all of it swirled together and indistinguishable and as perfect as a mere mortal could achieve.

The power of it floored me, and I had my own epiphany: All I could think about were the times I'd made her life tougher, caused her to doubt what she was attempting without considering the consequences, failed to truly understand the nature of the end toward which she was proceeding. I'd never felt quite so wretched and wondered if she'd ever forgive me.

Cherie's seeming trance lasted only a few seconds, and then she began casting her eyes around frantically. It took me a beat to realize she was looking for me, and when I waved and she spotted me, her features exploded into a smile that could have warmed a small planet. She fought her way through the limping and exhausted mass of bodies, desperate to share the moment with me, and as she gushed her gratitude for how selflessly I'd supported her, I realized that she'd barely noticed, if at all, what I believed to have been those times when I'd not been supportive at all.

Which of course only made me feel worse, and that was the very moment during which I made a solemn vow to go along with every single thing she felt she needed to do in order to continue a pursuit that made her happier than anything else she'd ever tried.

It was the second smartest decision I ever made, and, as happens to us so often, I discovered for myself something so simple and universal that in retrospect it seems blindingly obvious: When she was happy, I was happy. Whatever I could do to smooth the way turned out to be a purely selfish act. Her triumphs became mine, as did her setbacks, but of even greater importance, I finally understood the heart of an athlete who fiercely wanted to be extremely good at what she did. That the pursuit of athletic excellence is as much about mind as body is no longer a cliché for me, but a palpably real truth, and while her ability to get up before dawn and drive down an icy, snow-blown mountain road to a swimming pool an hour away still astonishes me, the reason for it is no longer obscure.

And it's a damned good thing I came to these realizations *before* she got into triathlon.

* * *

Now, what's all of this got to do with you? Maybe nothing, but maybe the same thing it has to do with my parents.

They'd never seen Cherie race, and in muted tones occasionally asked the same kinds of questions we've heard so many times before, variations of "So, how long does she plan to keep this up?" as though triathlon was some kind of momentary aberration to be undertaken once and quickly abandoned, like bungee jumping or alligator wrestling.

This past summer, my parents came to Lake Placid along with my nephew to watch her compete in the inaugural Ironman USA. Despite having seen countless of my videotapes, they'd never had the full, on-site experience, and I think they still haven't quite gotten over it.

The weather for the week prior had been bleak, a disheartening and forbidding mixture of intermittent showers and thick, gloomy clouds. Every athletic shop in the county was sold out of arm warmers by Tuesday, and the talk amongst entrants congregating on the course for familiarization workouts ran exclusively to how to cope with slick roads, wet shoes and the kind of sodden cold that settles with malicious glee in the bones and joints.

Fortunately, the weather was about the only serious problem that threatened the event. Everyone expected the organization of such a complex undertaking in a first-time location to experience teething problems, but it seemed as though Lake Placid had been hosting the Ironman for years and had the routine down cold. Admittedly, this state of affairs was at least partially enabled by the fact that the site of the 1980 Winter Olympics was a near-perfect venue, but that in no way detracted from the admiration that rightfully accrued to the race organizers who, had they been running things in 1980, would undoubtedly have left the world with a better impression of those chaotic Games than it actually got.

I used to come to Lake Placid with my family when I was growing up, and it's always been difficult to convince the uninitiated that the same state in which New York City is ensconced could also be home to such pristine alpine splendor. Already word is passing that this might be the most beautiful and dramatic Ironman course outside of the Big Island, redolent of pine and intercut throughout with crystalline water cascading gently right beside many of the roads. Startling vistas appear around nearly every turn, and much of the landscape is dominated by two massive ski jump towers that jut up from the forest and serve as comforting beacons connecting racers out on the course with the central site.

And what could be more thrilling than ending an endurance event on the same speedskating oval on which Eric Heiden had stunned the world two decades before?

As race morning dawned, streaks of light in the eastern sky encouraged racers to dare hope that a break in the weather was imminent. When the clouds began to thin even further, even the most jaded rationalists among the crowd had cause to doubt their conviction that this had to be a coincidence. The sun, visible for the first time in a week, continued to burn through the gloom as it rose, and spirits rose right along with it.

My parents and nephew were mesmerized by the electricity crackling in the air, the raw strength of the athletes assembling on the shore of Mirror Lake, the dizzying blend of anxiety, excitement and anticipation. Later they rode with me as I put three hundred frenetic miles on the rental car circumnavigating the course and trying to intercept Cherie in as many spots as we could. They shared my exhilaration at the turnaround of the first bike loop because her time was so much better than she'd predicted, groaned in dismay as she appeared alarmingly late on the second loop, cheered themselves hoarse as though the sound might speed her through the bike-to-run transition, and ran through an entire roll of film to try to capture forever the singular moment in which she brushed past them on the run only an arm's length away.

Only later did the onlookers begin to discover, as the athletes already had, the almost supernatural phenomenon of the seemingly benign bike course metamorphosing into a snarling beast on the second loop. Even those racers who'd ridden parts of the course for practice were badly shaken as their jellified legs and searing lungs howled in protest during that traumatizing replay, and negative splits were as rare as personal bests would be on that cunningly deceptive course. During the run that followed, many of those who touched a genuine Olympic gold medal placed near the turnaround for luck assumed it had revitalizing powers they would have scoffed at under normal circumstances.

I think my family may have been somewhat troubled by the depth of punishment an Ironman entails, but they forgot it quickly when confronted later that afternoon by the breathtaking sight of their 55-year old daughter-in-law gracefully streaking into the Olympic stadium to a first-place finish in her age group, a loopy smile planted on her face while many around her could only grimace. That she'd missed her target time by about twenty minutes made for an uncomfortable moment initially, the four of us not yet having become fully aware of the toll the unforgiving course had taken on the entire field, but as results drifted in and what she'd accomplished started to make itself evident—her margin of victory over second place exceeded an hour and she'd posted her highest overall finishing position ever—I doubt very much if Cherie's joy could possibly have surpassed theirs.

They no longer ask me how long she's going to keep this up.

* * *

Stumbling Towards the Finish Line

The answer to the question of triathlon widowhood doesn't lie in logistics. It isn't about scheduling appointments with each other or apportioning the household tasks or ensuring parity or fairness or equality.

It's about first realizing that, if your loved one aspires to be a triathlete, and especially one of the long-distance variety, you are linked to someone extraordinary and should be mindful of the privilege you've been afforded.

You need to trust me on this one: When you see his face as he crosses the line, your life will change forever, and every obstacle you erected instead of pulling one down will light up in your brain like a billboard. There's already enough guilt and regret to go around...why not exploit an opportunity to avoid some that's so easily predictable?

In the entire history of human relationships, expressing resentment has never once returned a positive benefit. It has never resulted in the creation of desirable behaviors, but instead is usually the seed of increasing bitterness and the stuff of seething anger. Understand that a triathlete in training has an awful lot of time to think, and your influence over the nature of that thinking can be profound. But just as there is plenty of time for him or her to work a small slight into a major crisis, so is there time for her to dwell appreciatively on the small sacrifice you made so that she could ride eighty miles that night. Whether she spends her two-hour run nursing a growing rage at your sophomoric petulance or contemplating how you demonstrated your devotion when it actually cost you something to do so is, ultimately, entirely in your hands.

One of two people is going to be coming home from that run soon: Which one would you rather spend the night blissfully wrapped around?

Easy call, the way I see it.

Circling the Drain

Forgive me for being serious just this once. Thankfully, it doesn't happen often.

I'm not normally prone to a lot of touchy-feely romanticizing about spiritual matters that are largely the self-serving inventions of people to whom concepts like "evidence" and "science" are regarded with suspicion. The way I look at it, anybody who believes in homeopathy, astrology, oxygenated water or wheat grass deserves to get swindled.

But one thing I've come to believe in strongly—because the evidence for it is overwhelming—is the mind–body connection and the extraordinary degree to which the mental can affect the physical. The examples are legion, and there's no sense repeating the oft-told stories, so I'd just like to throw in another one that might have some relevance in the endurance sports world.

Last Thanksgiving [2007] my wife Cherie wrote a piece about her father for her monthly column on the BioBuilde website. Glenn is 96, and Cherie spoke movingly about how he still rode his bike every day, rain or shine, even though he lives in western Washington, where there's plenty of rain and little shine.

A few months after that article came out, Glenn was taken off his blood thinning medication so he could undergo cataract surgery. (That was so he could keep his driver's license, if you can believe that.) Somehow, he wasn't informed of the risks of going off the med or what signs to watch for. So a few days later when he developed a pain in his leg, he did what came natural: sucked it up and tried to ignore it. What he didn't know was that he'd developed clots that were blocking the flow of blood. Eventually the pain got too bad and he let someone know. Surgeons had to open his leg pretty much from top to bottom to get at the clots, but the damage to muscle tissue from all of those hours with no blood flow was irreversible.

Glenn spent three weeks in the hospital, looked after by Cherie's brother Larry, who lives just a few blocks from Glenn. We got several reports a day from Larry and didn't know from minute to minute whether Glenn would live or die. The assault on his aging body was just too much. Eventually he was cleared to enter a rehab facility and was transferred the same day Larry had to leave the country for five weeks, which meant that it was Cherie's turn to manage the situation.

Larry was familiar with the rehab facility and warned us to be prepared. "It's full of people who are just circling the drain," was how he put it (Larry has a way of cutting to the heart of a matter quickly) and, harsh as that metaphor was, it was apt. I went up there the day Glenn was moved in, and walking those halls was depressing as hell. Not only did the patients look like the only thing they had to look forward to were the last rites, the staff treated them the same way. And it was hard to blame them.

Glenn looked awful. He could barely hold his head up or keep his eyes open. He sat in a wheelchair, drooling and nodding off frequently, and it was all he could do to bring a spoonful of Jell-O to his mouth.

Stumbling Towards the Finish Line

How he was managing to stay alive was beyond me. I learned a lot those first couple of days, about DNR instructions and euphemisms like "keeping him comfortable," and how wills and probate were administered in the state of Washington. Glenn was definitely circling the drain.

Until a force of nature named Cherie Gruenfeld hit town a few days later. Now, if you don't know Cherie, let me tell you that she is the sweetest-natured human being you'd ever want to meet. She doesn't have a mean bone in her body, nor an enemy in the world. I mean that literally. She would no more cause another human being a moment's misery than jump off a cliff.

Which makes you wonder why the people running the rehab clinic were ready to kill her.

She touched down like a tornado and said, "You will not treat my father like he's waiting to die!" She got him up and dressed; she dragged the physical therapist down to his room and demanded a plan; and she went to meals with him and practically stuffed food into his mouth.

"You're going to kill him," they said. "It's too much. Trust us, we've been there many times."

"You think he's going to die anyway," she shot back, "so what's there to lose?"

I'm going to make a very long story very short. As of this writing, Glenn is back in his own apartment, completely on his own except for meals that are provided for all the residents. He voluntarily gave up his driver's license, but he's learned how to ride the bus. Cherie went up to visit a few weeks ago and asked Glenn if he wanted to try to get on a stationary bike.

"What the hell are you talking about?" he said. "I've been out riding my regular bike!"

So this guy who was circling the drain has his life back. He's not quite at the same level as before—the shock of the episode was too severe—but he's on his own, getting fitter every day and still enjoying a bourbon before dinner every night. He even had a follow-up skin graft last week and weathered it beautifully, whereas a few weeks ago the doctors were afraid to perform the procedure because they weren't sure he could take it.

In her recent book about Ironman, Cherie wrote, "Whether you think you can or you think you can't, you're probably right." I used to think that was a somewhat treacly sentiment, but now I look at it as one of the truest things I've ever heard. What gets people up Everest or through an Ironman or past the speed of sound or running a sub-four-minute mile is the unshakable belief that it's possible and the willingness to put your life on the line to prove it.

I've always wondered what it is that truly separates the champions from the merely good. Is it genes? Discipline? Hard work, competitive drive, the ability to withstand pain? Probably all of those things, in various combinations. But what I'm coming to believe more and more is that the most important thing is an almost delusional conviction that the highest goals are not only possible, but inevitable. When Kobe launches a three-pointer at the buzzer with his team down by two, he isn't hoping it's going to go in. He *knows* it is. Even if he's missed his last five attempts, there's not a doubt in his mind that this one will make it. It's why champions always want the ball in the clutch and are never afraid of looking bad.

Which brings us back to Glenn. Cherie isn't a faith healer and there were no miracles involved. What she brought to the table was an attitude adjustment. "We can assume he's as good as dead, or we can assume he's going to get better." Admittedly, Glenn had a few things going for him that made it easier than for most folks: He's always been incredibly disciplined and fiercely determined, and all he needed to channel those strengths in a productive direction was somebody to convince him that it would pay off.

He also needed someone to convince the people responsible for his day-to-day care that it would pay off, and that was a much tougher job. Candidly, I don't know if they bought into it at first, but they sure behaved as though they did, because the last thing they needed was The Beast getting up in their faces if they lapsed into treating the old man like a goner. It was a lot easier to just follow her plan, and if he keeled over in the process, well, it would be her fault, not theirs.

The best part of the experience for Cherie, not counting getting her father back in her life, was the look on the faces of the residents and staff when Glenn stood up and walked out of the rehab center under his own power. I like to think that a few of them were inspired by the sight. Maybe some of the staff won't be so quick to write off patients in the future, having seen first hand that attitude can play more of a role in recovery than any particular therapeutic modality. Maybe some of the patients will stop seeing themselves as "circling the drain" and come to believe that there can be more to their lives than staving off pain until they die.

The sub-four-minute mile was once thought to be impossible. It was finally achieved by someone who was convinced it could be done. Now it's not even news when high schoolers do it. Climbing Everest was another impossibility, but two weeks ago a 76-year-old made it to the top. Thomas Edison tried over a thousand substances before he hit on tungsten to make an electric light, keeping at it because he was dead convinced something would work and he'd eventually figure it out.

It doesn't always work. People die attempting foolhardy feats, and some waste their entire lives in pursuit of the unattainable. Sometimes it's hard to know what's really possible and what isn't.

But of one thing I'm fairly certain: Attitude really is everything.

Not a new sentiment, I know. But it's one worth repeating, especially if you or someone you love is circling the drain.

FINAL WORD

2009 Ironman World Championship Wrap-up

Experience is a harsh teacher—she gives the test before she gives the lesson—and once in a while we need a reminder that toeing the start line at Ironman isn't an automatic ticket to a lifetime of bragging rights.

We're creatures of adaptation, we humans. We become quickly inured to repetition, treating patterns as normalcy, routine as status quo. But whenever our natural human tendency toward complacency seems poised to redefine the comfort zone, a snap back to reality seems, in retrospect, almost inevitable. This explains the collapse of our economy, spacecraft crashes, Kansas City beating the Yankees and disappointing outcomes on the Ironman World Championship course.

The race in Kona isn't some pre-fab reality show with a guaranteed fairy-tale ending. What start out as heart-warming stories often result in heartbreak and, despite our attempts to put the most positive spin on plot lines we've been cheering for, the hard fact is that Ironman can be nasty, brutish and disappointing. The heart transplant recipient isn't following a script provided by a sentimental producer and ends up in tears on the swim exit stairs, frozen to the spot because nothing in his pre-race visualization told him what to do if the unthinkable happened. The double amputee's race isn't choreographed for the benefit of a television audience, and he never got to the part of the race that worried him the most because side winds on the return trip from Hawi conspired to ensure that he'd never even get to put his run legs on. A big guy who used to be bigger wants to celebrate his hard-fought weight loss with a hard-fought Ironman win, but he's a few minutes late and doesn't make the cutoff.

In a way, these disappointments are a good thing. We stand at the finish line cheering for hundreds of athletes as they cross the final timing mat with their arms in the air. After hours of this, their faces blur together in our minds, the gestures become clichéd, the various flavors of expressed pain and achievement become indistinguishable...we become numb and complacent. Finishing becomes routine. What's another body across the line after the hundreds who came before?

It's the disappointments that snap us back. They remind us that starting is no guarantee of finishing. They drive home that every one of these people has suffered, sacrificed and striven. They help us to understand that dreaming is not enough, that Kona is not Disneyland, and that none of those briefly spotlighted faces got here by wishing upon a star.

Disappointments remind us of the real effort behind the seemingly effortless Chrissie Wellington and Craig Alexander. They make us think hard about the fact that 70-74 isn't some "Isn't that sweet?" infomercial,

but one of the most fiercely competitive age groups in the race. They make our eyes widen in wonder at the ones who crash, puke and cramp, but only long enough to shake it off and keep on going.

They help us understand the immense achievement of challenged athletes like Sarah Reinertsen and Scott Rigsby and Rudy Garcia-Tolson, with one good leg among the three of them.

I've watched dozens of Ironman races around the world and it never gets old for me. Part of the reason is that, as a total non-athlete myself, I have learned that the "You can do anything you set your mind to" mantra is nonsense of the first order. I couldn't do this race if the fate of the entire galaxy hung in the balance. Very, very few people could, but it doesn't seem that way to us who are close to the sport because we've been privileged to witness that vanishingly small percentage of the populace who can.

I hope that I, and you, never lose that sense of wonder at these aliens who walk among us.

The author

Lee Gruenfeld was a partner in the international consulting firm Deloitte before chucking it all to become a full time writer. Since then he has written thirteen books, including novels, non-fiction, and biographies, that have been published in a dozen countries and translated into eight languages. In addition to his "Through the Eyes of Lee Gruenfeld" column for Ironman. com, he has written feature pieces about triathlon for *Competitor* and *Inside Triathlon* magazines. He lives in Palm Springs, California, with his wife and many-time Ironman world championship age group winner Cherie Gruenfeld, author of the book *Become an Ironman* (Meyer & Meyer, 2008). He has never done an Ironman, never will, and believes that anyone who does should be committed to an asylum.

About the editor

A pro triathlete for nine years, **Kevin Mackinnon** retired from pro racing three weeks after his daughter, Chelsea, was born. Two more children, Sean and Ian, followed over the next four years. Since "pretending to find a real job," Kevin has coached numerous professional and age group triathletes, managed the Triathlon Pro Tour, worked as the communications director for Ironman Canada and Ironman North America and is currently the managing editor of Ironman.com. He's also the editor of *Triathlon Magazine Canada* and the author of two books, *A Healthy Guide to Sport* and *A Healthy Guide to Competition*. He's also married to a world champion triathlete: His wife, Sharon, won the world sprint championship in 2008.

Credits

Cover design:	Cornelia Knorr
Cover photos:	© Thinkstock/iStockphoto/Fluid Illusion
Internal photos:	Lee Gruenfeld
Editing:	Sabine Carduck, Manuel Morschel
Copy Editor:	Liz Evans
Layout:	Claudia Lo Cicero

FURTHER READING

A FEW DEGREES FROM HELL

Scott Ludwig

SCOTT LUDWIG

A FEW DEGREES
FROM HELL
White Hot Tales From the
BADWATER ULTRAMARATHON

MEYE
&MEYE
SPOR

CHAPTER ONE – PAM REED

From Pam's 2003 Badwater Application

Age: 42
Tucson, Arizona

Why I want a slot on the start line of the 2003 Badwater Ultramarathon:

I want to break my own record and make sure the whole thing was real.

SOME LIKE IT HOT BY SCOTT LUDWIG

Pam Reed stood at the starting line of the 2003 Badwater Ultramarathon with a huge target on her back. As the defending champion, that's to be expected. But the figurative target on her back wasn't her primary concern. Pam had more important issues to contend with.

For the past year Pam had to contend with the rumors circulating on the Internet that her 2002 Badwater victory was a "fluke." After all, she did have the good fortune of the "easier" 6:00 a.m. start which allowed Pam four hours of running before the hot desert sun was out in force later in the day – which made the conditions more difficult for the 8:00 a.m. and 10:00 a.m. starters (the latter group theoretically containing the faster runners in the race). Running virtually alone (i.e. no other competitors in sight) the entire race, Pam did not feel the regular pressures of actually competing head to head with anyone in the field. At least that's what the rumormongers would have you believe.

The fact that Pam's winning time a year ago (27:56:47) was a new women's course record by almost two hours didn't seem to have an impact at dispelling the "fluke" theory circulating around the world. Neither did the fact that the second place finisher (first place male) in the 2002 race finished over 4 ½ hours behind Pam. Or that Pam's 2002 time would have been fast enough to win Badwater seven times in the past decade. Or that Pam ran 12 hours faster than the 2001 women's champion. No, it was easier to simply discount Pam's 2002 victory as a fluke than to actually analyze the evidence and realize that Pam was indeed something special.

As Pam Reed stood at the starting line of the 2003 Badwater Ultramarathon, she had something to prove. It would be tough, as talented runners Dean Karnazes and Chris Bergland were lined up with her in the 10:00 a.m. starting group. At least the Race Director realized that Pam was a force to be reckoned with, assigning her the top-seeded bib number 1 and placing her in the third and final starting group, a solid four hours behind the "easier" 6:00 a.m. starters. Prior to the starter's pistol, Pam was relying on her pre-race thoughts that doing well would be "an easy thing to do." After all, she knew that 2002 was no fluke.

Pam had the utmost confidence in her crew, headed by Chuck Giles. Giles served as a marshal for the Badwater Ultramarathon and witnessed a Russian woman break the course record by several hours. Through his experiences in Death Valley, Giles designed a spraying system that could be installed in a runner's support van to keep the runner cooled off as they ran through Death Valley (he also designed a sprinkler system for cyclists competing in the Race across America).

He approached Pam prior to the 2000 race and encouraged her to participate; she politely declined. However, Pam thought about his offer and in 2002 she simply "showed up and ran." After her historic victory, Pam felt that she believed she ran "a perfect race." Along the same lines of the internet rumors about her victory, television reporters from Brazil and Germany asked her point blank if she had cheated. How could she explain that such a simple thing – getting cooled down while she ran – played a significant role in her 2002 victory? Didn't anyone realize that no one else was doing it, which set her apart from everyone else in the race?

Pam had prepared well for this year's race. She had been running three times a day totaling 100 to 115 miles a week near her home in Tucson, Arizona. Her training called for incremental training runs to prepare her for longer distances: 13-mile training runs to prepare for marathons, marathons to train for 50-milers, and 50-milers to train for 100-milers. For this year's Badwater, Pam had run a 100-kilometer (62 miles) race – a mere 10 days before!

Pam, attired in her traditional shorts, cotton T-shirt and white running hat, was ready to defend her title. She wore her iPod every step of the way. (Oddly enough, the iPod didn't work during the race; however she was in a "zone" and didn't want to change anything, so she wore it anyway.) During the race Pam's diet consisted of a steady supply of Ensure, Red Bull and club soda. There would be no solid food until the race was over. Her crew worked around the clock throughout the race: provided her with much-needed calories, telling her stories as they bicycled next to her, and giving her the emotional support one needs to run through an incredibly hot desert and over unforgiving mountain ranges. The importance of a crew is summed up in the words of Chris Giles: "A crew can't win it for you but can certainly lose it for you." Pam, on the other hand attributes 100% of her success to her crew.

Once Pam ran the first few miles, she ran comfortably in third place behind Dean and Chris. Two thoughts – which are significant since Pam believes that Badwater is 90% mental and 10% physical – were going through her mind at this point:

I can't believe I'm doing this.

It's OK not to win.

Imagine her surprise when first Dean and then Chris were in Pam's rear-view mirror.

It didn't come easy, however. Pam had to live through her "lowest point" in the race as she was trying to catch up to the two front-runners on the second major climb. Mentally she had settled for third place. She was feeling low emotionally, wondering "what the hell was I thinking" when she decided to return to defend her championship.

But her perseverance and training paid off.

As Pam passed Dean around the 80-mile mark, she thought Dean "was done" as the heat really seemed to be taking its toll on him. She exchanged pleasantries with Dean as she moved into second place and wished him good luck. Now to find Chris.

Ironically, she caught up with Chris Bergland at almost the same spot in the race – around 110 miles – that she realized she would win the 2002 race as she was so far ahead of the field. Poetically, she realized that she would repeat as champion at virtually the exact same spot as she passed Chris.

However, her second victory wasn't secure. The Race Director caught up with Pam five miles from Lone Pine (approximately 117 miles into the race) and told her that Dean was only 25 minutes behind her.

In a race of this magnitude, 25 minutes can equate to something as simple as a bad spell requiring a short recuperative rest on the side of the road. But there would be no resting for Pam. Amazingly, Pam did not stop at all during the race. Most runners opt to rest periodically – some as frequently as once every mile – by sitting in a canvas chair placed on the side of the road by a crewmember. (Note: Pam did not sit during either of her two Badwater victories.). Her "game plan" for the 2003 race was to win by running relaxed for most of the race with the exception of walking that "last hill" (only someone from the west coast would refer to the intimidating Mount Whitney as a "hill"). She executed her game plan to perfection, and finished the race in 28:26:50, a few seconds shy of 25 minutes in front of Dean Karnazes. Pam's steady approach to navigating that 'last hill' was successful, as Dean was unable to make up any of his 25-minute deficit on the 13-mile climb up Mount Whitney.

After Pam Reed's historic victory in the 2002 Badwater Ultramarathon, her life changed as people respected her more and she in turn was able respect *herself* more as well. Winning provided her more confidence and helped her to become a better runner.

Following her (perhaps even more) historic victory in 2003, the name of Pam Reed was receiving universal acclaim and recognition. Pam appeared on television (the David Letterman show, the Wayne Brady show, the Tony Danza show), in magazines (*Running Times, Runner's World and Outside*, among others), and spoke at the ISPO, the famous annual winter sports forum in Germany.

When asked which victory meant more – 2002 or 2003 – Pam opted for the latter. In Pam's mind, she had faced and conquered the greatest challenge of her life.

Pam Reed was indeed no fluke. She was a champion. The confident, two-time champion of the toughest footrace on the planet.

2003 Finishing Time – 28:26:52
2003 Badwater Champion

ISBN: 978-1-78255-003-7

*Available in book stores and on **www.m-m-sports.com***